Electric Vehicles for Smart Cities

Electric Vehicles for Smart Cities

Trends, Challenges, and Opportunities

EVANTHIA A. NANAKI

Department of Business Development and Technology,
Centre for Energy Technologies, Aarhus University,
Herning, Denmark

ELSEVIER

Elsevier
Radarweg 29, PO Box 211, 1000 AE Amsterdam, Netherlands
The Boulevard, Langford Lane, Kidlington, Oxford OX5 1GB, United Kingdom
50 Hampshire Street, 5th Floor, Cambridge, MA 02139, United States

British Library Cataloguing-in-Publication Data
A catalogue record for this book is available from the British Library

Library of Congress Cataloging-in-Publication Data
A catalog record for this book is available from the Library of Congress

ISBN: 978-0-12-815801-2

For Information on all Elsevier publications
visit our website at https://www.elsevier.com/books-and-journals

Publisher: Joe Hayton
Acquisitions Editor: Brian Romer
Editorial Project Manager: John Leonard
Production Project Manager: Sreejith Viswanathan
Cover Designer: Christian J. Bilbow

Typeset by MPS Limited, Chennai, India

  Working together
to grow libraries in
developing countries

www.elsevier.com • www.bookaid.org

Dedication

To my son, Anthony

"The Science of today is the technology of tomorrow"
E. Teller

Contents

Acknowledgments

This book would not have been possible without the help and support of a certain number of people, and I would like to express in this paragraph my enormous gratitude to all of them. I would like to thank Brian Romer (Executive Editor, Elsevier), for providing me the motivation to start the project of this book. He gave me the right support and suggestions to work on this book. I would like to thank John Leonard (Editorial Project Manager, Elsevier), who provided great assistance in the production of this book and showed great patience in extending the deadlines! Finally, I would like to thank Assoc. Professor George Xydis (Department of Business Development and Technology, University of Aarhus), for his valuable advice and extensive discussions around my work. Many thanks also to my parents and my family for their continuous love and support.

CHAPTER 1

Introduction

1.1 Sensing the energy scenery in the post COVID-era

The World Health Organization (WHO) declared COVID-19 a pandemic on March 11, 2020 (WHO, 2020), causing a huge impact on people's lives, families, and communities. The coronavirus pandemic created an unprecedented global health and economic crisis. Apart from the toll of early deaths, economic activity has stalled and stock markets have tumbled, while a wide range of energy markets have been severely affected, including coal, gas, and renewables.

The COVID-19 pandemic and the containment policies aimed at controlling it have changed consumption patterns. Historical evidence indicates that such major disruptions in the societal axis are not always a temporary crisis and can fundamentally reshape social attitudes and habits, leading thus to new policies and ways of working, as well as consumer needs and behaviors. For instance, the impact of World War II on

Electric Vehicles for Smart Cities
DOI: https://doi.org/10.1016/B978-0-12-815801-2.00005-8

women's participation in the workforce accelerated the female workforce participation after the war (Goldin and Olivetti, 2013).

In regard to the energy sector, it is noted that the outbreak has contributed to a decreased demand in global oil demand—especially in the transport sector—aggravated by a supply shock due to the end of restraints on production from OPEC producers and Russia (OPEC $+$). The scale of the collapse in oil demand, in particular, is well in excess of the oil industry's capacity to adjust. As 3 billion people around the world were under lockdown, due to the pandemic's outbreak, low prices couldn't stimulate a reaction from consumers. On the contrary, a rapid buildup of oil stocks was starting to saturate available storage capacity, pushing down prices further. As a matter of fact, on April 21, 2020 US oil prices turned negative for the first time on record after oil producers ran out of space to store the oversupply of crude oil left by the coronavirus crisis, triggering an historic market collapse. The price of US crude oil sank from \$18 a barrel to $-$\$38 in a matter of hours, as rising stockpiles of crude threatened to overwhelm storage facilities and forced oil producers to pay buyers to take the barrels they could not store (The Guardian, 2020).

Moving forward, many queries in regard to the energy scenery of tomorrow are arising. These include, inter alia:

- How the energy supply chains of clean energy pathways will emerge as the pandemic reaches its turning point and the world begins to recover?
- Will the coronavirus weaken global investments in clean energy and broader efforts to reduce emissions?
- Is the energy demand going to be followed by a sustainable energy consumption?

Governments and policy makers should not lose sight of the climate challenge and clean energy solutions as they craft stimulus packages to counter the economic damage from COVID-19. As this crisis unfolds, a conversation around energy security, reliability, and energy scarcity might arise, as this crisis has brought into light the significant role of the electricity sector, and pointed out the need for policy makers to take all necessary measures to ensure that current and future systems will remain reliable (taking into consideration their transformation via the rise of clean energy technologies).

1.2 The future of mobility

As cities continue to grow, the need for a safe, reliable, and affordable sustainable transportation is a necessity. In order to address the issues of climate change and urban development it is imperative to shift to flexible and long-term sustainable policy instruments. The energy transition to a zero-carbon future necessitates the deployment and adoption of innovative strategic plans aiming to develop innovative technologies, to model techniques, to reduce greenhouse gas emissions (GHG), and to create a sustainable transport system that will support economic growth and other social and environmental cobenefits. In this direction, during the past years, there has been a growing interest in disruptive mobility technologies such as autonomous driving, connectivity, hydrogen, electrification, and shared mobility.

Taken into consideration the fact that the transition to zero/low carbon cities is characterized by a higher share of renewable energy sources and electric vehicles (EVs), it is remarked that the integration of renewable energy and electromobility should be a priority for the energy and transportation sectors. In this direction, governments have enacted subsidy programs, supporting the installation of charging infrastructure, and have developed regulatory initiatives to support the deployment and management of EVs. In fact, some governments—including the United Kingdom—have announced that they will ban the sale of new fossil-fueled automobiles after 2035 (Maclellan, 2020), 5 years earlier than originally planned, in an attempt to mitigate the adverse effects of air pollution. Furthermore, the car manufacturers that were initially skeptical about EVs are now committing billions of dollars to their production. It is estimated that by 2022 there will be 127 different fully battery-electric car models available for purchase in the United States (Lutsey and Nicholas, 2019). Moreover, the deployment of new disruptive technologies enables the exploitation of renewable energy as EVs can be charged using solar or wind power.

In this context, it can be stated that future mobility trends are going to be shaped by technological advancements in EV infrastructure and relative investments from automakers, driving by this way the growth of EVs. In addition, consumer behavior, technological advancements in battery technology, economies of scale in EV production, native EV design, as well as cooperation among original equipment manufacturers (OEMs) (aiming to reduce costs—which are currently still higher than for comparable internal combustion engine vehicles) are of paramount importance for the energy transition to low-carbon mobility. During the upcoming years market and competition will be a critical factor for the successful deployment of electromobility as stakeholders are going to operate in an economic slowdown, but at the same time they will need to reshape their business models in a time of heightened city regulation, technology disruptions, and changing consumer needs.

It should be noted that despite the fact that EV sales grew to more than two million units globally in 2018 (increase of 63% on a year-on-year basis), they still represent a fraction of the overall light-vehicle market (with a penetration rate of 2.2%) (Hertzke et al., 2019). Further to this, the COVID-19 outbreak, which resulted in significant restriction of electric vehicle production, is going to affect the global electric vehicle sales in major markets. The role of government stimulus packages (i.e., via infrastructure rehabilitation) in the future is expected to support and to boost the EV market.

In regard to the future of mobility, the decisive influence of cities is highlighted in the energy transition to zero-carbon mobility, given that they constitute the most important stakeholders, as their governments can reconstruct and remodel their mobility systems. This is especially true for cities under the framework of smart cities, which entail and integrate inter alia the concepts of sustainable urban mobility, sustainable built environment, infrastructures and processes in energy, information and communication technologies and transportation, policy and regulation, integrated planning and management, standards, as well as business models and funding.

In view of the above, many queries are raised regarding the future of mobility. Are conventional gasoline-powered cars going to be replaced by EVs? Will gasoline stations be superseded by fast charging stations? Will the transportation sector of the future be electrified? Are OEMs and their suppliers able to make their EV supply chains as efficient, robust, and sustainable as those of their conventional vehicles? And will the charging infrastructure keep pace with the growing EV demand? As these questions are at the core of the energy and transport debates the following sections will try to showcase how this book can contribute to this debate.

1.3 Motivation for the book

This book is a response to the high demand of people, scholars, academics, industries, policy makers, as well as all involved stakeholders that nowadays want to have knowledge about:

- Current trends in electric vehicle technology.
- Charging infrastructure within the concept of smart cities (smart grid and smart energy charging).

- Electric vehicle market penetration and relative business development opportunities.
- The climate change risks associated with the pollutants emitted from the use of conventional and EVs. Is the usage of EVs beneficial to the reduction of greenhouse emissions, as well as to the reduction of harmful pollutants emitted from tailpipes?
- The factors that have contributed to supporting establishment and growth in PEV markets in different regions and cities around the world. How these cities and regions have successfully developed and deployed electric vehicle mobility strategy plans and roadmaps.

Starting from a deep analysis of the above main issues, based on the status of the literature and ongoing research projects, this book presents an integrated path of new technologies that allow the design of innovative solutions for EVs.

This book addresses the abovementioned queries within an integrated approach, taking into consideration not only the electric vehicle technology but also the transport system's requirements in conjunction with the potential of smart energy systems within the framework of smart cities (Fig. 1.1). The deployment of EVs in cities is being investigated and information on basic research and application approaches is given. The benefits of the use of EVs in terms of reduction of greenhouse gases are also assessed. This book also discusses the business models that will initiate changes in the vehicle market and in people's personal choices on transportation means. Case studies are employed in order to illustrate how EVs can be used to substantially reduce carbon emissions and cut down reliance on fossil fuels. The book also traces trends, innovations, challenges, and relative opportunities for further development.

Business models enabling and facilitating the implementation of electromobility in the transportation fleet from different viewpoints, including environmental, economic, political, and other aspects, are presented. The incentives for the purchase of EVs in different developed countries including Europe, the United States, China, and Japan have been considered and the most important concerns about EVs from the customers' point of view have been highlighted. Furthermore, the challenges imposed on the power system, which are aggravated by increasing the penetration of the EVs in transportation fleet, are also explained.

Key issues, such as the assessment of alternative market deployment approaches, the interaction between grid infrastructure and vehicles and the operational reliability, the assessment of electromobility deployment in urban areas in terms of GHG emissions, as well as current trends of

Figure 1.1 Integrated approach for electric vehicles for smart cities.

development schemes, are addressed—within an integrated framework. In this context, this book investigates the role of EVs within the urban area and especially within the concept of the "smart city." As there is a lack of a systematic and integrative approach to the deployment of EVs, this book covers the need for an integrated system taking into account the energy system, the vehicle technology, and the transport system (Fig. 1.1).

Based on the abovementioned, the motivation for this book lies in:

• The significance of a multidisciplinary approach starting from conceptual designs (modeling) to the implementation of low/zero-carbon strategy plans for the establishment of carbon-free cities.

• The presentation of an integrated/holistic point of view with regard to the deployment of EVs in cities, which does not focus only on the technical details, but also on the social, political, and economic aspects.

- The determination of what has been done until now in the market of EVs around the world.
- The presentation of an overview of key concepts, theories, and discourses in regards to the impact of the auto industry and vehicles to climate change. This assessment and synthesis of the existing information is in line with the concept of life cycle analysis (LCA).
- The investigation of the potentiality of a new energy economy based on renewable sources, where the role of EVs is of great significance.
- The identification of the gaps in the existing research that this book is endeavoring to address, positioning this book in the context of previous research and creating a research space for it.
- The production of a rationale and to establish the need for this study and thus justify its originality.
- Bridging the gap between the academic understanding of EVs and their relative deployment with regard to a city's functions with the municipal planning of organizational structures.

1.4 Aim and objectives of the book

EVs within the scope of smart cities are gaining recognition as alternative ways through which a low-zero carbon society can be pursued. Discussion of the concept of electromobility and its interaction with the city and grid is made in order to point out the need for an integrated approach. In this context, the book tries to plot the plethora of possible pathways between what has already been achieved and what is still needed. This is achieved by exploring and assessing the ways through which EVs can be integrated into a city's transportation system and how this may create a complete set of new technologies and service offerings, offering at the same time a better quality of life.

The goal of this book is to constitute a valuable tool that can be helpful to stakeholders and decision-makers in the process of regional and strategic planning, with reference to sustainable transport design. It aims to be helpful along the way in policy, practical, conceptual, and visionary ways. Thus it aims to help in decision-making, with regard to the national and sustainable energy designs, and to demonstrate how EVs can best be utilized within cities. The book's objective is to provide useful insight to policy makers, urban planners, engineering consultancies, scientists, researchers, students, as well as citizens interested in supporting a smooth transition to the future energy landscape. Furthermore, the book aims to point out that the combination of external factors, such as stringent emissions regulations, rising fuel prices, financial incentives, intelligent load management, and exploitation of local renewables, can contribute to a decarbonized urban energy future.

1.5 Structure of the book

The book discusses the challenges and future trends of electromobility—within the concept of smart cities—encompassing aspects such as smart charging, market development and market introduction, climate change mitigation, as well as successful case studies of electrical vehicle capitals around the world. The book is structured into six sections that are briefly described here below; Fig. 1.2 shows the book's flowchart. It is noted that the book is designed in such a way that it allows each chapter to be read alone, while at the same time all chapters can be grouped together, in order to aid the reader (Fig. 1.2).

Following this introductory chapter, Chapter 2, Electric Vehicles presents the background of the basic principles of electric vehicle technologies, the current status of key automotive technologies, and a brief presentation of different types of EVs (including battery electric vehicles—BEVs; hybrid electric vehicles—HEVs; plug in hybrid electric vehicles—PHEVs; and fuel cell electric vehicles—FCEVs); the charging power levels and infrastructure are also introduced. The chapter provides the necessary background for understanding these concepts, as well as basic principles, general definitions, and practical applications. The scope of this chapter is to provide basic information about current technologies, so as to be able to outline the drivers that will shape future demand and trends.

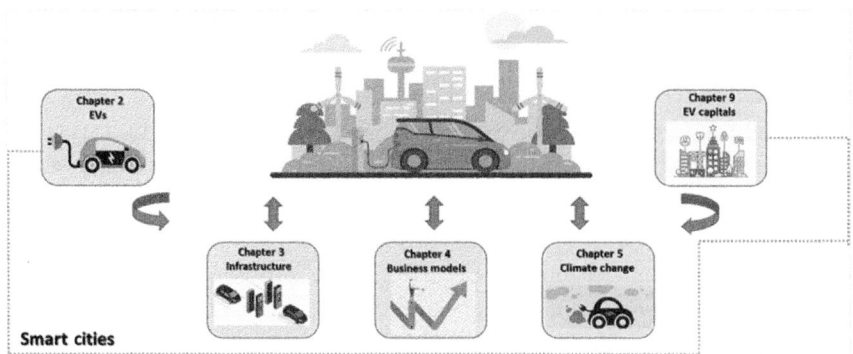

Figure 1.2 Flowchart of the book's structure.

Chapter 3, Electric Vehicle Charging Within Smart Cities elaborates on the transition to a new age of mobility and the challenges of electromobility within the concept of the smart city. Smart cities play an important role toward the transition to a lower-carbon urban environment by providing all the necessary technological advancements for adequate recharging infrastructure. This chapter reviews the concept, framework, advantages, challenges, and optimization strategies of vehicle to grid (V2G). The benefits, services, and potential barriers of the V2G technology implementation are discussed. In addition, various V2G optimization techniques are analyzed. In addition, different standards and various applications of the main results of smart grid projects are presented.

Chapter 4, Market Introduction of Electric Vehicles to Urban Areas then details several of the more innovative approaches to mobility, which have the potential of disrupting traditional value chains and could enable further uptake of EVs. In addition, this chapter reviews the latest developments in new registrations and the stock of EVs, looking primarily at electric cars and focusing on the developments that took place in 2019 as well as trends since 2010. Stock and sales figures are assessed against policy support schemes and country commitments on EV deployment. This chapter aims to provide readers with a useful insight into the market and of the business models they require to excel in today's rapidly shifting automotive industry—an industry fit for the 21st century, which embraces and embodies the concepts of electrification and sustainability. Further to this, the term of *integrated innovative business models for EVs* (e-IIBMs) is being introduced. Finally, many case studies of business models employed worldwide as well as their relative impacts are presented (car leasing, car sharing, V2G, battery second usage, etc.).

Chapter 5, Climate Change Mitigation and Electric Vehicles points out the significant role that electromobility plays in mitigating climate change—based on the Paris Declaration on Electro-Mobility and Climate Change and Call to Action, which brings together individual and collective commitments to increase electromobility to levels compatible with a less-than 2-degree pathway. Emissions of EVs are assessed by the employment of LCA. This chapter allows a researcher/practitioner to conduct site and user-specific LCAs which reflect the prevailing conditions and individual use patterns. For this reason, the basics on LCA in regards to EVs are also presented. The goal of the chapter is to analyze existing vehicle technologies (conventional versus alternative) and highlight their environmental burdens. Relevant guidelines and studies on life cycle assessment of EVs are presented. In this direction, a case-driven LCA for EVs is presented in detail. The corresponding solutions are discussed; the potential benefits in terms of climate change mitigation as well as the relative impacts of each LCA stage are analyzed.

Chapter 6, Electric Vehicle Capitals—Case Studies reports some successful case studies from electric vehicle deployment in cities all over the world. This chapter focuses on and refers to statistical data evidencing the high percentages of alternative vehicle penetration as well as charging infrastructure in cities such as Los Angeles, Amsterdam, Oslo, Shanghai, and Tokyo. The chapter demonstrates the utilization patterns of EVs in many cities and explores fleet integration aspects all over the world. In addition to analyzing the electric vehicle sales and charging infrastructure in these markets, this chapter identifies and discusses the unique policies, actions, and programs in place that have enabled this success.

In summary, this book addresses key issues such as the assessment of alternative market deployment approaches, the interaction between grid infrastructure and vehicles and the operational reliability, the assessment of electromobility deployment in urban areas, as well as the costs and benefits of development schemes within an integrated framework. In this context, this book investigates the role of EVs within the urban area and especially within the concept of the "smart city." As there is a lack of a systematic and integrative approach to the deployment of EVs, this book covers the need for an integrated system taking into account the energy system, the vehicle technology, and the transport system (Fig. 1.1).

1.6 Concluding remarks

Everything is connected to everything else; therefore in order to bring a zero-carbon emission shift in transportation, it is imperative to think holistically. Cities are physically formed of and around energy infrastructure: they are increasingly connected and sophisticated bundles of generation, distribution, networking, and storage systems bridging power, thermal energy and mobility, storage, and networks. Urban centers and their neighborhoods and districts, but also their wider regions are of crucial importance in the energy transition, which is going to define the 21st century. In this manner, EVs are only part of this equation, as smart cities—via a holistic system operation—should shape the future mobility pathways.

Cities should scale up green public transportation and public transport on demand, and increase the focus on pedestrians and cyclists, as well as autonomous vehicles and "mobility as a service". Increasing freight by railway and introducing green freight distribution in the city, zero-emission heavy-duty vehicles and zero-emission taxis should be part of a city's holistic approach to becoming fossil fuel-free. Green public procurement, goods and services delivered by zero-emission vehicles, and good park and ride solutions, in combination with EVs, and an increased use of intelligent traffic systems (ITS) and artificial intelligence (AI) to make the EV use swift, efficient, and user-friendly, are equally necessary. Furthermore, this energy transition to a zero-carbon future, should be accompanied with the use of renewable electricity, as well as with the necessary right regulatory framework and financial incentives, as well as with the public—private cooperation and the resilience to succeed.

In summary, the global energy future depends on a lot of variables, including the political willingness to use green taxes, regulations, and other incentives to make the shift to zero-carbon energy alternatives; technological developments for vehicles, batteries, chargers, autonomous vehicles, AI, and ITS; global price developments for alternative fuels such as gasoline and diesel; national and transnational cooperation, involving local government, national government, and private businesses; global cooperation and free exchange of examples and ideas; and sound business models that can help finance the green shift in transport.

References

Goldin and Olivetti, 2013. Shocking labor supply: a reassessment of the role of World War II on U.S. women's labor supply. <https://www.nber.org/papers/w18676>.

Hertzke, P., Müller, N., Schaufuss, P., Schenk, S., Wu, T., 2019. Electric-Vehicle Adoption Despite Early Growing Pains. McKinsey and Company. Available from: https://www.mckinsey.com/industries/automotive-and-assembly/our-insights/expanding-electric-vehicle-adoption-despite-early-growing-pains.

Lutsey, N., Nicholas, M., 2019. Update on Electric Vehicle Costs in the United States through 2030. The International Council on Clean Transportation. Available from: https://theicct.org/sites/default/files/publications/EV_cost_2020_2030_20190401.pdf.

Maclellan, K., 2020. Electric dream: Britain to ban new petrol and hybrid cars from 2035. Reuters. <https://uk.reuters.com/article/us-climate-change-accord/electric-dream-britain-to-ban-new-petrol-and-hybrid-cars-from-2035-idUKKBN1ZX2RY> (accessed 21.05.20.).

The Guardian, 2020. Oil prices dip below zero as producers forced to pay to dispose of excess. <https://www.theguardian.com/world/2020/apr/20/oil-prices-sink-to-20-year-low-as-un-sounds-alarm-on-to-covid-19-relief-fund> (accessed 22.4. 20.).

World Health Organization—WHO, 2020. <http://www.who.int>.

CHAPTER 2

Electric vehicles

2.1 Introduction

Over the past decades, the growing concern over climate change, energy independence, and security of energy supply have accelerated the path to the decarbonization of the transport sector. To be more specific, road transport accounted for 21% of global energy consumption and 17% of global carbon dioxide (CO_2) emissions in 2013 (IEA, 2015). Carbon emissions from road transport have been growing steadily and will continue to do so if road transport is not progressively decoupled from fossil fuels (EIA, 2014). It is evident that stabilizing global temperature increase to below 2°C relative to preindustrial levels necessitates a combination of improved fuel efficiency and deployment of alternative fuels in road transport, particularly advanced biofuels, electricity, and hydrogen (IEA, 2015).

For the reasons noted, this growing concern about climate change triggered agreements between EU countries to cut their emissions by 80% by 2050, to stabilize atmospheric CO_2 at 450 ppm, in order to keep global warming under 2°C. It is noted that through these agreements the road transport sector is expected to reduce its emissions by 95% (Poullikkas, 2015; Wager et al., 2016). Furthermore, as urban pollution due to vehicle use is responsible for serious health problems, the creation of a low-carbon transportation system is of great significance for a sustainable future (Nanaki et al., 2015; Nanaki and Koroneos, 2016). In this direction, alternative vehicle technologies (AVT), such as electric vehicles (EVs), are a promising technology that can tackle increased CO_2 emissions and air pollutants, as well as noise coming from passenger cars and light commercial vehicles. Road transport electrification is expected to play a major role in achieving these goals, given that the electric power train is significantly more energy efficient than the conventional one and the electricity used could come from renewable energy sources.

Governments around the world are implementing different initiatives, policies, and programs for wider uptake of EVs. Incentives to EVs' purchase costs, development of charging infrastructure, and the increase of public awareness of EVs' benefits are among the actions taken to promote

Electric Vehicles for Smart Cities
DOI: https://doi.org/10.1016/B978-0-12-815801-2.00006-X

EVs. For instance, in order to accelerate the uptake of AVTs, the European Union (EU) plans to accompany its political decision with a regulatory framework, which will combine the decided CO_2 targets for 2025 and 2030 with a technology-neutral incentive mechanism for zero- and low-emission vehicles in order to accelerate their penetration. The incentive covers both zero-emission and low-emission vehicles (with tail-pipe emissions of less than 50 g CO_2 per km). Under this framework, manufacturers achieving a share of zero- and low-emission vehicles, which is higher than the agreed benchmark level for 2025 and 2030 (proposed benchmark values are 15% and 30% for 2025 and 2030, respectively), will be rewarded in the form of a less strict CO_2 target.

Since the 19th century EV technologies have gone through a series of technological developments; aiming to be competitive with the dominant internal combustion engine (ICE) vehicles. The invention of the electric motor benefited the use of electric powered vehicles. Robert Anderson, during the period 1832—39, invented the first prototype electric-powered carriage, which was powered by nonrechargeable primary cells (Guarnieri, 2011); nonetheless only in the late 19th century were some units produced in North America, United Kingdom, and France. In addition, the first hybrid car was reported in 1899 by the Pieper establishment of Liege, Belgium (Khan and Kar, 2009); and in 1900 Dr. Ferdinand Porsche developed the world's first series hybrid electric vehicle (HEV). Due to limitations imposed by high initial costs and limited autonomy, the EVs were removed from the market in the 1930s, and only after the 1970s did the interest in this technology return (Chan et al., 2010).

During the past decades, attention has been paid to improving EV technologies, aligned with carbon emission restrictions. In the last 10 years EV technologies have benefited from European and US programs for the development of clean technologies to reduce CO_2. The power train, the battery, the charging infrastructure, the global vehicle market, the energy prices, climate policy, and the electricity sector are the main components that experienced a major shift along the EV development process. The continual development of EV technologies is of critical importance in the improvement of EV's performance and the increase of their competitiveness. Nonetheless, it should be mentioned that the electrification of the transportation sector is beneficial to the reduction of emissions, although how much it helps depends significantly upon the source of the electricity used to charge vehicles: renewable sources, nuclear power, or fossil fuel (Nanaki et al., 2015).

This chapter aims to present an overview of different EV technologies. The chapter covers a range of topics related to EVs, including inter alia the presentation of basic types of EVs and their technical characteristics, charging mechanisms, and the architecture of vehicle to grid and grid to vehicle. To be more specific, the general classification of EV technologies is discussed in Section 2.2, whereas different configurations are presented through Sections 2.2.1–2.2.5. Section 2.3 describes the batteries used as energy storage to store the vehicle's power. It is noted that despite the fact that batteries are the most used, ultracapacitors (UCs) and flywheels are also considered potential energy storage systems (ESS). In addition, Section 2.3 presents different energy generation systems that are commonly used in order to extend the range of EVs. Different charging voltages and charger configurations as well as power conversion systems are presented in Section 2.4 and Section 2.5 presents the impacts of EV charging on the power grid.

2.2 Electric vehicle technologies

EVs can either run on electric propulsion or they can have an ICE working alongside. The motive and auxiliary power comes from the power stored in the energy storage unit, which is recharged from grid electricity and brake energy recuperation. Electricity, necessary for the movement of the vehicle, may come from generation plants as well as renewable energy sources and is stored in batteries, fuel cells (FCs), and UCs. Unlike conventional vehicles, the EV uses a more efficient power source and electrical motor than the power train of ICEs (Hannan et al., 2014). Energy waste is reduced with the use of regenerative braking and thermoelectric generators. The braking process of the vehicle absorbs its energy, converts it back to electrical energy, and returns the energy to the batteries, while the thermoelectric generator converts heat from the engine and machine systems to electricity automatically (Chan and Chau, 2002; Tie and Tan, 2013). EVs normally do not need a gearbox as the electric motors have high torque at a wide range of speed.

The configuration of an EV drive train consisting of three major subsystems: electric motor propulsion, energy source, and auxiliary. The electric propulsion subsystem comprises vehicle controller, power electronic converter, electric motor, mechanical transmission, and driving wheels. The energy source subsystem involves the energy source, the energy management unit, and the energy refueling unit. The auxiliary subsystem consists of the power steering unit, the hotel climate control unit, and the auxiliary supply unit. Based on the control inputs from the accelerator and brake pedals, the vehicle controller provides proper control signals to the electronic power converter, which functions to regulate the power flow between the electric motor and energy source. The backward power flow is due to the regenerative braking of the EV and this regenerated energy can be restored into the energy source, provided the energy source is receptive. Most EV batteries, as well as UCs and flywheels, have the ability to accept regenerative energy. The energy management unit cooperates with the vehicle controller to control the regenerative braking and its energy recovery. It also works with the energy refueling unit to control the refueling unit and to monitor the usability of the energy source. The auxiliary power supply provides the necessary power with different voltage levels for all the EV auxiliaries, especially the climate control and power steering units.

Based on the power supplement and propulsion characteristics, EVs are available in various drivetrain architectures, enabling different mobility features and energy management. These technologies vary in the way the onboard electricity is generated and/or recharged, and the way the internal electric motor and combustion engine are coupled. The mix of battery capacities, charging capabilities, and technological complexity give the consumers a choice of options with regard to vehicle ranges, refueling options, and price. These can be categorized:

• Battery electric vehicle (BEV)
• Hybrid electric vehicle (HEV)
• Plug-in hybrid electric vehicle (PHEV)
• Fuel cell electric vehicle (FCEV)

Table 2.1 summarizes a brief classification of different types of EVs. The BEV is purely fed by electricity from the power storage unit, while its propulsion is provided by an electric motor. The driving system of HEV combines the electric motor and the engine, while the power sources involve both electricity and gasoline or diesel. FCEV is driven by an electric motor and could be directly or indirectly powered using hydrogen, methanol, ethanol, or gasoline.

2.2.1 Key technologies of electric motors

The electric motors play a crucial role in EV technologies, as the motor converts the electrical energy from the battery into mechanical energy, which enables the vehicle to move. It also acts as a generator during regenerative action which sends energy back to the energy source. Direct current (DC) motor drives are not considered to be an attractive choice, due to their lack in efficiency, bulky structure, and lack of reliability (Chan, 2002; Gao et al., 2005). During the past decades, different types of electric motors have been developed (AC and DC) in order to meet the needs of the automotive sector; induction and permanent magnet (PM) types are the most favored ones (Rajashekara, 2013).

DC motors used to be considered to be the most suitable technology for EVs due to their simple control electronics; nonetheless as they require regular maintenance they are not suitable for mass-scale EV adoption. AC motors require complicated and costly power electronics, including an inverter, as the power source—the batteries—provides DC current (Guzzella and Sciarretta, 2013). The overall cost of AC motors is higher. Their advantages are a higher power density, which is very important in an automotive application as it allows the use of a smaller and lighter motors, and higher efficiency, which maximizes the range for a given battery capacity.

The following types of electric motors suitable for the abovementioned EVs technologies can be distinguished:

- Brushed DC motor
- Permanent magnet brushless DC Motor (BLDC)
- Permanent Magnet Synchronous Motor (PMSM)
- Induction motor (IM)
- Switched reluctance motor (SRM)
- Synchronous reluctance motor (SynRM)
- PM assisted synchronous reluctance motor
- Axial flux ironless PM motor

The typical requirements for motor and drive technology take into consideration the following: high torque density and power density; wide speed range including constant torque and constant power (CP) operations; high efficiency over wide speed range; high reliability and robustness; all at a reasonable cost. Induction machines are used for EVs, HEVs, and FCVs, due to their simplicity, robustness, and wide speed range. It is noticed that the efficiency of an IM is lower than that of a PM due to the inherent rotor loss. For this reason, the size of an IM is bigger than that of a PM (of the same power and speed rating). On the other hand, PMs are characterized by high efficiency, high torque, and higher power density, thus making them a preferable choice for many EVs. Nonetheless, PM

Table 2.1 Major characteristics and features of electric vehicles.

Type of EVs	BEV	HEV	FCEV
Energy source	Battery	1. Battery/ultracapacitor 2. Internal combustion engines	FCs
Propulsion technique	Electric motor drives	1. Electric motor drives 2. Internal combustion engines	Electric motor drives
Characteristics and features	1. Zero emission 2. Short driving range 3. Higher initial costs	1. Low emission 2. Longer range 3. Complex	1. Zero emission 2. Medium driving range 3. Highest initial costs
Major techniques	1. Electric motor control 2. Battery management 3. Charging device	1. Electric motor control 2. Battery management 3. Managing multiple energy sources 4. And optimal system efficiency 5. Components sizing	1. Fuel processor 2. Fueling system 3. FC cost
Regenerative braking	Yes	Yes	Yes
Major issues	1. Battery sizing and management 2. Charging facilities 3. Cost 4. Battery lifetime	1. Battery sizing and management 2. Control, optimization, and management of multiple energy sources	1. FC cost, life cycle and reliability 2. Hydrogen production and distribution infrastructure 3. Cost

BEV, Battery electric vehicle; *EVs*, electric vehicles, *FCEV*, fuel cell electric vehicle; *HEV*, hybrid electric vehicle.

motors inherently have a short CP range—coming from the presence of the PM field, which can only be weakened through production of a stator field component, which opposes the rotor magnetic field. In the case of a stator winding short circuit fault, the system can run into problems due to the existence of a rotor PM field. The SRM can be used for electric propulsion for EVs, HEVs, and FCVs due to its simple and rugged construction, simple control, ability of extremely high speed operation, and hazard-free operation (Chan, 2002).

2.2.2 Battery electric vehicles

In BEVs an electric motor powered by a battery replaces the ICEV and the tank (Tie and Tan, 2013). To be more specific, BEVs or full electric vehicles (FEVs) or all electric vehicles (AEVs) (Fig. 2.1) consist of an electric drive and an electric battery for energy storage, the DC/DC converter adjusts the voltage of the electric current provided to a 2-quadrant inverter or a 4-quadrant bidirectional inverter with a dedicated power electronics controller, which controls the power provided to (and from, in case of regeneration capability, that is, 4-quadrant inverter) the electric motor. The 4-quadrant inverter utilizes inertia for regeneration (recharging) during deceleration and breaking. The battery is normally recharged through a plug and a battery charging unit, which can either be carried on board or fitted at the charging point. The large battery packs can be recharged through regenerative braking on drive and externally charged when the vehicle stops. The power electronics controller regulates the power supplied to the motor and hence it controls the vehicle speed forwards and backwards as well as the system of regenerative braking (frictionless deceleration) as mentioned above. EV has an all-electric propulsion system and always operates in charge-depleting mode.

Two types of BEVs, according to the mode of transmission of the electric power developed by the electric motor to the drive wheel, can be discerned: (1) in the first type the electric motor replaces the classic ICE. The power produced by the electric motor is transmitted to the wheels via the transmission (gearbox). (2) In the second type, each drive wheel is

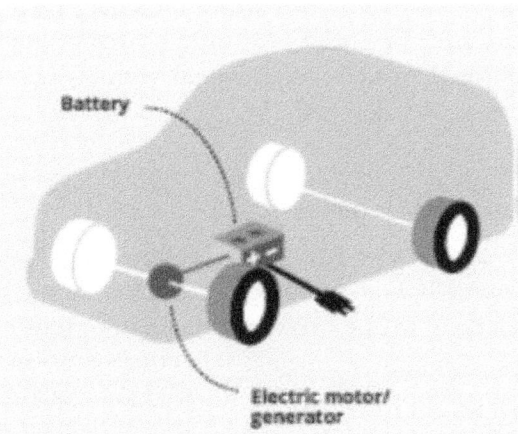

Figure 2.1 Battery electric vehicle.

fitted with an electric motor (hub motor). Using a gearbox results in a decrease of the overall efficiency (due to inherent friction in the mechanisms that compose it). The regenerative breaking technology can be employed in order to address the abovementioned mechanical losses (Varga, 2012; Damiani et al., 2014).

The electric motor can be either a DC or AC. A DC motor typically ranges between 20 and 30 kW and requires full battery voltage of up to 200 V. A DC motor usually is coupled to a DC controller, which is in the range of 40–60 kW. An AC motor uses a three-phase motor running at 240 V AC with a 300 V battery voltage and typically has higher rated power. Taken into consideration the fact that BEVs rely on the energy stored in their battery packs, their range is correlated with the battery capacity. BEVs can cover approximately 100–250 km on one charge; whereas top-tier models can cover 300–500 km (Grunditz and Thiringer, 2016). The driving range is also affected by the driving condition and style, vehicle configurations, road conditions, climate, battery type, and age. For this reason, the selection of a proper drive and optimal control strategy are of crucial importance to the optimization of battery energy management (Sutikno et al., 2014).

BEVs have many advantages: they are efficient due to the high torque of the electric motor that is transmitted to the wheels resulting to smoother acceleration; they do not emit noise while operating; they are environmentally friendly, due to zero tailpipe emissions; and they can be charged overnight on low-cost electricity coming from any type of power station, including renewables (EEA, 2016). On the other hand, there are some disadvantages to using BEVs, such as the high production costs, the limited autonomy and top speed, the large charging times, the reduced overall size (compared to vehicles equipped with ICE), and the lack of electric motor noise can cause traffic accidents.

2.2.3 Hybrid electric vehicles

HEVs (Fig. 2.2) propel through a combination of two different power sources (conventional ICE and a battery/electric motor). The electric battery supplies electricity to the drivetrain, so as to optimize the operating efficiency of the combustion engine. The battery in an HEV can be charged by the engine or through captured kinetic braking energy from regenerative braking. Since 1995, when HEVs experienced a renewed interest from competing manufacturers, several variations to the HEV

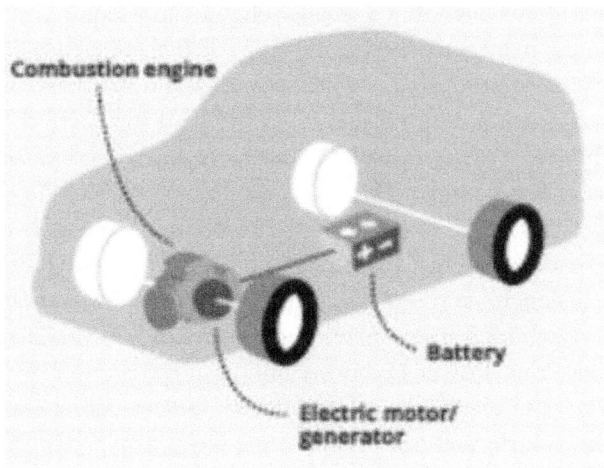

Figure 2.2 Hybrid electric vehicle.

technology have been developed. These include micro HEVs, mild HEVs, full HEVs, and PHEV (Duoba, 2011).

- *Micro HEVs*: A micro HEV is a vehicle with an electric motor in the form of an integrated alternator/starter that uses start/stop technology, in order to shut down the engine, when the vehicle comes to a complete stop, and start it up when the driver releases the brake pedal. During cruising, the vehicle is propelled only by the ICE. Examples of micro hybrids on the road today are the BMW 1 and 3 series, Fiat 500, SMART car, Peugeot Citroen C3, Ford Focus and Transit, and Mercedes-Benz A-class (Technology CfAA, 2018).
- *Mild HEVs*: The mild HEV has a lot of similarities to a micro HEV, but with an increased size of the integrated alternator/starter motor and a battery which permits power assist during vehicle propulsion. Typical fuel efficiency increases for mild HEVs are around 20% − 25% for real-world driving compared to a nonhybrid. Examples of mild HEVs on the market include the BMW 7 Series Active Hybrid, Buick La Crosse with e-Assist, Chevrolet Malibu with e-Assist, Honda Civic and Insight Hybrid, and the Mercedes-Benz S400 Blue Hybrid (Technology CfAA, 2018).
- *Full HEV*: In full HEVs, the electric motor and batteries are significantly bigger than those of the micro HEVs and mild HEVs. As such, depending on the vehicle power demand, the electric motor can be used as the sole power source. Compared to micro HEVs and mild

HEVs, full HEVs have much smaller engines and require more sophisticated energy management system. Typical fuel efficiency increases for full HEVs are around 40% − 45% for real-world driving compared to a nonhybrid. Examples of full HEVs on the road today are the Chevrolet Tahoe Hybrid, Toyota Prius and Camry Hybrid, Ford C-Max, Honda CR-Z, and Kia Optima Hybrid (Technology CfAA, 2018). The full hybrid vehicles can be further subdivided into Synergy Hybrid and Power Hybrid. Synergy Hybrid compromises the drive performance, energy efficiency, and emission reduction. In this subcategory, the engine is downsized as compared with conventional vehicles, such as in the Toyota Prius. Power Hybrid is aiming to have better driving performance, thus the engine is not downsized, and in conjunction with the motor, the vehicle will have better drive performance as compared with a conventional vehicle, such as in the Toyota Highlander.

- *PHEVs*: PHEVs essentially possess the same configuration as full HEVs but with the addition of an external electric grid charging plug, much bigger electrical components (electric motor and battery) and a downsized engine. Owing to the high-capacity electrical components, PHEVs are able to run on electric power for long periods of time. Examples of PHEVs on the road today are the Chevy Volt, Ford C-Max Energi and Fusion Energi, Fisker Karma, Porsche Panamera S E-Hybrid, and Toyota Prius Plug-in (Technology CfAA, 2018).

HEVs have many advantages including fuel savings resulting from the ability to use both the electric motor and the ICE to deliver kinetic power (Takaishi et al., 2008). The regeneration of kinetic braking energy, which usually is lost as heat to mechanical brakes in conventional vehicles, is utilized in HEVs (Axsen and Kurani, 2013). In addition, HEVs have the possibility of cranking the engine with the electric motor, resulting in an improved cranking technique (inertia cranking) (Mercier, 2012). Furthermore, in full HEVs, fuel consumption during idling can be eliminated by the use of the engine shutoff/startup feature (Bitsche and Gutmann, 2004). On the other hand, there are some concerns with regard to HEVs. These include the increased cost, the ESS and power converters; reliability and warranty related issues; safety concerns due to the introduction of high voltage in the vehicle system; and electromagnetic interference (EMI) caused by high-frequency high-currents switching in the electric power train system. It should be noted that in order to achieve the abovementioned advantages a real-time control strategy is of great importance.

2.2.3.1 Configuration

According to the design of the power flow from the sources of energy, HEV's configurations can be classified as hybrid and parallel hybrid (Chau and Wong, 2002; Guzzella and Sciarretta, 2007). The power flow in the *series HEV* is passed down to the transmission over a single path (electrical path); whereas *parallel HEVs* allow power flow through two paths (electrical and mechanical path) from the energy sources to the transmission (Husain, 2010).

The series HEV is composed of ICE, generator, power converter, motor, and battery (Fig. 2.3). There is no direct mechanical connection between the ICE and the transmission. Consequently, the ICE can be controlled independently of the vehicle power demand and close to its peak-efficiency region. The series HEV could thus be described as being powered primarily by the electric motor and secondarily by the ICE.

The parallel HEV allows both the electric motor and ICE to deliver power in parallel to drive the vehicle, that is, both the engine and the electric motor are able to work independently or cooperatively to provide traction. Different from the series HEV, the engine is mechanically connected to the driving wheels via a gearbox, while the electric motor is used to support the engine during accelerations. Depending on the power of the motor, it could also be used as the sole power source of the vehicle while idling and during startups. The engine used in the parallel HEV configuration is usually bigger than those used in the series configuration, while the electric motor is comparatively smaller and less powerful (Fig. 2.4). Parallel HEVs come in two sub configurations: the pretransmission parallel and the posttransmission parallel.

All other configurations different from the above two types of series and parallel HEV can be referred to as complex HEVs. One variation of the complex HEV is the *series—parallel HEV*, which incorporates the

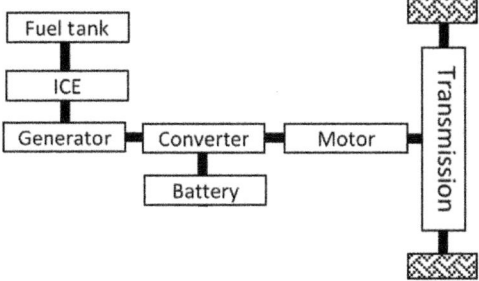

Figure 2.3 Configuration of series HEV. *HEV*, Hybrid electric vehicle; *ICE*, internal combustion engine.

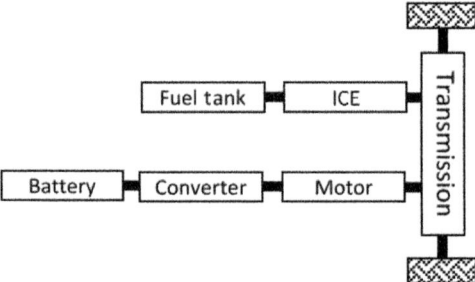

Figure 2.4 Configuration of parallel HEV. *HEV*, Hybrid electric vehicle; *ICE*, internal combustion engine.

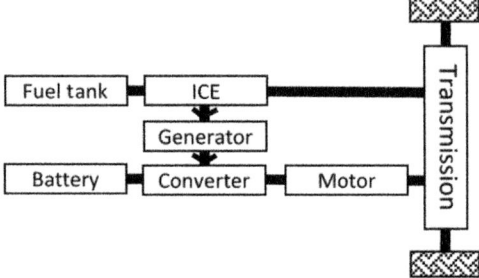

Figure 2.5 Configuration of series—parallel HEV. *HEV*, Hybrid electric vehicle; *ICE*, internal combustion engine.

features of both series and parallel HEVs by adding an additional mechanical linkage and a generator between the ICE and converter in a parallel HEV (Fig. 2.5). The series—parallel HEV has the possibility of having the engine completely decoupled from the vehicle, thus making it possible for the vehicle to be powered using just the electric motors (Liu et al., 2005). It also offers the possibility of operating the ICE around its peak-efficiency region due to flexibility in both torque and speed changeability at the ICE output. These advantages become partially offset when energy losses during conversion of mechanical energy to electrical energy is taken into account. High complexity and cost are drawbacks of this system, but it is adopted by some vehicles to use dual-axle propulsion (Chan, 2002). It should be mentioned that the popular Toyota Prius (model NHW20, 2004—09) adopted this configuration.

2.2.4 Plug-in hybrid electric vehicles

PHEVs are defined as HEVs that have a battery storage system of 4 kWh or more, a means of recharging the battery from an external source, and

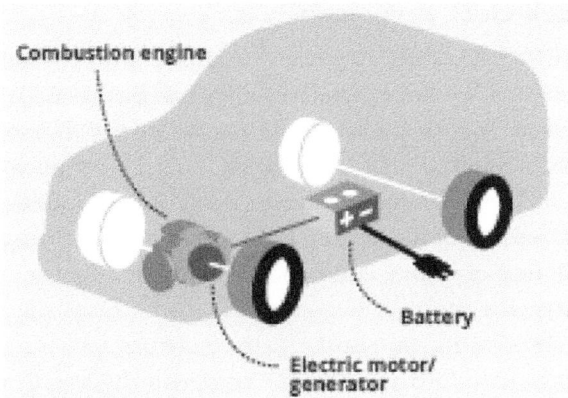

Figure 2.6 Plug-in electric vehicle.

the ability to drive at least 16 km in electric mode (Pollet et al., 2012). The concept of PHEV was developed, in order to extend the all−electric range of HEVs (Gao and Ehsani, 2010). As a matter of fact, a PHEV is similar in concept to an HEV, but with a larger battery and a grid connection. The grid connection allows the battery to be charged with electricity and the larger battery size enables the car to drive a significant distance in all-electric mode. An all-electric range of 20 miles can be denoted through the notation PHEV-20, and a 40-mile all-electric range would be PHEV-40. PHEV uses both an ICE and an electrical power train; nonetheless the PHEV uses the electric propulsion as main driving force (Fig 2.6).

For this reason, PHEVs require a bigger battery compared to HEVs. Depending on the state of charge (SOC) of the battery, PHEVs operate in two different modes. The first is charge−−depleting (CD) mode, during which the battery discharges from its beginning state (e.g., 100% charged). After reaching the end of its CD range, a PHEV will switch to charge-sustaining (CS) mode, during which the PHEV operates using the regenerative braking and power from the engine to keep the average SOC constant. The switch to CS operation is triggered by the battery reaching the specified SOC.

PHEVs can be a viable solution for the creation of a low-carbon transportation system, provided that the electricity mix is coming from alternative energy sources (Nanaki and Koroneos, 2016). In addition, PHEVs have significant benefits compared to a HEV, as a PHEV may offer 25%−55% reduction in NOx, 35%−65% reduction in greenhouse gases, and 40%−80% reduction in gasoline consumption (Amjad et al., 2010).

2.2.5 Fuel cell electric vehicles

FCEVs are AEVs; therefore they share a similar power train with BEVs, except for the energy source, which is a *FC stack* (Fig. 2.7). Taking into consideration the fact that FCEVs are powered by hydrogen-induced electrolysis, with water and heat being the only by-products of this process, FCEVs are zero-emission vehicles and can be considered a viable solution for a zero-carbon transportation sector. FCEVs carry the hydrogen in special high-pressure tanks mounted in the vehicle; whereas the oxygen required for the power generation comes from the air from the environment. Hydrogen can also be extracted from fuel using a fuel processor. Compressed hydrogen gas and cryogenic hydrogen (supercooled liquid hydrogen) are the two types of hydrogen fuel tanks. Since hydrogen gas is the more common of the two, most common fuel tanks are set up for hydrogen gas storage. The gas is stored in a compressed state in high-pressure tanks, located either in the trunk or under the floor of the vehicle. Hydrogen fuel is sourced from these tanks to feed the FCs. These tanks are connected to the fuel port (into which the gas is dispensed from refueling stations).

Electricity generated from the FCs goes to an electric motor which gives power to the vehicle. Excess energy is stored in storage systems like batteries or supercapacitors (SCs). The power control unit manages the flow of electricity generated in the FC according to the driving conditions. Fig. 2.8 illustrates a FCEV power train configuration with an optional fuel processor (Yang, 2000). The power train of FCEVs is ideal

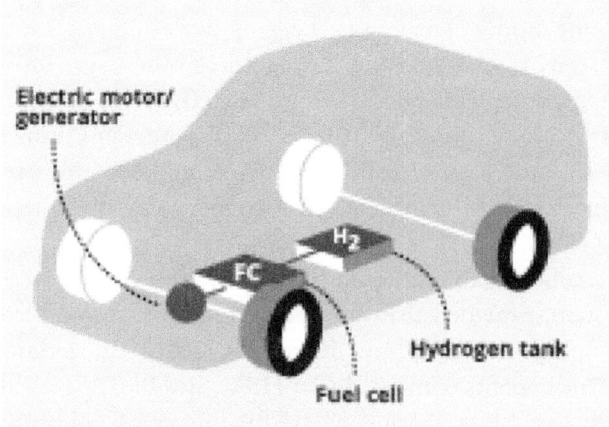

Figure 2.7 Fuel cell electric vehicle.

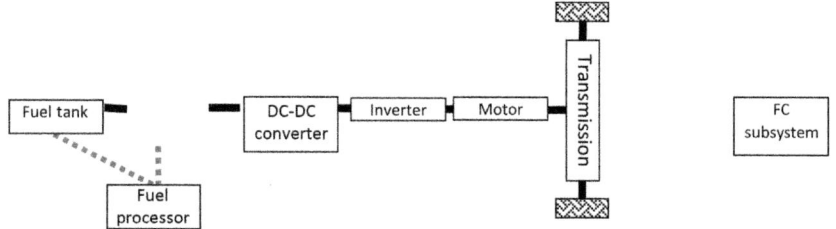

Figure 2.8 Configuration of fuel cell electric vehicle.

for a CP supply, but not proper for an abrupt change in power demand. Therefore low-speed vehicles are suitable for such an application; it is pointed out that in order to produce high-speed vehicles, different modifications can be made to the basic power train.

In many cases, in order to reduce losses attributed to voltage drop in internal resistances, energy storage units, such as batteries or UCs, are used alongside FCs. For instance, the Toyota Mirai uses batteries to power its motor and the FC is used to charge the batteries (www.toyota.com). The batteries receive the power reproduced by regenerative braking as well. This combination provides more flexibility as the batteries do not need to be charged, only the fuel for the FC has to be replenished and it takes far less time than recharging the batteries.

The main power supplier is a FC, which has the following components: anode, an anode layer, electrolyte, cathode, and a cathode catalyst layer. The FC stack consists of hundreds of single cells, which convert chemical energy into electrical energy. However, the fuel is not contained in the electrode, but supplied to the electrode from a separate subsystem. As long as fuel and oxidant are supplied to the FC in sufficient quantities, the generation of electrical energy is ensured. The challenge consists of evenly supplying all single cells of the stack with fuel and also in removing the reaction (or waste) products properly. The polymer electrolyte membrane fuel cell (PEMFC) is the most preferred FC due to its high-power density, low operating temperature (60°C−80°C) and low corrosion in comparison to other FC solutions (Uzunoglu and Alam, 2007; Mekhilef et al., 2012). It is noted that when using a hydrogen PEMFC, the waste product is just pure water. Other types of FCs include direct methanol fuel cells (DMFC), PEMFC, alkaline electrolyte fuel cells (AFC), phosphoric acid fuel cells (PAFC), molten carbonate fuel cell (MCFC) and solid oxide fuel cells (SOFC).

The use of FCEVs offers significant advantages such as reduced emissions of air pollutants, due to zero tailpipe emissions and due to the fact that hydrogen can be produced from renewable energy sources. In addition, their refilling requires the same amount of time as the filling of a conventional vehicle at a gas pump. This makes the adoption of these vehicles more likely in the near future (Camacho and Mihet-Popa, 2016). However, the scarcity of hydrogen fuel stations and the high initial cost are significant challenges for their successful deployment (Rao and Wang, 2011).

2.3 Energy sources in electric vehicles

2.3.1 Energy storage unit

One of the biggest challenges for the deployment of electric mobility is the storage of electrical energy. For this purpose, different ESS of high energy and power density can be employed in order to get the required energy. Fast charging, long service and life cycle, low purchase and maintenance costs are significant factors for their selection. High specific energy is required from a source to provide a long driving range, whereas high specific power helps to increase the acceleration. Moreover, ESS should be sized in order to store sufficient energy (in kilowatt hours) and provide adequate peak power (in kilowatts) for the EVs to have a specified acceleration performance and the capability to meet appropriate driving cycles. From the above, it is evident that a "perfect" energy source should have many and diverse characteristics, which can be used in different combinations, aiming to satisfy the desired power and energy needs. Therefore many requirements are considered for electric energy storage in EVs. The management system, power electronics interface, power conversion, safety, and protection are the significant requirements for efficient energy storage and distribution management of EV applications (Madanipour et al., 2016; Xing et al., 2011). ESS is classified into mechanical, electrochemical, chemical, electrical, thermal, and hybrid (IEC, 2011). Flywheels, secondary electrochemical batteries, FCs, UCs, superconducting magnetic coils, and hybrid ESSs are commonly used in EV powering applications (Hannan et al., 2014; Azidin et al., 2013; Madanipour et al., 2016).

2.3.1.1 Batteries

Batteries are storage devices that consist of one or more electrochemical cells that convert the stored chemical energy into electrical energy. Batteries are classified as primary or secondary. The primary types are not rechargeable but the secondary batteries, which are preferred for vehicular applications, are rechargeable. The capacity of batteries is measured in ampere hours (Ah) and the energy in the batteries is measured in watt hours (Wh). It should be mentioned that the energy stored in the battery (capacity × average voltage during discharge), which is measured in Wh, should be carefully calculated. The useable SOC of the battery, which is represented in percentage, is equally important as it indicates the status of charge available in the battery. Battery management is of great importance in order to operate in the window of SOC or SOC swing in order to prolong the life cycle of the battery. The capacity is proportional to the maximum discharge current. The maximum discharge current is typically represented by the index of C. For instance, a discharge rate of 1 C indicates that the battery is depleted in 1 hours while 2 C indicates that the battery is depleted in only half an hour.

Batteries have been the major energy source for EVs for a long period of time; though during the past decades they have gone through significant changes as new battery technologies have been invented and adopted, pursuing by this way new performance goals. Various types pf batteries with different capacity and characteristics are available; from these the following types are suitable for vehicular purposes: lead—acid batteries, nickel batteries, zinc batteries, lithium batteries, and metal—air batteries. Table 2.2 summarizes the technical characteristics of main battery types used in EVs.

The initial battery technology used in transportation was the lead—acid (Pb—acid) battery. The name of lead—acid comes from the combination of lead electrodes and acid used to generate electricity. The lead—acid battery is a matured and affordable technology, with apparent drawbacks

Table 2.2 Technical characteristics of main battery types used for EV (Suberu et al., 2014; Husain, 2010; Helmers and Marx, 2012).

Battery technology (type)	Specific energy (Wh/kg)	Energy/ volume coefficient (Wh/L)	Power/ weight coefficient (W/kg)	Self- discharge coefficient (% per 24 h)	Number of recharging cycles
Pb-acid	40	70	180	1	500
Ni—Cd	60	100	150	5	1350
NiMH	70	250	1000	2	1350
Li-ion	125	270	1800	1	1000
Li-ion polymer	200	300	3500	1	1000
Na—NiCl	125	300	1500	0	1000

associated with the handling of acid substances, the presence of lead in its construction, a low stored energy/weight ratio, and low stored energy/ volume ratio. The lead—acid battery was replaced by nickel-based batteries, such as nickel—cadmium (Ni—Cd) and nickel—metal hydride (Ni—MH). Nickel—cadmium (NiCd) is characterized by a long life cycle (approximately 1500 cycles); nonetheless the use of a heavy metal (cadmium) in its construction led to EU directives limiting the use of this type of battery, so as to protect human and animal health (Matheys et al., 2008). Furthermore, drawbacks such as poor charge and discharge efficiency, high self-discharge rate, memory effect, and poor performance in cold weather make this type of technology not suitable for EVs. Zero-emissions batteries research activity (ZEBRA) battery or the sodium—nickel chloride (Na—NiCL$_2$) was introduced into the EV industry at the same time as the Ni—MH battery. This type of battery uses sodium salt as the electrolyte and has the advantage of having a high stored energy density. ZEBRA batteries have lower life cycle costs than those of lead—acid batteries (Dustmann, 2004). They also have advantages such as higher or equal energy density compared with lithium batteries, lowest cost of any modern EV battery technology, high calendar life, ruggedness, fail-safe to cell failure (overcharging or overdischarging), and resistant to overcharge and overdischarge. However, due to their high operating temperatures (245°C—350°C), significant operational safety issues have arisen (Cluzel and Douglas, 2012).

Lithium-based batteries are promising energy storage devices for EVs, as they have many advantages, such as light weight, high specific energy, high specific power, and high energy density. In addition, lithium batteries have no memory effect and do not contain any poisonous metals, such as lead, mercury, or cadmium. Every lithium battery needs a protection circuit in every pack in order to maintain safe operation. As Table 2.3 indicates lithium-based batteries are used in the majority of EVs. Lithium-ion (Li-ion), lithium-ion polymer (LiPo), and lithium-iron phosphate are the most common lithium-based batteries. The main disadvantage is the high production cost compared with NiCad and Ni—MH battery packs. In a lithium battery, the lithium metal is the most expensive them but is less safe than a Li-ion battery. LiPo can adapt to a wide variety of packaging shapes, has good reliability and ruggedness, but it has poor conductivity and a low power density. For a high power density lithium battery, lithium-iron phosphate is a popular choice, in other words it has higher discharge current then most other lithium batteries.

Table 2.3 Different battery types for selected EVs (Young et al., 2013).

Company	Country	Vehicle model	Battery type
GM	United States	Chevy-Volt, Spark	Li-ion
		Saturn Vue Hybrid	NiMH
Ford	United States	Escape, Fusion, MKZ HEV	NiMH
Toyota	Japan	Prius, Lexus	NiMH
		Scion iQ EV, RAV4 EV	Li-ion
Honda	Japan	Civic, Insight	NiMH
Hyundai	South Korea	Sonata	Li polymer
Chrysler/ Fiat	United States	Fiat 500e	Li-ion
BMW	Germany	X6	NiMH
		Mini E, ActiveE	Li-ion
Mitsubishi	Japan	iMiEV	Li-ion
Nissan	Japan	Altima	NiMH
		Leaf EV	Li-ion
Tesla	United States	Roadster, Model S	Li-ion
Iveco	Italy	Electric Daily	Sodium−Ni−Cl

Battery technologies in the experimental phase, such as lithium−sulfur (Li−S), zinc−air (Zn−air) and lithium−air (Li−air) are promising solutions for high energy density and decreased cost. However, the Li−S battery has a high discharge rate and a short life cycle (Kolosnitsyn and Karaseva, 2008). On the other hand, Zn−air battery has very high energy density, yet it is characterized by low power density and a short life cycle. Similarly, the Li−air battery is still in the prototype stage and has not been commercialized yet.

2.3.1.2 Ultracapacitors

UCs or SCs, also known as double-layer capacitors, are electrochemical capacitors of high power density (compared to other energy storage devices). They consist of an electrical double layer and a separator. The separated charges provide a small amount of potential energy, as low as 2−3 V. The double layer is made of a nanoporous material, such as activated carbon that can improve the storage density. The capacitance values of SCs can reach 3000 F. Their characteristics include inter alia maintenance-free operation, longer operation cycle life (500,000 cycles), and insensitivity to environment temperature variation (Datasheet K2 Series Ultracapacitors, 2015). Moreover, due to their longer life cycle, high rate of charge/discharge, and low internal resistance, UCs have minimum heat loss and good reversibility (Burke, 2000). Depending on different energy storage mechanisms and electrode materials three types of UCs technologies are employed in EVs:

- Electric double-layer capacitors (EDLC)
- Carbon/carbon, pseudocapacitors
- Hybrid capacitors

The specific power density for these three types of UC is approximately 1000−2000 kW/kg for 95% efficient pulse but EDLC has a more power density than other types of UCs. Specific energy density of EDLC is the lowest (5−7 Wh/kg). It should be highlighted that the amount of energy stored per unit weight of SCs is between 3 and 5 Wh/kg, whereas that of a Li-ion battery is approximately 130−140 Wh/kg (Farcas et al., 2009). Therefore, the combination of SCs with FCs, which have low power density but high energy density, is a practical alternative to improve the efficiency and performance of HEVs. In addition, SCs have a high charging rate, which allows regenerative braking to be used more efficiently.

2.3.1.3 Flywheel energy storage

Flywheel energy storage (FES) systems are suitable for the application of EVs and power systems due to advanced power electronics and material engineering (Liu and Jiang, 2007). The efficiency and rated power of FESs fall within the range of 90%−95% and 0−50 MW, respectively (Xu et al., 2016). The flywheel comprises a rotating cylindrical body in a chamber, coupled bearings, and an energy transmission device, that is, generator/motor together mounted with a common shaft (Bolund et al., 2007). The energy maintained by the constantly rotating flywheel is converted to electrical energy by a transmission device. The advantages of FES compared to other storage forms for EV use can be summarized as follows: they are lighter; faster and more efficient at absorbing power from regenerative braking; they are economically affordable; they have a long life; there is no depth of discharge effect; and theoretically infinite charge and discharge cycles (Liu and Jiang, 2007). Nevertheless, high self-discharging features are attributed to windage and bearing friction losses. There are two types of FES: high- and low-speed FES systems (Bolund et al., 2007). A high-speed FES system transmits energy to drive the load via a generator, whereas a low-speed FES system receives energy to be charged from the power source via a motor. It is highlighted that with advanced technologies of materials and designs, FES systems are employed for energy storage application of EVs (Xu et al., 2016).

2.3.2 Energy generation unit

After using a battery as energy storage instead of a fuel tank, more of the electric generator can be built in the vehicle, in order to extend the range of a vehicle. Several types of energy generators including FCs, automotive thermoelectric generator (ATEG), as well as regenerative braking.

2.3.2.1 Fuel cell

FCs generate electricity by an electrochemical reaction, as chemical energy is converted into electric energy via the process of electrolysis. An FC has an anode (A), a cathode (C), and an electrolyte (E) between them. Fuel is introduced to the anode, gets oxidized there, the ions created go through the electrolyte to the cathode and combine with the other reactant. The electrons produced by oxidation at the anode produce the electricity. The by-product of an FC is heat and water. As already mentioned in Section 2.2.5 there are many types of FCs (i.e., DMFC, PEMFC, AFC, MCFC, SOFC). DMFC is used in portable electronics (mobile phones, tablet, laptops, and others) due to its low temperature operation, fast recharge, and greater energy capacity. The energy density of methanol is 4390 Wh/L compared with a Li-ion battery with a density of 620 Wh/L. DMFC, PEMFC, AFC, and PAFC are categorized as low operating temperature FCs. These FCs are currently used in transportation such as the Citaro fuel-cell bus and Honda FCX Clarity (passenger vehicle). The MCFC and SOFC are high operating temperature FCs, which are normally used in electric utility and distributed generation due to their high power output.

2.3.2.2 Automotive thermoelectric generator

An ATEG is a device that converts heat energy into electricity using the Seebeck effect. It can be employed either to ICEs or EVs, in order to achieve the optimum fuel economy. A typical ATEG consists of four main elements: a hot-side heat exchanger, a cold-side heat exchanger, thermoelectric materials, and a compression assembly system (Wikipedia, 2019). The lifetime of ATEG is around 10−20 years without maintenance with low $/watt installed capability. Table 2.4 sums up the characteristics of ATEG materials (Crane, 2006). The higher the ZT (thermoelectric material effectiveness) the more heat energy can be converted into electric energy. Materials of high Seebeck effect are semiconductors (attributed to high electrical conductivity and low thermal conductivity). The most common materials used are Bi_2Te_3, PbTe, and SiGe, whereas materials such as n-type BiSb, p-type, and $FeSi_2$ have good thermoelectric properties, but

Table 2.4 Characteristics of thermoelectric generator materials.

Temperature (°C)	Type	TEG material	ZT (maximum)
< 150	P	Bi_2Te_3	0.8
	N	Bi_2Te_3	0.8
150–500	P	Zn_4Sb_3	—
	p, n	PbTe	0.7, 0.8
	P	TeAgGeSb (TAGS)	1.2
500–700	P	$CeFe_4Sb_{12}$	1.1
	n	$CoSb_3$	0.8
700–900	p, n	SiGe	0.6–1.0
	p	LaTe	1.4

are less used. It is highlighted that automakers such as Nissan, GM, and BMW are testing ATEG with their vehicles.

2.3.2.3 Regenerative braking

Regenerative braking is an energy recovery mechanism, which slows a vehicle by the use of the vehicle's momentum to recover energy that would be otherwise lost to the brake discs as heat. When a vehicle is in coasting and braking modes, the kinetic energy from a moving car generates electricity back to the supply side, known as regenerative braking. There are four ways to capture the energy generated by regenerative braking:

1. Storing the generated electricity directly into ESS.
2. The hydraulic motors store energy in a small canister through compressed air.
3. Storing the generated electricity in FES as rotating energy.
4. Storing the generated electricity as gravitational energy (potential energy) through spring.

Table 2.5 depicts the different methods of recovering the braking energy. Regenerative braking operates together with the friction brake in some ratio when the vehicle starts to slow down. This is because the regenerative braking system does not generate enough energy to physically stop the vehicle. It also serves as a safety purpose of the vehicle.

2.4 Current charging technology and available charging infrastructure worldwide

2.4.1 Electric vehicles charging technology

The promotion of common open standards, interoperability and efficient data exchange is one of the most important steps toward facilitation of the

Table 2.5 Different methods of recovering the braking energy (MacKay, 2009; Valente and Ferreira, 2008).

Energy storage mechanism	Energy converter	Recovered energy from braking	Example current application	Fuel EPA
Electric energy storage	Electric motor/ generator	~50%	HEV, AEV	20%
Compressed gas energy storage	Hydraulic motor	>70%	Heavy-duty delivery vehicles	40%−50% improve
Flywheel energy storage	Rotational kinetic energy	>70%	F1	43%
Gravitational energy storage	Spring storage system	−	Train	5%

EV adoption. Energy and electric mobility service providers should work together with the EV industry in order to create a technological language in the field of EV charging that will shape the new e-mobility behavior and culture. Toward this direction the international standardization organizations have issued a series of standards that study, suggest, regulate, and coordinate the EV charging technology development worldwide. In this direction, the Electric Power Research Institute (EPRI) as well as the Society of Automotive Engineers (SAE) have set specific standards regarding the charging of EVs.

Charging of EVs can be employed via DC or AC systems. Different current and voltage configurations for charging, mentioned as "Levels" determine the time required for a full charge. These Levels vary in each country depending on frequency, voltage, electrical grid connection, and transmission standards. Wireless charging has also been investigated. Charging follows standards related to safety, installation, and connection of the EV supply equipment (EVSE) to the EV. EVSE is the "point-of-fueling" infrastructure that is used in order to deliver electrical energy from an electricity source to an EV charger. EVSE is also known as an electric recharging point including cords, connectors, and interfaces into utility power to deliver energy to an EV battery (Gordon-Bloomfield, 2010). EVs typically charge from conventional power outlets or dedicated charging stations, a time-consuming process; nonetheless this can be done overnight.

The safety standards that should be complied with by the chargers are the following (Williamson et al., 2015):

- SAE J2929: Electric and Hybrid Vehicle Propulsion Battery System Safety Standard
- ISO 26262: Road Vehicles—Functional safety
- ISO 6469-3: Electric Road Vehicles—Safety Specifications—Part 3: Protection of Persons Against
  Electric Hazards
- ECE R100: Protection against Electric Shock
- IEC 61000: Electromagnetic Compatibility (EMC)
- IEC 61851-21: EV Conductive Charging system—Part 21: EV Requirements for Conductive Connection to an AC/DC Supply
- IEC 60950: Safety of Information Technology Equipment
- UL 2202: EV Charging System Equipment
- FCC Part 15 Class B: The Federal Code of Regulation (CFR) FCC Part 15 for EMC Emission Measurement Services for Information Technology Equipment.
- IP6K9K, IP6K7 protection class
- −40°C−105°C ambient air temperature

It is pointed out that currently, the charging networks offer conventional AC charging outlets, based on the prevailing national vehicle charging specifications, standards, and protocols. During conventional AC charging, energy is transferred to the vehicle's onboard charger. In the United States, the AC charging standard used is the SAE J1772 standard, which is the same standard used in electrical outlets in homes in the United States and Japan, and is either 120 V 16 A, called Level 1, or 220 V 32 A, called Level 2 outlets. In Europe, the AC charging standard used is the IEC62196, Mode 1 which is a 230 V 16 A outlet. In Australia, the standard used is the AS 3112 with 230 V 15 A outlets. Finally, in the United Kingdom, charging stations use the BS 1363 standard 230 V 13 A outlets. It is noted that current trends with regard to the charging technology and infrastructure are explored in more detail in Chapter 3, Electric Vehicle Charging Within Smart Cities.

2.4.2 Charging power levels and infrastructure

As per EPRI'S and SAE's guidelines, charging can be categorized to AC Level 1, AC Level 2, and DC fast charging (DCFC) Level 3, along with the subsequent functionality requirements and safety system (Electric

Transportation Engineering Corporation, 2009). As per the new revision of SAE standards, DCFCs are categorized into DC Level 1 and DC Level 2 (Massachusetts Division of Energy Resources, 2014). In addition, as per International Electrotechnical Commission (IEC)'s guidelines four modes of EV charging can be discerned, namely, AC Mode 1 (slow), AC Mode 2 (slow), AC Mode 3 (slow/fast), and DC Mode 4 (fast) based on IEC 61851-1 (IEC, 61851-61851, 2010). The conversion from AC to DC for these charging levels occurs in the vehicle onboard charger (Metha, 2010).

2.4.3 Types of charging systems

A battery charger is a device used to transfer energy to a rechargeable EV battery by processing and controlling the electric current through it. An EV charger incorporates a rectifier to recharge an EV battery by converting AC to DC. Currently the charging of EV batteries is made by the following methods: (1) conductive charging method using plug connection, which is the most utilized method today; (2) inductive charging method; and (3) battery swapping (Nguyen et al., 2014; Zheng et al., 2014).

2.4.3.1 Conductive charging

Conductive charging suggests the direct connection of charger and vehicle. The charging is achieved through a cable connection that allows contact between the power supply and the battery. It consists of a rectifier and converter with some power factor correction and they are classified as onboard and offboard chargers. The onboard charger, which is embedded in the vehicle, contains the rectifier and the battery regulation system, whereas in the offboard charger these systems are placed on the charging station or the EVSE. Conductive charging is available in the Nissan Leaf, Tesla Roadster, and Chevy Volt (Metha, 2010).

2.4.3.2 Inductive charging

Inductive charging, also known as wireless charging, uses an electromagnetic field to transfer electricity to an EV battery. This system does not require the plugs and cables required in wired charging systems, there is no need to attach the cable to the car. The benefit of inductive charging is that it provides electrical safety under all weather conditions. Nonetheless this technology is not currently available for commercial EVs due to health and safety concerns. The specifications are determined by different standardization organizations in different countries: Canadian Safety Code 6 in Canada

(Consumer and Clinical Radiation Protection Bureau, 2009), IEEE C95.1 in the United States (IEEE, 1999), ICNIRP in Europe (Ahlbom et al., 1998), and ARPANSA in Australia (ARPANSA, 2002).

Depending on the operating frequency, efficiency, associated EMI, and other factors, there are different technologies to provide wireless charging. These include inductive power transfer (IPT), which is a mature technology, but it is contactless, not wireless; capacitive power transfer, which has significant advantages at lower power levels due to low cost and size (yet it is not suitable for higher power applications like EV charging); permanent magnet coupling power transfer, which is low in efficiency; resonant inductive power transfer (RIPT) and on-line inductive power transfer (OLPT), which seem to be the most promising techniques; however their infrastructure is quite challenging; resonant antennae power transfer has a similar concept to RIPT, but the resonant frequency in this case is in the MHz range and might cause health problems if not shielded properly.

2.4.3.3 Battery swapping

Battery swapping is a scheme that is used, so that the users can swap their empty battery with a fully charged one from a battery swapping station (BSS). BSSs have several benefits, such as long battery lives, less time consuming, and comparatively minimal cost to manage, given that batteries are collected and managed in centralized locations. Different charging techniques are available to charge an EV battery. Conventional charging methods are constant current (CC), constant voltage (CV), CP, taper charging, and trickle charging (www.mpoweruk.com). Advanced charging involves a combination of the above methods, such as CC/CV. Pulse current (PC)-charging and negative pulse-charging are also good charging strategies for fast charging of an EV battery (www.mpoweruk.com).

CC charging is the simplest technique as it employs a single low-level current to the discharged battery. In practice, the current level is set as 10% of the maximum rated capacity of the battery. This type of charging is best suited to nickel−cadmium and nickel−metal hydride batteries. CV applies constant charging voltage to the battery by varying the charging current, until the charging current drops to almost zero. This charging system is usually used for emergency power backup systems and is suitable for lead−acid batteries. Taper charging is done through an unregulated constant voltage source and the charging current reduces in an uncontrolled way due to an increase in the cell voltage as the charge builds up (Lynch and Salameh, 2007). It is noted that the taper charging method posts danger to the battery in the case of overcharging.

The CC−CV charging technique is utilized for the majority of commercial chargers, in order to charge a Li-ion battery as this battery has higher power and energy densities than others. The advantages of the CC−CV technique include limited charging current and voltage through battery controller utilization; thus overvoltages are prevented and thermal stress is reduced. First, a CC is applied to charge a battery until a predefined voltage level is achieved, and then a CV is used until a termination condition is reached. CC charging mode is faster than CV charging mode. The CV mode is used to prevent overvoltage charging, which can increase the loss of battery life (Lan-Ron and Jieh-Hwang, 2010).

PC-charging charges a battery by feeding charge current in pulses. The charging rate can be controlled by changing the width of pulses. Precise pulse control plays an important role in this charging method. It is estimated that the PC charging speed is more than two times faster than the speed of the CC−CV charging system (Hu et al., 2015). Chen (2009) proposed a new pulse-charging method, which is duty-varied voltage pulse-charging. This method instead of using the constant pulse width, detects and supplies the suitable charge pulse with varying pulse width to the battery to increase the charge speed and charge efficiency.

2.5 Impact of electric vehicles charging on electric power grid

Charging of EVs puts additional loads on the power grid, having adverse effects on the existing distribution network. The impact of charging EV fleets on the power grid is affected by a number of factors, such as the EV penetration levels, the EV battery characteristics, the charging patterns, the charging locations, the charging modes, the charging times, the battery SOC, EV driving patterns, fleet charging profiles, driving distances, demand response strategy, as well as tariffs. Additionally, the various possible charging rates in conjunction with the dynamic behavior of EVs complicate the potential impacts. This section summarizes the impacts of charging EVs on the grid:

- *Increased peak demand—impacts on load profile*: The deployment of EVs will have a significant impact on the load profile of the power grid. This is attributed to the fact that EVs are considered additional loads to be connected to the power grid. Furthermore, as it is estimated,

EVs are charged during residential peak load periods as EV owners tend to start charging their EVs once they reach home after work (Weiller, 2011). As a result, large fleets of EV charging will increase the peak load of the power grid load profile (Goncalves et al., 2013; Liu, 2012). A number of alternatives can deal with this issue [i.e., implementation of time-of-use (TOU) tariff system, which shifts the EV loads from peak hours to off-peak periods].

- *System components*: Charging of large EV fleets might cause overloading of power grid components (i.e., transformer and cable) due to inappropriate design. Akhavan-Rezai et al. (2012) have described the stress on distribution transformers attributed to the large penetration of PHEVs in a medium-voltage distribution system. A PHEV circuit impact model was proposed to randomly distribute the PHEV loads throughout the circuit. EV integration to a distribution network may significantly increase the transformer loading. In order to address this challenge, proper selection of the transformer, network planning, and load management are important to reduce the negative impacts of charging. Furthermore, the smart metering approach has been suggested (Masoum et al., 2010) as an answer to the maintenance of better power quality and reduction of THD in the distribution network to enhance transformer life.

- *Power quality—voltage profile*: Voltage drop can be caused by system congestion induced by simultaneous EV charging. A typical charging load is between 10 and 30 kW, so a simultaneous charging of multiple vehicles in the same distribution branch might cause congestion. Under these circumstances, the voltage at customer premises might drop below acceptable and/or statutory limits. EV charging from the power grid will cause voltage drop and voltage deviation on the EV interconnection point. Hence, large fleets of EV charging may make the network voltage violate the safe regulatory voltage requirements.

  - *Voltage instability*: Voltage variation in a three-phase system is a condition in which the differences between voltage magnitudes or phase angles are not equal. It occurs only in a polyphase (e.g., three-phase) system because of unequal loads in distribution lines. A number of studies suggests that the impacts of EVs are significant (Wang et al., 2012; Li et al., 2012), whereas others indicate that the effects are insignificant (Farkas et al., 2013). Nonetheless, all of these results are influenced by several factors, such as the strength of the test network, EV interconnection point, EV penetration levels, as well as the EV charging characteristics. In order to lessen the voltage instability, a smart charging plan is suggested as a viable solution (Li et al., 2012). This strategy can also significantly alleviate security problems even with large adoption of EVs.

- *Voltage sag*: Voltage sag is a reduction of RMS voltage at the power frequency for a period of 0.5 cycles to 1 minutes (IEEE, 1995). Voltage sag in a distribution network is attributed to short circuit, overload, or starting of electric motors. Lee et al (2014) modeled an EV charger and power converter utilizing an electromagnetic transient program, in order to estimate the voltage sag, which exceeded the limits at 20% EV penetration. A smart grid with a load management strategy provides tremendous prospects that can improve the voltage sag and the overall power quality of the distribution networks (Masoum et al., 2010).
- *Harmonics*: As per IEEE's guidelines, harmonics stand for the component of voltage and current spectrums whose frequencies are an integer multiplication of the reference frequency (i.e., 50 or 60 Hz) (IEEE, 1995). Total current harmonic distortions and total voltage harmonic distortions are expressed as percentages. It is noted that high harmonic distortion may lead to system components derating. A number of studies indicate that EV charging has no significant harmonic impact on the power grid; nonetheless, others indicate the opposite (Nguyen et al., 2014). An inclusion of a filtering device might address the harmonic distortion into the power grid.
- *System power losses*: Uncoordinated charging can result in great power losses and unacceptable voltage deviations. For this reason, alternatives should be found, so power utilities are able to bear these losses. In this direction, Nyns et al. (2010) suggested an objective function based on coordinated EV charging to reduce the system power loss. Similarly, it has been suggested (Deilami et al., 2011; Sortomme et al., 2011) that a coordinated charging strategy significantly minimizes power system losses.
- *Voltage instability*: The ability of an electric power grid to bring the operation back to steady-state condition after the occurrence of disturbance or transient is of great significance for a reliable power supply. As the EV load characteristics are different from the traditional household or industry (nonlinear), a number of studies have assessed their impact on voltage stability (Dharmakeerthi et al., 2014; Shi et al., 2012; Wu et al., 2012). A wide area control method that damps out

the oscillations during charging and discharging of an EV battery as well as bus voltage control method via a tap changing transformer have been suggested in order to overcome the voltage instability problem caused by EV penetration (Mitra and Venayagamoorthy, 2010; Rajakaruna et al., 2015). Another study proposed the use of a wide-area controller to provide auxiliary control signals to the power grid components for power system stability improvement during the EV charging and vehicle-to grid operation (Wu et al., 2012).

2.6 Impact of vehicle to grid technology to power grid

Vehicle-to-grid (V2G) refers to the technology of bidirectional flow of electricity between the EV and the grid. V2G technology describes a system in which EVs communicate with the power grid to sell demand respond services by either returning electricity to the grid or by throttling their charging rate (Robledo et al., 2018). V2G storage offers the possibility to store and discharge electricity generated from renewable energy sources such as solar and wind, with output that fluctuates depending on weather and time of day (Lindeman et al., 2018).

V2G services are beneficial both for EV owners and for power grids as they can help to increase the performance of a supply grid in terms of system efficiency, reliability, stability, and generation dispatch of distribution networks (Srivastava et al., 2010). In this context, EVs can serve both as a load and as a distributed storage device. When EVs are attached to distribution network, the battery of a vehicle can be used to deliver power to a grid at peak hours of load and thus enhance the reliability of a system. Further to this, V2G systems can provide sufficient voltage support to subsequently moderate the use of voltage regulators at distribution networks (Ohtaka et al., 2004; Wade et al., 2009). Additionally, V2G reduces distribution line loss, circumvents voltage drop, and achieves protective relay tripping (Ehsani et al., 2012). Summing up, it can be stated that V2G technology not only has the potential to stabilize grids in terms of peak-load savings (Rüther et al., 2014) but also it can reduce power system operating costs and secure distribution networks (Ma et al., 2013). Nonetheless, in order to extend the battery life, which will be affected by the frequent charging and discharging, intelligent charging systems should be employed (Mwasilu et al., 2014). This is further analyzed in Chapter 3, Electric Vehicle Charging Within Smart Cities.

2.7 Concluding remarks

As the world is in an energy transition to a low-carbon future reality the nature of the transportation systems as well as their connective infrastructure will also have to adapt. With the ever more stringent constraints on energy resources and environmental concerns, EVs will attract more interest from the automotive industry and the consumer. In this direction, four main types of EVs, namely, the BEVs, HEVs, the PHEVs, and the FCEVs have been discussed in detailed. The main difference lies in the fact that BEVs operate only on battery charge and therefore always employ the charge-depleting mode of operation requiring high power and high-energy battery packs. On the other hand, PHEVs offer the possibility of onboard battery charging and the option of charge depleting or charge sustaining modes of operation. Nonetheless issues regarding the energy storage, the system stability of power grid, the uninterruptible power availability, the dynamic resource allocation, the power quality, and range autonomy should be further developed, in order to facilitate EV deployment.

List of abbreviations

AC	alternating current
AFC	alkaline electrolyte fuel cells
AVT	alternative vehicle technologies
Bi_2Te_3	bismuth telluride
BSS	battery swapping station
CC	constant current
CD	charge depleting
$CoSb_3$	cobalt antimonide
CP	constant power
CS	charge sustaining
CV	constant voltage
DC	direct current
DCFC	direct current fast charging
DMFC	direct methanol fuel cells
EDLC	electric double-layer capacitors
EDVs	electric-drive vehicles
EI	electromagnetic interference
EPRI	electric power research institute
ESS	energy storage system
EVs	electric vehicles
EVSE	electric vehicle supply equipment
FC	fuel cell

FCEVs	fuel cell electric vehicles
FES	flywheel energy storage
HEVs	hybrid electric vehicles
ICE	internal combustion engine
IEC	International Electrotechnical Commission
IPT	inductive power transfer
MCFC	molten carbonate fuel cells
PAFC	phosphoric acid fuel cells
PbTe	lead telluride
PEMFC	proton exchange membrane fuel cells
RIPT	resonant inductive power transfer
SAE	Society of Automotive Engineers
SiGe	silicon germanium
SOC	state of charge
SOFC	solid oxide fuel cells
TOU	times of use
UCs	ultracapacitors
V2G	vehicle to grid
Zn_4Sb_3	zinc antimonide
ZT	thermoelectric material effectiveness

References

Ahlbom, A., Bergqvist, U., Bernhardt, J.H., Cesarini, J.P., Court, L.A., Grandolfo, M., et al., 1998. Guidelines: for limiting exposure to time-varying electric, magnetic and electromagnetic fields (up to 300 GHz). Health Phys. 74, 494–521.

Akhavan-Rezai, E., Shaaban, M.F., El-Saadany, E.F., Zidan, A., 2012. Uncoordinated charging impacts of electric vehicles on electric distribution grids: normal and fast charging comparison. In: Proceedings of the IEEE Power and Energy Society General Meeting, pp. 1–7.

Amjad, S., Neelakrishnan, S., Rudramoorthy, R., 2010. Review of design considerations and technological challenges for successful development and deployment of plug-in hybrid electric vehicles. Renew. Sustain. Energ. Rev. 14, 1104–1110.

Australian Radiation Protection and Nuclear Safety Agency (ARPANSA), 2002. Radiation Protection Standard: Maximum Exposure Levels to Radiofrequency Fields—3 kHz to 300 GHz; Radiation Protection Series Publication No. 3. ARPANSA, Melbourne, Australia.

Axsen, J., Kurani, K.S., 2013. Hybrid, plug-in hybrid, or electric – what do car buyers want. Energy Policy 61, 532–543.

Azidin, F.A., Hannan, M.A., Mohamed, A., 2013. Renewable energy technologies and hybrid electric vehicle challenges. Prz. Elektrotech. 89 (8), 150–156.

Bitsche, O., Gutmann, G., 2004. Systems for hybrid cars. J. Power Sources 127, pp. 8-1.

Bolund, B., Bernhoff, H., Leijon, M., 2007. Flywheel energy and power storage systems. Renew. Sustain. Energ. Rev. 11 (2), 235–258.

Burke, A., 2000. Ultracapacitors: why, how, and where is the technology. J. Power Sources 91, 37–50.

Camacho, O.M.F., Mihet-Popa, L., 2016. Fast charging and smart charging tests for electric vehicles batteries using renewable energy. Oil Gas Sci. Technol. 71, 13–25.

Chan, C.C., 2002. The state of the art of electric and hybrid vehicles. Proc. IEEE vol. 90 (no. 2), 247–275.

Chan, C.C., Chau, K.T., 2002. Modern Electric Vehicle Technology. Oxford University Press, New York.

Chan, C.C., Boucayrol, A., Chen, K., 2010. Electric, hybrid, and fuel-cell vehicles: architectures and modeling. IEEE Trans. Veh. Technol. 59, 589−598.

Chau, K.T., Wong, Y.S., 2002. Overview of power management in hybrid electric vehicles. Energ. Convers. Manag. 43, 1953−1968.

Chen, L.R., 2009. Design of duty-varied voltage pulse charger for improving Li-ion battery-charging response. IEEE Trans. Ind. Electron. 56 (2), 480−487.

Cluzel, C., Douglas, C., 2012. Cost and performance of EV batteries. Final Report Element Energy Limited, Cambridge, p. 21.

Consumer and Clinical Radiation Protection Bureau, 2009. Limits of human exposure to radiofrequency electromagnetic energy in the frequency range from 3 kHz to 300 GHz. Environmental and Radiation Health Sciences Directorate, Healthy Environments and Consumer Safety Branch, Health Canada. Safety Code, 6, 10−11.

Crane, D.T., 2006. Progress towards maximizing the performance of a thermoelectric power generator. In: Proceeding of the 25th International Conference on Thermoelectrics, Vienna, Austria, BSST LLC.

Damiani, L., Repetto, M., Prato, A.P., 2014. Improvement of power train efficiency through energy breakdown analysis. Appl. Energy 121, 252−263.

Datasheet K2 Series Ultracapacitors, 2015. Maxwell Technol. <http://www.maxwell.com/docs/DATASHEET_K2_SERIES_1015370.PDF>.

Deilami, S., Masoum, A.S., Moses, P.S., Masoum, M.A.S., 2011. Realtime coordination of plug-in electric vehicle charging in smart grids to minimize power losses and improve voltage profile. IEEE Trans. Smart Grid 2 (3), 456−467.

Dharmakeerthi, C.H., Mithulananthan, N., Saha, T.K., 2014. Impact of electric vehicle fast charging on power system voltage stability. Int. J. Elect. Power Energy Syst. 57, 241−249.

Duoba, M., 2011. Engine design, sizing and operation in hybrid electric vehicles. Argonne National Laboratory, Presentation at University of Wisconsin−Madison, ERC 2011 Symposium, June 8.

Dustmann, C.H., 2004. Advances in ZEBRA batteries. J. Power Sources 127 (1−2), 85−92.

EEA, 2016. Electric vehicles and the energy sector—impacts on Europe's future emissions, EEA briefing. <http://www.eea.europa.eu/themes/transport/electric-vehicles/electric-vehiclesand-energy>.

Ehsani, M., Milad Falahi, M., Lotfifard, S., 2012. Vehicle to grid services: potential and applications. Energies 5 (10), 4076−4090.

EIA, 2014. International Energy Outlook 2014. U.S. Energy Information Administration.

Electric Transportation Engineering Corporation, 2009. EV Charging Infrastructure Deployment Guidelines, BC, pp. 1−51.

IEC 61851−61851, 2010. Electric Vehicle Conductive Charging System-Part 1: General Requirements. 2.0 ed.

Farcas, C., Petreus, D., Ciocan, I., Palaghita, N., 2009. Modeling and simulation of supercapacitors. Design and technology of electronics packages (SIITME), Gyula, Hungary.

Farkas, C., Szucs, G., Prikler, L., 2013. Grid impacts of twin EV fast charging stations placed alongside a motorway. In: Proceedings of the IYCE 2013: 4th International Youth Conference on Energy, June 6−8, pp. 1−6.

Gao, Y., Ehsani, M., 2010. Design and control methodology of plug-in hybrid electric vehicles. IEEE Trans. Ind. Electron. 57, 633−640.

Gao, Y., Ehsani, M., Miller, J.M., 2005. Hybrid electric vehicle: overview and state of the art. In: Proceedings of the IEEE International Symposium on Industrial Electronics, Dubrovnik, Croatia, June 20–23, pp. 307–316.

Goncalves, R.L., Saraiva, J.T., Sousa, J.C., Mendes, V.T., 2013. Impact of electric vehicles on the electricity prices and on the load curves of the Iberian electricity market. In: Proceedings of the EEM 2013: 10th International Conference on the European Energy Market, May 27–31, pp. 1–8.

Gordon-Bloomfield N. What is EVSE and why-does-your-electric-car-charger-need-it. Greencar Reports 2010. <https://www.greencarreports.com/news/1050948_what-is-evse-and-why-does-your-electric-car-charger-need-it>.

Grunditz, E.A., Thiringer, T., 2016. Performance analysis of current bevs based on a comprehensive review of specifications. IEEE Trans. Transp. Electr. 2, 270–289.

Guarnieri, M., 2011. When cars went electric, part one [historical]. IEEE Ind. Electron. Mag. 5 (1), 61–62.

Guzzella, L., Sciarretta, A., 2007. Vehicle Propulsion Systems: Introduction to Modelling and Optimization, second ed., Springer, Berlin.

Guzzella, L., Sciarretta, A., 2013. Electric and hybrid-electric propulsion systems. Vehicle Propulsion Systems Introduction to Modeling and Optimization. Springer, Berlin Heidelberg, pp. 67–162.

Hannan, M.A., Azidin, F.A., Mohamed, A., 2014. Hybrid electric vehicles and their challenges: a review. Renew. Sustain. Energ. Rev. 29, 135–150.

Helmers, E., Marx, P., 2012. Electric cars: technical characteristics and environmental impact. Environ. Sci. Eur. 24, 14–29.

Hu, S., Wang, X., Wang, R., Wu, J., He, X., 2015. Hybrid sinusoidal-pulse charging strategy for Li-ion battery in electric vehicle application. In: Proceedings of the 2015 IEEE Applied Power Electronics Conference and Exposition (APEC), pp. 3117–3123.

Husain, I., 2010. Electric and Hybrid Vehicles: Design Fundamentals, second ed. CRC Press, Boca Raton FL.

IEA, 2015. World Energy Outlook 2015. International Energy Agency.

IEEE, 1995. Standards Coordinating Committee 22 on Power Quality, IEEE Std 1159. IEEE Recommended Practice for Monitoring Electric Power Quality.

IEEE, 1999. Standard for Safety Levels with Respect to Human Exposure to Radio Frequency Electromagnetic Fields, 3 kHz to 300 GHz, IEEE Std C95.1, IEEE, New York.

Khan, M.C., Kar, N., 2009. Hybrid electric vehicles for sustainable transportation: a Canadian perspective. World Electr. Veh. J. 3.

Kolosnitsyn, V.S., Karaseva, E.V., 2008. Lithium-sulfur batteries: problems and solutions. Russ. J. Electrochem. 44 (5), 506–509.

Lan-Ron, D., Jieh-Hwang, Y., 2010. ILP-based algorithm for lithium-ion battery charging profile. 2010 IEEE International Symposium on Industrial Electronics (ISIE) 2286–2291.

Lee, S.J., Kim, J.H., Kim, D.U., Go, H.S., Kim, C.H., Kim, E.S., et al., 2014. Evaluation of voltage sag and unbalance due to the system connection of electric vehicles on distribution system. J. Electr. Eng. Technol. 9, 452–460.

Li, H.L., Bai, X.M., Tan, W., 2012. Impacts of plug-in hybrid electric vehicles charging on distribution grid and smart charging. In: Proceedings of the IEEE POWERCON 2012: International Conference on Power System Technology, October 30–November 2, pp. 1–5.

Lindeman, T., Pearson, J., Maiberg, E.l., 2018. Electric school buses can be backup batteries for the US power grid. <https://www.vice.com/en_us/article/bj3x74/electric-school-buses-vehicle-to-grid-v2g-power-grid>.

Liu, J., 2012. Electric vehicle charging infrastructure assignment and power grid impacts assessment in Beijing.

Liu, H., Jiang, J., 2007. Flywheel energy storage — an upswing technology for energy sustainability. Energy Build. 39 (5), 599—604.

Liu, J, Peng, H, Filipi, Z., 2005. Modeling and control analysis of toyota hybrid system. In: 2005 IEEE/ASME International Conference Advanced Intelligent Mechatronics Proceedings, pp. 134—139.

Lynch, W.A., Salameh, Z.M., 2007. Taper charge method for a Nickel-Cadmium electric vehicle traction battery. In: Proceedings of the IEEE Power Engineering Society General Meeting, June 24—28, pp. 1—5.

Ma, Z., Callaway, D.S., Hiskens, I.A., 2013. Decentralized charging control of large populations of plug-in electric vehicles. IEEE Trans. Control. Syst. Technol. 21 (1), 67—78.

MacKay, D.J.C., 2009. Sustainable Energy—Without the Hot Air. UIT Cambridge, Cambridge, pp. 125—126.

Madanipour, V., Montazeri-Gh, M., Mahmoodik, M., 2016. Multi-objective component sizing of plug-in hybrid electric vehicle for optimal energy management. Clean. Technol. Env. Policy 18 (4), 1189—1202.

Masoum, M.A.S., Moses, P.S., Deilami, S., 2010. Load management in smart grids considering harmonic distortion and transformer derating. In: IEEE Innovative Smart Grid Technologies Europe (ISGT Europe), Gaithersburg, MD, pp. 1—7.

Massachusetts Division of Energy Resource, 2014. Installation Guide for Electric Vehicle Supply Equipment, pp. 1—26.

Matheys, J., Van Mierlo, J., Timmermans, J.-M., Van den Bossche, P., 2008. Life-cycle assessment of batteries in the context of the EU directive on end-of-life vehicles. Int. J. Veh. Des. 46, 189—203.

Mekhilef, S., Saidur, R., Safari, A., 2012. Comparative study of different fuel cell technologies. Renew. Sustain. Energ. Rev. 16, 981—989.

Mercier, C., 2012. Advanced power train controls. Lecture at IFP School PSA Peugeot Citroën.

Metha, S., 2010. Electric plug-in vehicle/electric vehicle status report. Electr. Eng. 1—15.

Mitra, P., Venayagamoorthy, G.K., 2010. Wide area control for improving stability of a power system with plug-in electric vehicles. IET Gener. Transm. Distrib. 4 (10), 1151—1163.

Mwasilu, F., Justo, J.J., Kim, E.K., Do, T.D., Jung, J.W., 2014. Electric vehicles and smart grid interaction: a review on vehicle to grid and renewable energy sources integration. Renew. Sustain. Energ. Rev. 34, 501—516.

Nanaki, E.A., Koronos, C.J., 2016. Climate change mitigation and deployment of electric vehicles in urban areas. J. Renew. Energ. 99, 1153—1160.

Nanaki, E.A., Xydis, G.A., Koronos, C.J., 2015. Electric vehicle deployment in urban areas. J. Indoor Built Environ. 25 (7), 1065—1074. doi: 10.1177/1420326X15623078 ibe.sagepub.com.

Nguyen, T.D., Li, S., Li, W., Mi, C.C., 2014. Feasibility study on bipolar pads for efficient wireless power chargers. In: Proceedings of the Twenty-Ninth Annual IEEE Applied Power Electronic Conference and Exposition (APEC), pp. 1676—1682.

Nyns, K.C., Haesen, E., Driesen, J., 2010. The impact of charging plug-in hybrid electric vehicles on a residential distribution grid. IEEE Trans. Power Syst. 25 (1), 371—380.

Ohtaka, T., Uchida, A., Iwamoto, S., 2004. A voltage control strategy with NAS battery systems considering interconnection of distributed generations. In: Proceedings of the International Conference on Power System Technology (PowerCon). pp. 226—231.

Pollet, B.G., StaffellI, Shang, J.L., 2012. Current status of hybrid, battery and fuel cell electric vehicles: from electrochemistry to market prospects. Electrochim. Acta 84, 235—249.

Poullikkas, A., 2015. Sustainable options for electric vehicle technologies. Renew. Sustain Energy Rev. 41, 1277−1287.

Rajashekara, K., 2013. Present status and future trends in electric vehicle propulsion technologies. IEEE J. Emerg. Sel. Top. Power Electron. 1, 3−10.

Rao, Z., Wang, S., 2011. A review of power battery thermal energy management. Renew. Sustain. Energy Rev. Vol. 15 (No. 9), 4554−4571.

Robledo, C.B., Oldenbroek, V., Abbruzzese, F., van Wijk, A.J.M., 2018. Integrating a hydrogen fuel cell electric vehicle with vehicle-to-grid technology, photovoltaic power and a residential building. Appl. Energy, 215.

Rüther, R., Drude, L., Pereira Jr, L.C., 2014. Photovoltaics (PV) and electric vehicle-to-grid (V2G) strategies for peak demand reduction in urban regions in Brazil in a smart grid environment. Renew. Energy 68, 443−451.

Shi, R., Zhang, X.P., Kong, D.C., Deng, N., Wang, P.Y., 2012. Dynamic impacts of fast-charging stations for electric vehicles on active distribution networks. In: Proceedings of the IEEE PES ISGT 2012: Innovative Smart Grid Technologies Asia, May 21−24, pp. 1−6.

Sortomme, E., Hindi, E.M.M., MacPherson, S.D.J., Venkata, S.S., 2011. Coordinated charging of plug-in hybrid electric vehicles to minimize distribution system losses. IEEE Trans. Smart Grid 2 (1), 198−205.

Srivastava, A.K., Annabathina, B., Kamalasadan, S., 2010. The challenges and policy options for integrating plug-in hybrid electric vehicle into the electric grid. Electr. J. 23 (3), 83−91.

Suberu, M.Y., Mustafa, M.W., Bashir, N., 2014. Energy storage systems for renewable energy power sector integration and mitigation of intermittency. Renew. Sustain. Energy Rev. 35, 499−514.

Sutikno, T., Idris, N.R.N., Jidin, A., 2014. A review of direct torque control of induction motors for sustainable reliability and energy efficient drives. Renew. Sustain. Energy Rev. 32, 548−558.

Takaishi, T., Numata, A., Nakano, R., Sakaguchi, K., 2008. Approach to High Efficiency Diesel and Gas Engines, 45, Mitsubishi Heavy Industries, Ltd Technical Review.

Technology CfAA, 2018. HEV levels. <http://autocaatorg/Technologies/Hybrid_and_Battery_Electric_Vehicles/HEV_Levels/> (accessed January 2019).

The International Electrotechnical Commission (IEC), 2011. Electrical Energy Storage. White paper, Geneva, Switzerland.

Tie, S.F., Tan, C.W., 2013. A review of energy sources and energy management system in electric vehicles. Renew. Sustain. Energy Rev. 20, 82−102.

Uzunoglu, M., Alam, M.S., 2007. Dynamic modeling, design and simulation of a PEM fuel cell/ultra-capacitor hybrid system for vehicular applications. Energy Convers. Manag. 48, 1544−1553.

Valente, S., Ferreira, H., 2008. Braking Energy Regeneration Using Hydraulic Systems. Polytechnic Institute of Porto (IPP), Portugal.

Varga, B.O., 2012. Energy management of electric and hybrid vehicles dependent on power train configuration. Cent. Eur. J. Eng. 2, 253−263.

Wade, N., Taylor, P., Lang, P., Svensson, J., 2009. Energy storage for power flow management and voltage control on an 11kV UK distribution network. In: Proceedings of the 20th International Conference and Exhibition on Electricity Distribution, pp. 1−4.

Wager, G., Whale, J., Braunl, T., 2016. Driving electric vehicles at highway speeds: the effect of higher driving speeds on energy consumption and driving range for electric vehicles in Australia. Renew. Sustain. Energy Rev. 63, 158−165.

Wang, H., Song, Q., Zhang, L., Wen, F., Huang, J., 2012. Load characteristics of electric vehicles in charging and discharging states and impacts on distribution systems.

In: Proceedings of the SUPERGEN 2012: International Conference on Sustainable Power Generation and Supply, September 8—9, pp. 1—7.

Weiller, C., 2011. Plug-in hybrid electric vehicle impacts on hourly electricity demand in the United States. Energy Policy 39 (6), 3766—3778.

Wikipedia, 2019. Thermoelectric generator. <https://en.wikipedia.org/wiki/Automotive_thermoelectric_generator> (accessed February 2019).

Williamson, S.S., Rathore, A.K., Musavi, F., 2015. Industrial electronics for electric transportation: current state of-the-art and future challenges. IEEE Trans. Ind. Electron. 62, 3021—3032.

Wu, D., Chau, K.T., Liu, C., Gao, S., Li, F., 2012. Transient stability analysis of SMES for smart grid with vehicle-to-grid operation. IEEE Trans. Appl. Supercond. 22 (3), 5701105.

Xing, Y., Ma, E.W.M., Tsui, K.L., Pecht, M., 2011. Battery management systems in electric and hybrid vehicles. Energies 4, 1840—1857.

Xu, Y., Pi, H.W., Ren, T.Q., Yang, Y., Ding, H.F., Peng, T., et al., 2016. Design of a multipulse high-magnetic-field system based on flywheel energy storage. IEEE Trans. Appl. Supercond. 26 (4), 5207005.

Yang, W.-C., 2000. Fuel cell electric vehicles: recent advances challenges-review. Int. J. Autom. Technol. 1, 9—16.

Young, K., Wang, C., Strunz, K., 2013. Electric vehicle battery technologies. Electric Vehicle Integration into Modern Power Networks. Springer, New York, pp. 15—56.

Zheng, Y., Dong, Z., Xu, Y., Meng, K., Zhao, J., Qiu, J., 2014. Electric vehicle battery charging/swap stations in distribution systems: comparison study and optimal planning. IEEE Trans. Power Syst. 29 (1), 221—229.

CHAPTER 3

Electric vehicle charging within smart cities

3.1 Introduction

Over the past decade, increasing concern over the depletion of fossil fuels as well as the adverse effects of climate change have impelled the transition to zero-carbon emission energy systems. Especially in the case of transportation energy systems, electric vehicles (EVs) are considered to be an efficient transportation technology, in order to mitigate greenhouse gas emissions (GHGs) and regional emissions in urban areas such as cities (Nanaki and Koroneos, 2016). Many governments have taken measures to encourage the use of EVs both in the private and public sectors. Worldwide the market growth has been higher than 30% for 5 consecutive years, leading to an accumulated number of 5 million EVs on the road by 2019 (IEA, 2019). The successful deployment of EVs entails the development of a charging infrastructure that is accessible, easy to use, and relatively inexpensive.

However, the electrification of transport constitutes a considerable additional load for the electricity grid, leading to power grid problems (i.e., voltage falls, power losses, etc.). As a matter of fact, the impact of electric mobility may amount up to an additional 15% of average annual electricity demand of households (Figenbaum, 2017). Taking into consideration the fact that the charging profiles of EVs tend to overlap with household consumption profiles, the power consumption peaks are expected to increase significantly as a result of EV charging (Muratori, 2018) reaching the limits of the grid capacity (Daina et al., 2017). As such, electric mobility provides a substantial challenge to grid operators to facilitate sufficient capacity for charging EVs and to maintain grid stability and security, while limiting investment in grid reinforcements.

In this context, in order to optimize EVs charging a well-coordinated and controlled infrastructure is needed. Controlled charging of a large numbers of EVs can be well supported with the help of the smart grid. Amplification of peak demand and voltage fluctuations, demand smart charging approaches to control the electrification of EVs. Smart charging deals with challenges like stability, infrastructure modifications, and load management. Smart cities, which rely on the deployment of information

Electric Vehicles for Smart Cities
DOI: https://doi.org/10.1016/B978-0-12-815801-2.00001-0

and communication technology, provide a new opportunity for the development of smart charging approaches. Optimally charged EVs not only enhance the smart grid power efficiency but can also provide other advance features like ancillary services, such as vehicle-to-grid (V2G).

This chapter aims to present different charging mechanisms and strategies as well as tools within the smart city concept. The objective is to illustrate the state-of-the-art, to identify the challenges as well as to explore the implications of these practices for policy makers and regulators. The concept of the smart charging concept and the two main control architectures of smart charging (centralized and decentralized control) are presented. Innovative concepts such as building-to-grid (B2G), V2G, sun-to-vehicle (S2V), and vehicle-to-infrastructure (V2I) are also mentioned. A brief overview of some existing smart charging projects around the world is also presented. Open issues, challenges, and future research directions related to EVs charging are also highlighted.

3.2 The concept of the smart city

The concept of the smart city has received much attention during the past decade. Smart cities are key enablers of the energy transition to zero-carbon cities. Many definitions have been suggested, including the terms of intelligent city, digital city, future-forward city, connected city, etc. Despite the large number of terms, it can be stated that a smart city incorporates the use of smart technologies aiming to improve economic, social, and environmental standards (Nanaki and Xydis, 2019). To be more specific, a smart city places emphasis on:

- the utilization of networked infrastructure to improve economic and political efficiency and enable social, cultural, and urban development;
- business-led urban development;
- the aim of achieving the social inclusion of various urban residents in public services;
- the crucial role of high-tech and creative industries in long-term urban growth;
- the role of social and relational capital in urban development; and
- the role of social and environmental sustainability.

In this manner, the main objective of smart cities is to improve the quality of life through the deployment and use of smart technologies; while supporting the economic productivity through a sustainable industrial ecosystem development.

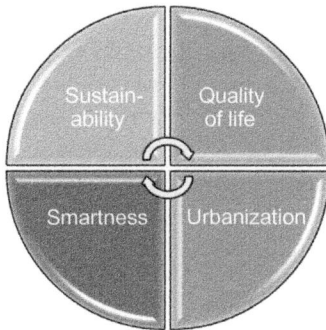

Figure 3.1 Characteristics of smart cities.

As per European's Smart Cities initiative the six key characteristics of smart cities (Giffinger et al., 2007) include smart governance, smart people, smart mobility, smart economy, smart environment, and smart living. Many studies (i.e., Batty et al., 2012) have employed these characteristics, in order to develop indicators as well as frameworks and strategies.

Based on the above, it can be stated that the characteristics of the smart city are those that can address in a "smart way" the challenges of urbanization such as waste management, air pollution, traffic congestion, health effects, resource scarcity, and infrastructure aging (Fig. 3.1). Finally, it is highlighted that the process of developing the abovementioned characteristics should take into consideration the need for government leadership and organizational change, the city plan, the existence of a robust legal framework, the presence of a technological model, and the reinforcement of business models that will ensure the effectiveness of the measures adopted.

3.3 Charging infrastructure

Charging infrastructure is of great significance for the successful deployment of EVs in urban areas. Charging stations, charging points, and charging modes constitute the basic parts of the charging architecture. The term "charging station" usually refers to a single piece of PEV charging equipment, whereas a "charging point" refers to the individual connectors that can charge a PEV at any given time. Box 3.1 summarizes basic definitions of charging architecture.

Charging modes, which are specified in IEC 61851 (I. T. C. 69, 2010), involve the level of communication between the vehicle and the charging station (Meissner and Richter, 2003). With regard to connectors,

BOX 3.1 Basic charging definitions

Charging post: a facility where an e-car can be charged with electricity. A charging post can have multiple (often two) charging points.

Charging point: a plug-in connection (a charging post generally has two).

Normal charging: charging at a relatively low voltage with the charger in the car, suitable for charging while parked (i.e., at the work place).

High-speed charging: charging with a high voltage whereby the charger is in the high-speed charging post. The charging strength begins at 50 kW and rises to 350 kW for ultrafast charging. Particularly suitable when parking for shorter periods (approx. 20 minutes).

Flexible charging: the speed with which a car is charged during a session varies in the course of the day. The charging posts take account of expected peaks and dips on the electricity grid.

Smart charging: the charging speed depends on the total energy demand on the network and the supply of locally generated renewable energy. The vehicle's battery can also contribute to the grid during peak demand. This also requires smart charging posts where the owner of the vehicle can control the process, including the level of the tariff.

these are regulated by IEC 62196 (IEC, 2014) and modified by IEC 62196-2 and IEC 62196-3 (IEC, 2011). The Schuko connector is most widely used to charge electric motorcycles and bicycles. Table 3.1 lists the main characteristics of existing charging modes and charging types.

Charging points include all the necessary protections and one or more outlet bases or cable-connector sets for charging in mode 1 or 2, whereas an electric vehicle charging system (EVCS) comprises a set of equipment installed to provide electrical power to recharge an EV, including charging station protections, the connecting cable, and the electrical outlet or connector. This system enables the communication between the EV and the fixed installation, and it is used for charging in mode 3. UNE/EN standard 61851 incorporates the abovementioned elements. It is highlighted that EVCSs can be categorized to charging posts (outdoor use) and wall boxes (indoor use).

3.3.1 Types of charging systems

Depending on the mode of energy transfer the charging of batteries can be categorized to the following:

- *Conductive charging*: This type of charging is a simple and highly efficient, as it transfers power through direct contact. A conductor is used

Table 3.1 Main specifications of charging modes and charging types.

Term	Definition	Options
Charging mode	The charging mode describes: • the speed at which a vehicle is charged; • defines the required voltage, current and speed which charging cables of a particular mode have to provide; • defines the level of communication between the vehicle and the power outlet. The modes are defined in the international industry norm DIN19 IEC20 61851	*Mode 1*: Slow AC charging household charging using home plugs, charging device integrated in vehicle (250 V 1-phase or 480 V 3-phase; max. 16 A; 3.7–11 kW). *Mode 2*: Slow AC charging with semi-active connection to vehicle to communicate for safety purposes if 32 A can be drawn (250 V 1-phase or 400-V 3-phase; max. 32 A; 7.4-22 kW). *Mode 3*: AC charging with active connection between charger and vehicle, that is, to ensure safety and communicate smart charging (250 V 1-phase or 480 V 3-phase; max. 32 A; 14.5–43.5 kW). *Mode 4*: DC fast charging, active connection between charger and vehicle.
Charging type	The charging type describes the plug that connects the vehicle and the charging point.	*Type 1* (Yazaki, SAE21 J1772-2009): Allows slow charging (North America). *Type 2* (Mennekes, VDE22-AR-E 2623-2-2): EU standard for slow charging. *Type 3* (EV Plug Alliance): Allows slow charging, found in Italy and France. Not installed since 2012. *Type 4* (CHAdeMO, JEVS23 G105-1993): Allows slow and fast charging, found in Japan and Europe. *CCS* (Combined Charging System, Type 2 and Combo 2): EU plug standard for Type 2 slow charging and Combo 2 fast charging. *Tesla Charger*: International slow charging for Tesla vehicles. *Tesla Supercharger*: International fast charging for Tesla vehicles.

in order to connect the electronic devices to the extent of energy transfer. This type of charging is available in the Nissan Leaf, Tesla Roadster, and Chevy Volt (Metha, 2010).

- *Inductive charging*: This type of charging is also known as wireless charging, and employs an electromagnetic field to transfer electricity to an EV battery. In this type of charging, a primary coil is placed on the surface or beneath it, and the secondary coil is placed under the vehicle. The mutual coupling within inductively coupled power transfer systems is generally weak. To deliver the necessary power and ensure equipment sizes remain manageable, it is necessary to operate at high frequencies. At present, the operational frequency for high-power applications is limited to below 100 kHz as a result of switching losses. Moreover, resonant circuits are normally employed in the primary and/or secondary networks to further boost the power transfer capability, while minimizing the required voltage and current ratings of the power supply (Wang et al., 2005). The charging process starts by placing the vehicle on the charging station and ends when the battery is fully charged or if the vehicle is removed. Contactless energy transfer technology is spreading in city transportation applications because of their high mobility and flexibility in loading (Jiang et al., 2016). This method provides electrical safety under all weather conditions. However, current state-of-the-art inductive chargers are low efficiency and have a high power loss. Nonetheless, a commercial inductive charger can deliver high power at an efficiency of up to 86%.
- *Battery swapping*: This type of charging involves exchanging the empty battery with a fully charged one at a battery swapping station (BSS). The battery exchange system or "battery swap" is based on paying for a monthly rental of a battery, which may be exchanged after it is exhausted for a fully charged battery in any of the stations planned for this service. This scheme has many advantages, including long battery lives, low time consumption, as well as minimal cost to manage. This type of charging gives the chance to avoid the peak demand of the grid (Zheng et al., 2014). On the other hand, issues such as the high investment cost and huge space that are required for BSS construction, as well as battery safety issues constitute the drawbacks of this type of charging (Liu et al., 2011).

3.3.2 Charging power levels

The charging equipment or "electric vehicle supply equipment" (EVSE) is differentiated based on the charge power, which is used to charge the

PEVs and BEVs (the capacity of which range usually between 5−15 kWh and 25−40 kW, respectively) (Broussely, 2010). The categories are as follows:

- *Level 1* (<3.7 kW): This type of charging enables the vehicle to plug directly into a standard AC outlet and the vehicle's onboard charging equipment converts the power into DC. In most European countries, the charging power reaches 3.7 kW, that is, 230 V and 16 A. However, there are other European countries with lower power, such as the United Kingdom (230 V and 13 A) and Switzerland (230 V and 10 A). This type of charging is often used to charge the vehicles overnight at home or at the workplace. Charging can take 8−10 hours. Slow charging is sometimes called Mode 2 charging, a reference to the type of cable used (AFD, 2020).

- *Level 2* (>3.7 kW and <22 kW): These type of chargers tend to be installed in car parks, supermarkets, leisure centers, and houses with off-street parking. Charging requires approximately 3−4 hours.

- *Level 3* (>22 kW and <43.5 kW for AC) and (<400 kW for DC): This type of charging is performed using external chargers, due to the charger size and cooling requirements of the electronics integrated. This type of charging can employ either an AC three-phase charger or a DC. The goal of a DC charger is to be able to provide up to 80% of the PEV's charging levels in 20 minutes or less. With batteries becoming larger (i.e., increased electrical storage capacity), DC charging will move to higher power levels to continue to meet this goal. At present, fast charging puts a strain on batteries, especially if fast charging is carried out often. As a matter of fact, only a limited number of cars have batteries that allow for ultrafast or high-power charging, potentially leading to different battery costs (NREL, 2017). So far, only the Porsche Taycan has a battery that can handle 800 V or 240 kW (at 300 A) (Porsche, 2018).

It should be highlighted that fast charging poses significant challenges to power sector operators, as the additional loads to the electricity network can increase the peak loads, thereby stressing power system flexibility. In this direction, measures aimed to limit the impact of fast chargers during peak hours are considered. For instance, the City of Amsterdam aims to constrain the maximum capacity of chargers during peak hours and Tesla plans to offset part of the potential power system constraints by adding large solar arrays to its supercharger network and upcoming mega chargers (ElaadNL, 2018) (Table 3.2).

Table 3.2 Charging characteristics of different types of EVs (Rajakaruna et al., 2015; Schey, 2013).

Model	Vehicle type	Battery size (kW h)	Energy available (kW h)	Range (km)	Energy consumption (kW h/kW)	AC Level 1		AC Level 2		DC Level 3	
						Demand (kW)	Charge time(h)	Demand (kW)	Charge time(h)	Demand (kW)	Charge time(h)
Nissan Leaf	EV	24	19.2	160	0.12	1.8	11	6.6	2.9	50	0.4
Mitsubishi i-MiEV	EV	16	12.8	150	0.086	1.5	9	3.6	4	50	0.26
Toyota RAV4	EV	41.8	32.18	160	0.20	1.9	17	9.6	3.35	50	0.64
Cooper (BMW)	EV	28	21.5	160	0.13	1.9	11	7.6	2.8	50	0.43
Sabaru Stella	EV	9.2	7.1	80	0.09	1.8	4	3.8	2	47	0.15
Tesla Roadster	EV	53	37.1	340	0.11	1.8	21	16.8	2.2	100	0.37
Chevrolet Volt	PHEV	17.1	13.7	64	0.21	1.4	10	3.6	4	N/A	N/A
Toyota Prius	PHEV	5.2	4.1	25	0.16	1.8	3	3.2	1.5	N/A	N/A

3.3.3 Standardization: Current trends

Harmonized charging standards are of crucial importance for the energy transition to zero-emission cities, as they ensure accessibility for EV charging networks and drastically reduce investment risks for the stakeholders. Table 3.3 summarizes the charging standards in a number of countries. Currently, 41 countries have specified a hardware charging standard. In 2019 the trends with regard to hardware charging involve inter alia the following:

A Memorandum of Understanding (MoU) between the Japanese CHAdeMO Association and the China Electricity Council (GB/T standard) (CHAdeMO, 2018b), was signed in 2018 and involves the development of a common ultrafast charging standard (up to 900 kW) including V2G functionality, as well as the development of a new standard for two-wheelers and low-speed electric vehicles (IEEE, 2018).

- CCS Combo 2 and CHAdeMO have become the mandated plugs for DC fast chargers in India. The IEC 62196-2 Type 2 is retained as the main AC fast charging standard, as well as the Bharat standard for AC (IEC 60309) and DC slow charging (Government of India, 2018).
- The United States released the Society of Automotive Engineers (SAE) J3068 standard that specifically targets medium- and heavy-freight trucks (SAE International, 2018).
- Singapore confirmed IEC 62196-2 Type 2 as its standard for AC charging and CCS Combo2 as standard for DC charging (CharIN, 2019).
- CHAdeMO released its new protocol (CHAdeMO 2.0) that enables high power charging up to 400 kW (CHAdeMO, 2018a).
- Tesla released its version 3 (V3) of the supercharger network (March 2019), which allows charging up to 250 kW (doubling the recharging speed relative to V2 network) (Tesla, 2019). New Model 3 Tesla vehicles can be charged via the V3 network, whereas other Tesla models can be upgraded via a software update. In addition to the current accessibility to CHAdeMO standard via adapters, Tesla is making the combined charging system (CCS) standard accessible in several countries and regions. In Europe, where the CCS Combo 2 is mandatory according to the provisions of the EU Alternative Fuels Infrastructure (AFI) Directive (EC, 2014), the new Tesla Model 3 will make use of CCS Combo 2 for fast charging (Electrek, 2018).

Table 3.3 Charging standards in selected countries.

Selected countries	Conventional plugs Level 1	Slow chargers Level 2	Fast chargers Level 3	
Australia	AC Type 1	AC IEC 62196–2 Type 2	AC three-phase	DC • Accepts all IEC 62196 standards • TESLA has its own connector
China	Type 1	GB/T 20234 AC		GB/T 202034 DC
European Union	Type C/F/G	IEC 62196-2 Type 2	IEC 62196–2 Type 2	• Requires CCS Combo 2(IEC 62196–3) and accepts all IEC 62196–3 standards • TESLA has its own connector

Japan	Type B	• SAE J1772 Type 1 • Tesla has its own connector		• Accepts all IEC 62196-3 standards • TESLA has its own connector
North America	• Type B • SAE J1772 Type 1	• SAE J1772 Type 1 • Tesla has its own connector	SAE J3068	• Accepts CCS Combo • TESLA has its own connector

3.3.4 Communication protocols

Standard communication protocols carry out the communication between the vehicle, the charging stations, the grid, and the roaming platforms. Communication functions include identification, authorization, battery status, etc. The communication methods of the various charging protocols rely on different physical connections; thus a variety of different communication protocols can be encountered worldwide. The standard IEC 61815 is derived from SAEJ177 adopted to Asian and European line voltage levels. The IEC 61815 possesses three modes of operation corresponding to three level of SAEJ1772. The Mode 1 of IEC 61815 relates to residential charging with unique grounding requirements, as the current is slightly higher in this standard, compared to SAEJ1772. The Mode utilizes the same voltage levels as Mode 1 with 32 A of current, while Mode 3 allows current up to 250 A.

In general, the IEC 61851-1 standard (IEC, 2017) sums up the basic charging requirements for nearly all chargers. Level 1, level 2, and Tesla AC connectors have no direct communication in their cables and require off-board controls for authentication, payment, and smart charging, such as via an app. Level 3 AC chargers require external controls for communication as they have basic signaling. In the case of DC fast chargers, CCS connectors are coupled with power line communication (PLC) protocols, while CHAdeMO, Tesla, and GB/T use controller area network (CAN) communication.

Furthermore, recent developments with regard to communication protocols include protocol ISO/IEC 15118, which provides more functionality to enable V2G communication. It is noted that CAN communication, which necessitates a minimum for peripheral communication (e.g., authentication, verification and payment) in DC charging, emphasizes on the charger, whereas the use of the more complex PLC protocol in the CCS standard emphasizes on the role of the vehicle.

Currently a number of adapters (conversion device between standards) have been developed between charging standards (and therefore also the capacity for EVs to handle the related communication protocols), aiming to tackle the issue of the double standardization and the related differences on communication protocols (CAN vs PLC).

3.4 Charging economics

The costs associated to charging infrastructure can be categorized to fixed and variable costs. Fixed costs include the costs related to purchase of the equipment that is required to recharge the vehicle, whereas variable costs refer to the power that is consumed.

The fixed costs associated with different types of electric vehicle supply equipment (EVSE) consist of:

- *The cost of installation and site preparation* (including electrical service extension, permitting, labor costs, and trenching to lay cables): These costs are minimal for residential Level 2 unless the installation of new circuitry is required. Installation costs are substantially higher for commercial or public Level 2 chargers. Commercial Level 2 EVSE usually require some form of wiring extensions, the installation of signage, and trenching to install the additional connections to the grid.

- *Costs regarding utility infrastructure upgrades*: In some cases, these costs are minimal or unnecessary, whereas in others they are a major component of the overall cost. For instance, in cases where more than one charger is located in the same place, the infrastructure requirements may be correspondingly greater, since the peak demand is larger. A single Level 2 EVSE is unlikely to require a transformer upgrade; however, when many of them operate simultaneously on the same circuit, there is the chance of overload of the existing transformer.

- *Cost of the charging equipment*: These costs vary across different charger types manufacturers, and specifications.

With regard to variable costs these are differentiated according to their use (residential or commercial). Usually the charge for residential use of Level 1 and Level 2 is at a fixed, residential rate per kWh consumed, although some utilities offer EV-specific time-of-use (ToU) rates, in order to promote charging at night or during off-peak periods. These rates offer low prices at off-peak times (usually at night) and significantly higher prices during peak times (mid-afternoon and early evening). Users can choose to charge in the afternoon at a premium rate, or overnight at a discounted rate. ToU rates can have multiple price brackets depending on the utility and service area, with mid-range prices for partial peaks, and higher peak prices in the summer than the winter. The electricity demand is expected to increase a household's electricity demand by 25%–40% (Salisbury and Toor, 2016).

In most cases, the electricity used by commercial chargers is calculated using commercial and industrial electricity rates, which include a per-peak-kW demand charge and a volumetric per-kWh energy tariff. Commercial tariffs typically offer lower volumetric charges, however, demand charges are also applied. Demand charges are indicative of the

BOX 3.2 Demand charge—examples from the United States
- The demand charge for commercial customers in the United States is $8.62 kW^{-1} of peak demand (Kettles and Raustad, 2017).
- In California, the Southern California Edison (SCE) sets an EV-specific demand charge of $13.20 kW^{-1} (SCE, 2015), whereas Pacific Gas and Electric (PG&E) sets a winter peak demand charge of $10.47 and summer charge of $17.84 (PG&E, 2017).
- The average demand charge faced by EVSE operators is $13 kW^{-1} (Clint et al., 2015).

generation and distribution costs required to cover the peak demand from both a framework and a distributional level. Taken into consideration the fact that the charge is based on maximum, not average, load, it favors heavy, consistent loads and penalizes the short bursts of high power. Demand charges can be higher during the summer, and may also be layered into noncoincident charges (reflecting maximum demand at any time) for recovering local distribution system costs, and additional coincident charges (applied during peak times) for recovering infrastructure and generation costs incurred in meeting system peaks. Box 3.2 illustrates some examples of demand charge in the United States. It is highlighted that the demand charge rises proportionally for additional chargers, since it depends only on maximum demand.

3.5 Smart charging

The increased electrification of the transportation sector is expected to affect the load profile of the power grid—given that EVs are additional loads that are connected to the power grid in order to be charged. It has been estimated that charging of large EV fleets will increase the peak load of the power grid load profile (Liu, 2012; Goncalves et al., 2013). In this direction, the concept of smart charging offers viable solutions and charging strategies that aim to monitor, manage, and restrict the use of charging devices and to optimize energy consumption. As a matter of fact, smart charging entails the synergistic approach of the available technology, regulations, and functions in order to achieve reliable operation of a network in an environmentally and economically sustainable manner. In this manner, smart charging can manage the user's charging time and power and/or other interactions with the electrical system through regulating the electricity demand (Paschero et al., 2013). This can be achieved with the employment of optimization or heuristic algorithms that aim to avoid saturation of transformers and lines, reduce GHG emissions, minimize generation costs, etc.

In this way, the smart charging facilitates a certain level of control over the charging process. In order to realize the smart grid concept, automatic control and bidirectional communication are of paramount significance. Advanced meter infrastructure plays a key role on the grid monitoring, which allows the customers to act as prosumers and take part in several operational schemes (i.e., demand response, electricity pricing, distributed automation). Demand flexibility is an intended interaction between the customers and the supply companies. According to this interaction the customers may differentiate their demand profile, or the companies may have access to modify the customers demand profile in order to optimize the grid operation by following a preestablished contract agreement. In this operational manner, EVs either may absorb energy acting as typical passive units (DC loads) in a G2V function or they may release energy acting as active units (DC sources) in a V2G function. Based on the above, it is obvious (as illustrated in Fig. 3.1) that EVs not only avoid adding stress to the local grid but also provide services to fill flexibility gaps both on the local level and on the system level. Consequently, the EVs might be used as controllable electrical loads or controllable electrical sources, and therefore they may offer supportive services to the electrical smart grid concept (Box 3.3).

There are many approaches, which incorporate different pricing and charging options, toward smart charging. Fig. 3.2 summarizes different smart charging approaches, including:

- *Time-of-use (TOU)*, which encourages consumers to move their charging from peak to off-peak. As a matter of fact, this is one of the most used market systems in which the EV can be integrated. This system breaks down the day into a series of intervals, usually three (peak, shoulder, and off-peak), assigning a different price to each one. Vehicles can be classified according to the charging priority, assuming higher prices at higher priority. This control allows a lower variation of the voltages in the nodes and transmission losses across the network (Chunlin et al., 2017).

- *Direct control mechanisms*, such as switching on and off the charging. These mechanisms enabled by the EV and the charging point will be necessary as a long-term solution at higher penetration levels and for delivery of close-to-real-time balancing and ancillary services.

BOX 3.3 Key technical terms

Ancillary services (system and local levels/transmission and distribution system operators): Supporting real-time balancing of grids by adjusting the EV charging levels to maintain steady voltage and frequency. While flexibility has been well-developed at the system level by transmission system operators (TSOs), distribution system operators (DSOs) are mostly not yet equipped with flexibility from distributed energy resources for operating their grids.

Aggregator: A legal entity that aggregates the load or generation of various demand and/or generation/production units. Aggregation can be a function that can be met by existing market actors, or can be carried out by a separate actor.

Behind-the-meter optimization and backup power (local level/consumers and prosumers): Increasing self-consumption of locally produced renewable electricity as well as lowering dependence on the electricity grid and reducing the energy bill by buying cheap electricity from the grid at off-peak hours and using it to supply home when the electricity tariff is higher (during evenings).

Demand side management: A global or integrated approach aimed at influencing the amount and timing of electricity consumption in order to reduce primary energy consumption and peak loads.

Distribution generation: Generation plants connected to the distribution system.

Distributed system operators: A natural or legal person responsible for operating, ensuring the maintenance of and, if necessary, developing the distribution system in a given area and, where applicable, its interconnections with other systems and for ensuring the long-term ability of the system to meet reasonable demands for the distribution of electricity.

Peak shaving (system level/wholesale): Flattening the peak demand and filling the "valley" of demand by incentivizing late morning/afternoon charging in systems with large penetration of solar and nighttime charging that could be adjusted following nighttime wind production as cars are parked for longer time than they need to fully charge.

Transmission system operators: A natural or legal person responsible for operating, ensuring the maintenance of and, if necessary, developing the transmission system in a given area and, where applicable, its interconnections with other systems, and for ensuring the long-term ability of the system to meet reasonable demands for the transmission of electricity.

- *Unidirectional control of vehicles (V1G)* that allows increasing or decreasing the rate of charging. In this type of operation between the PEV and the grid the direction is from the grid to vehicle. V1G or Grid to Vehicle (G2V) enables grid supplementary services by employing a

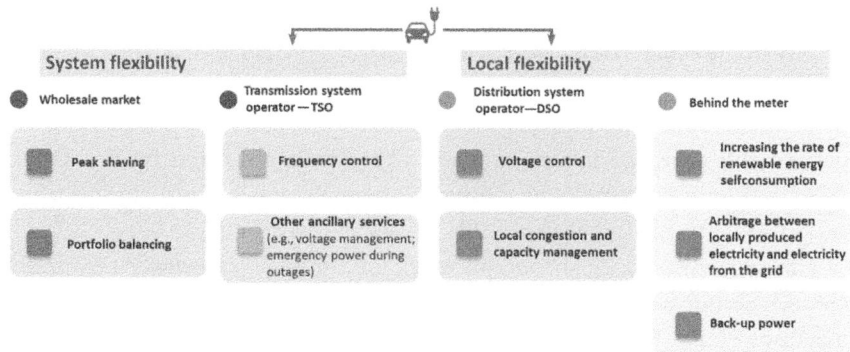

Figure 3.2 Indicative flexibility services provided by EVs.

variable EV charging rate dependent on the power generation needs. This is managed by EV aggregators which act as intermediary bodies between the power grid and collection of EVs. These supplementary services allow EVs to act as distributed energy resources. The services include grid management through frequency regulation, appropriation of spinning reserve as backup for the unexpected power loss, reactive power compensation, etc.

- *Bidirectional charging*, which refers to a power flow that can be given from the grid to the vehicle, used to charge its batteries, or given from the vehicle to another entity (grid, building, home, etc.). A bidirectional controlled approach such V2G allows the EV to provide services to the grid in the discharge mode, whereas in V2H and in V2B, EVs are used as a residential backup power supply during periods of power outage or for increasing self-consumption of energy produced onsite (demand charge avoidance).

3.5.1 Smart charging strategies

The integration of charging needs with power demand is a necessity, especially when power generation is transitioning toward high integration of renewable energy sources (RES). In this direction, controlled charging of a large number of electrical vehicles (EVs) can provide aggregated power system services, supporting their smooth integration. EV aggregators aim at facilitating EV smart charging services (management of optimal charging of higher number of EVs, even distribution of the load, flexibility when the number of EVs increases), while participating in the electricity market via complex interactions with other market entities.

To be more specific, the aggregator unit (AU), which is used as the central control device (Bessa and Matos, 2012), provides also the ancillary services (such as frequency regulation, voltage regulation, reduction of power losses, load leveling, and minimization of load variance) and contributes to the profit of the smart grid. The AU is regulated by the DSO, which acts as the central unit between the transmission and the distribution power system (Lopes et al., 2011).

The strategies that can be followed, in order to optimally cover the demand response through smart charging are the following (García-Villalobos et al., 2014) (Fig. 3.3):

- *Centralized strategy*: This approach focuses on the aggregation of charging operations, where emerging market entities temporally and spatially manage the charging load of a large EV fleet with advanced optimization models (Nguyen and Le, 2014; Wu et al., 2012). In this strategy, the AU collects all the charging related information, such as

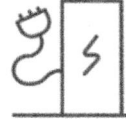

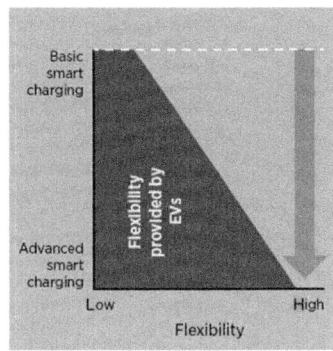

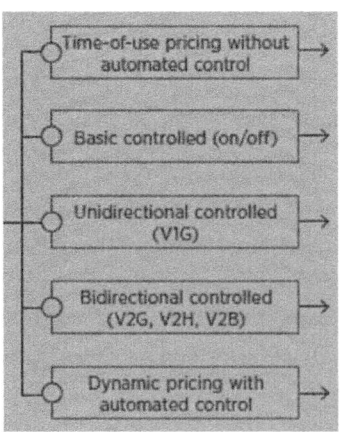

Figure 3.3 Smart charging approaches.

SOC of batteries, location of EVs, and their parking time, with the help of the charging post manager (CPM). CPM facilitates the AU in controlling the number of different cars in the parking area. In this approach, the AU participates in the management of the power grid, as well as safeguarding the smooth operation of the distribution system (in case of any fault in distribution system, the AU halts all the charging sessions and takes part in the actions to remove faults in the distribution system). It is noted that the centralized approach provides also ancillary services. However, issues such as the sophisticated communication infrastructure, which adds complexity in the system; the provision of alternative arrangement (in case the AU fails), which increases the cost, and ensuring security and privacy constitute the drawbacks of this charging approach.

- *Decentralized strategy*: This approach focuses on individual scheduling and demand response of EV agents (i.e., Hu et al., 2014; Tan et al., 2014; Qi et al., 2014). This strategy requires some type of computational intelligence on the part of EV or customer. It addresses the data security issues that the centralized approach faces in charging the EVs. In this way, each vehicle performs its operation based on a series of internal and/or external signals. This approach adds more flexibility and scalability to the system. As the number of cars increases, this approach distributes the computational load on the customer which minimizes the overall processing and computational load on the charging network. Taken into consideration the fact that this charging approach allows the customer to decide the charging approach (i.e., to what extent and to when the vehicle is going to be charged), this approach has gained much attention from users compared to the centralized approach. The main limitation of this approach is the avalanche effect that minimizes the system performance. The avalanche effect is the increase in the load when a large number of cars are charged at low electricity rates.

- *Hybrid strategy*: This approach employs both of the abovementioned approaches (i.e., centralized and distributed) for the charging of EVs. The main advantage of hybrid EVs charging is that it addresses the various limitations of centralized and distributed EVs charging approaches.

3.5.2 Smart grid

An electrical power grid, which utilizes automation and remote control in order to improve the reliability, efficiency, and sustainability of the power supply can be characterized as a smart grid (Ancillotti et al., 2013). Smart grids are characterized by a two-way communication between utility and customers enabling different energy paths to provide greater interoperability between various components of the system (Bhatt et al., 2014). The collected information along with autonomous and intelligent monitoring control is employed, in order to supervise and optimize the overall operations of the interconnected components. The smart grid allows the consumers to take part in the grid operation, as they can access the real-time information about the electricity usage, tariff, and incentive through the use of advanced metering infrastructure. In this manner, consumers play a vital role for the balancing of the energy supply and demand by deciding their electricity usage patterns and preferences.

It is highlighted that in comparison to the conventional grid, the crucial feature of a smart grid is the inclusion of the extensive bidirectional communication paths connecting various components. These two-way communication paths have enabled the development of various applications in a smart grid, such as advanced metering infrastructure, home automation network (HAN), demand response, integration of distributed generations, and V2G.

The implementation of the smart grid can improve the grid reliability and power quality. Smart grid technologies are shown in Table 3.4.

3.5.3 Vehicle-to-grid

The V2G technology was proposed by Amory Lovins in 1995 and further research was carried out by Prof. William Kempton (Lam et al., 2012; Richardson, 2013). The V2G concept constitutes a form of smart charging that allows EVs to both deliver and extract energy from the grid. As a matter of fact, V2G technology can transfer energy from the power grid to charge EVs, as well as discharge the charge of EVs batteries into the power grid for grid support. This technology is used to sell demand response services by throttling the charge rate, shifting the charging time or returning electricity to the grid. To be more specific, the services that can be provided to the smart grid, include inter alia reactive power compensation, peak load shaving, spinning reserve, smart grid regulation, as well as load leveling.

In this type of charging the EV receives charging from the power grid whenever the charge level of EV battery is low. In V2G operation, the charge level of the EV battery is continuously monitored and can be discharged to the smart grid. EVs can be considered as dynamic distributed energy storages (Fig. 3.2). In this type of smart charging the charger, which

Table 3.4 Smart grid technologies.

Technology	Description	Communication	Advantages
Advanced metering infrastructure	Electronic device that records and collects the real-time information regarding the electricity usage	Two-way communication between power utility and the customers	• Better monitoring • Management of electricity billing (López et al., 2014)
Supervisory control and data acquisition	A centralized system, which collects real-time data from the monitoring devices and control various equipment remotely	Two-way communication system for transferring data and control signals	• Advanced control technology • Implementation in many power grids
Home automation network	Enables the communication of different electric appliances within a home with the purpose of creating a safe, energy efficient and economical living environment	Two-way communication	• Automated monitoring, management, and control to all connected electric appliances • Response and control of the connected electric appliances according to the customer preference and real-time grid condition (Li et al., 2014)
Demand response	The customers participate in improving the operation of power grid, and in return they are rewarded with incentives	Two-way communication	• Avoidance of the additional power generation to meet the peak load demand or emergency situation • Cost-effective alternative to sustain the power grid operation (Siano, 2014)
Integration of Distributed Generators	It allows the consumers at distribution level to generate power and supplies to nearby loads	Two-way communication	• Reduction of power losses • Adoption of renewable energy sources (i.e., solar photovoltaic and wind)
Vehicle-to-grid	Control and management of the energy exchange between the power grid and EV battery The charge level of the EV battery is monitored and can be discharged to the smart grid	Bidirectional communication	• Active power regulation • Reactive power regulation • Ancillary service support

receives (in EV charging mode) and supplies (EV discharge mode) electric energy to and from the net, is bidirectionally connected to the network. The aggregator plays a significant role in this type of charging, since AUs can act as new suppliers of both primary and secondary reserve services to TSOs. Furthermore, DSOs can use EVs as free floating storage for net balance services at a local level, producing in this way decentralized sustainable energy. Using EVs for demand response means that EVs can supply electricity back to the grid locally at moments of scarcity. Vehicles can act as temporary storage of locally produced energy during the day that is used in the evening to help fill in peak energy demand. Taken into consideration the fact that V2G concept is associated with significant financial benefits, it can be considered as an alternative option to economic incentives for the promotion of EV deployment (Rotering and Ilic, 2011).

As presented in Box 3.4, V2G technology offers opportunities and new business models for TSOs, DSOs, and local private energy networks. EVs through V2G can be used as a home energy storage system helping homeowners to perform cost-effective management of power resources. In addition, through the discharging facility, ancillary services can be provided (i.e., frequency control, load balance, and spinning reserve services) ensuring by this way the maintenance of the balance on the grid network (Pillai and Bak-Jensen, 2010). Furthermore, the use of such a system could be used for "valley filling" (timing devices to draw power at times of low grid demand) and "peak shaving" (reducing the peak energy demand on the grid). Moreover, V2G can be used, in order to compensate for deviations caused

---

BOX 3.4 V2G business model—the case study of San Diego Gas and Electric Vehicle—Grid Integration Pilot

San Diego Gas & Electric (SDG&E) launched a VGI pilot project that is testing making fleets of EVs available as dispatchable distributed energy resources to improve the stability of the grid. SDG&E will install and operate 3500 charging stations throughout the San Diego region, mainly Level 2 (slow) charging stations, with a large share at multiunit dwellings (Barnes, 2019).

The program explores dynamic pricing and, through an app, incentivizes charging activities at moments of high renewable energy. Dynamic hourly rates are posted on a day-ahead basis, and they reflect both the system and local grid conditions. An app matches customer preference with those prices. For simple ToU, bigger effects were recorded for customers with separate EV-only meters.

by intermittent RES, such as wind power and solar photovoltaic (PV) (Druitt and Früh, 2012). V2G can also play a significant role in avoiding startups of carbon intensive units, thus contributing to the reduction of the carbon intensity of electricity. It is highlighted that the financial gains of the aggregator are proportional to the power, since the supply market is based on power, instead of energy (Harris and Webber, 2014).

However, V2G has drawbacks with regard to the extra energy cost resulting from the extra charging, which would be required for the maintenance of the required state of charge (SOC). It should be noted that the V2G concept requires integration work and potentially additional investments in the vehicles and in the power system as the frequent V2G operation will increase the electrical stress on the batteries, reducing their lifetime. In this direction, the integration of wind and solar power is expected to make the large-scale V2G concept economically attractive.

3.5.3.1 Regulation services

Several regulation services can be found on the market, with the frequency and voltage regulation being the most relevant for EVs. It is noted that these services can be employed in order to develop and deploy viable business models taking into consideration factors such as minimum bid size, participating capacity, SOC, etc. (Peng et al., 2017). In order to create a profitable business model within this area, it is important that the service providers create value for the three main stakeholders—grid, aggregator, and EV owner (Fig. 3.4).

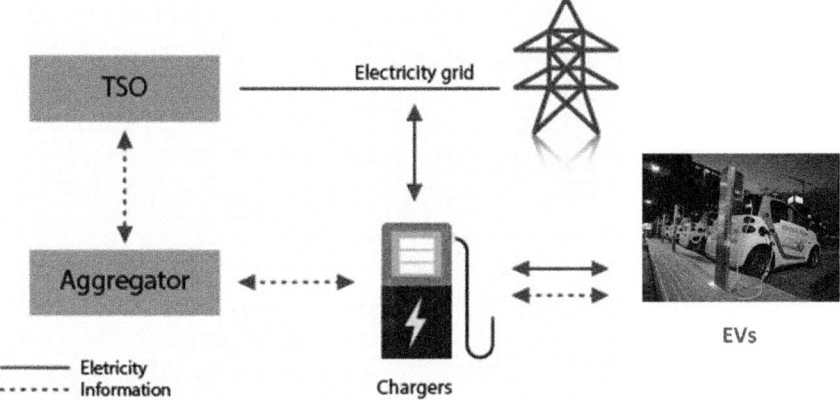

Figure 3.4 Vehicle-to-grid concept.

1. *Frequency regulation*

One of the most critical and extended ancillary services regarding the synergies between EVs and markets is the frequency regulation, as it is beneficial to the battery cycle lifetime without compromising the potential economic benefits (Li et al., 2015). In most cases, a frequency regulation strategy consists of the aggregator dispatching the bidirectional charging according to the grid frequency deviation (Peng et al., 2017).

Deviations in the grid frequency can be corrected by varying the power generation or consumption. In most cases, generators coupled to the network (spinning reserve) are responsible for this regulation, assuming greater contamination and degradation of equipment (Kaur et al., 2018). Unlike the sale of electric power, which is billed by the amount of energy, the provision of frequency regulation is remunerated based on available installed power (Rehman and Riaz, 2018).

The basic methods of frequency regulation consist of:
- Classical frequency regulation system, which is called droop method (Liu et al., 2013).
- The "adaptive droop method," creates a state called battery state holder (BSH), transferring the dead nand to the abscissa axis.

With regard to operation strategies, these can be summarized as the following:
- Early deadline first (EDF): in this strategy the vehicle with the least available time for charging has the highest priority. During the parked time, there are four modes of operation: immediate charging, charging when there is available power, charging with price limit, and charging with provision of frequency regulation (Han et al., 2010). Although the simulation example considers the joint operation of several homes, the methodology is proposed to be used with Home Energy Management System (HEMS) and aims to be upgraded to a decentralized or multiagent strategy.
- A strategy based on the coordination of several agents, where the creation of different entities depending on the number of vehicles to be controlled is proposed (given that each aggregator will cover a large area). These entities are based on a controller called the Micro Grid Aggregation Unit (MGAU) for every 400 vehicles located in the MV/LV transformation centers and a Central Aggregation Unit (CAU) located in the HV/MV transformation centers for every 20,000 vehicles. For large consumption points, such as shopping centers, they recommend feeding the EVs directly from the MV network. As in

unidirectional mode, the DSO can interrupt charging in the case of abnormal system operation, while the frequency regulation is based on droop method.
• A strategy aiming to minimize network frequency deviations, to maximize the V2G contribution respecting the preferences of the user, to minimize the battery degradation, and to maximize the user retribution has also been proposed (Kaur et al., 2018).

Finally, the frequency stabilizing effect that can be found in EVs enables the creation of virtual power plants (VPPs) (Luo et al., 2014). VPPs encompass a series of generators and/or storage systems, of a single or a combination of several technologies, under the same electric entity without the need for being located in the same geographical location.

2. *Active/reactive power for voltage regulation*

As the large scale of EV charging is a massive challenge to the power grid, safeguarding power efficiency and voltage stability are power qualities that need to be regulated throughout the power grid operation for grid reliability. The most common method of voltage regulation and power factor correction is the installment of the static volt−ampere reactive compensator, which supplies reactive power support to the power grid (Jiang and Fei, 2013). With the implementation of V2G technology, the reactive power compensation service for grid voltage regulation and power factor correction can be accomplished with the grid-connected bidirectional EV chargers. The DC-link capacitor connected in a bidirectional EV charger is able to provide reactive power support to the power grid with an appropriate switching control for the EV converter.

3. *Load profile—harmonic filtering*

The implementation of V2G technology may affect the power quality of the smart grid, taking into consideration the fact the EV chargers can be considered a harmonic source (due to the use of converter switching), which generates current harmonics (Gallardo-Lozano et al., 2012). In this direction EV chargers with appropriate control can be employed as the active filter, in order to filter out the harmonics generated by EV chargers and other nonlinear loads (Boynuegri et al., 2014). The converter of the EV charger can operate as variable impedance for each individual harmonic frequency and solve the harmonic problem with proper filtering strategy (Rauchfuss et al., 2014).

Furthermore, as the large-scale integration of EVs into the energy grid is expected to increase load, which could cause system overload during peak periods it is highlighted that V2G in conjunction with demand side management (DSM) has the potential to flatten the demand curve to an average value by responding as generators at peak demand (Shinde and Swarup, 2016). Based on the above, V2G operators could develop a business model, which will dispatch intelligent signals that regulate when different EVs charge to reduce peak load. If the system is built appropriately, it might be possible to reduce the dimension of the energy distribution network, which could be an economically viable alternative. However, currently in most European countries, such a marketplace for DSO does not exist, which is a barrier toward providing this service, as DSOs' strategies are based on making long-term investments in grid expansions in order to absorb larger peaks.

4. *Spinning reserve*

While uncontrolled charging should be avoided, smart charging (with or without V2G or ancillary services) reduces the cost of system operation and allows integration of more RES. Shifting responsibility regulations from traditional units to EVs allows the exploitation of generation sources at the point of maximum efficiency, leading to economic and environmental benefits (Pavić et al., 2015).

3.5.3.2 Vehicle-to-grid—renewable energy sources

The energy transition to a low-carbon electrical power system can be achieved with the integration of RES into the power grid. Despite the environmental benefits that the integration of RES present, the power generation is intermittent and is dependent on the weather. For instance, variations of wind speed and solar irradiance result in fluctuations in power generation for wind turbines and solar PVs. In order to find a solution for this issue, stationary energy has been suggested as a possible solution (Mwasilu et al., 2014); nonetheless this solution for the RES intermittency issue requires a high investment cost, which causes the delay of RES deployment.

A viable solution to this issue is the adoption of an appropriate V2G control strategy, the EVs can be used in order to provide a solution to the renewable energy intermittency issue (Fazelpour et al., 2014). To be more specific, EVs are charged from the power grid when renewable distributed generation generates excessive power and discharged to the power grid when renewable distributed generation does not generate enough power. Furthermore, the EV battery can be used as the energy storage system to regulate the voltage of a power grid with renewable energy integration.

To sum up, taken into consideration the fact that EVs can charge power from and discharge power into the power grid via V2G technology, they can be considered distributed energy storage systems. In this direction, EVs energy storages can be used to stabilize the inconsistent generation of RES and accommodate more RES integration. On the other hand, EVs charging from the power grid with high penetration of RES will be beneficial to life cycle emissions (see Chapter 5: Climate Change Mitigation and Electric Vehicles). Therefore the interaction of EVs with RES can achieve mutual benefits enabling the power grid to move toward sustainability.

3.5.3.3 Vehicle-to-building

The vehicle-to-building (V2B) technology combines local (usually renewable) generation technologies and storage systems (including EVs). The concept was introduced in 2008 as a variant of V2G aiming to flatten the demand curve of a building by applying DSM, and thus optimizing energy consumption. This can be achieved by applying the optimal management of buildings and considering a fleet of vehicles such as offices or car-rental companies. The concept of V2B is based on the concept that surplus solar energy can be stored in the batteries of electric cars during the day, and the energy is returned to the building energy system when solar generation is insufficient to serve the total energy demand at a given moment in time. At times of power system blackouts, vehicles are ready to serve as a backup instead of diesel generators. The latter are employed to islands that are not interconnected to the mainland grid and have to be self-supporting.

3.5.3.4 Vehicle-to-home

Vehicle-to-home (V2H) falls under V2G technology and its application is within a HAN. In a HAN, EVs act as energy storage systems able to store the excessive power generation from the home solar PV unit and discharge it to supply the other smart appliances. It is noted that this technology is beneficial with regard to the reduction of home electricity bills (by shifting the peak load). Furthermore, it can be used as a source of emergency power when the grid is down. It can be employed, in order to reduce both the demand charge (monthly fixed-rate cost) and the energy charge rate (cost per kWh). When this technology is combined with the renewable distributed generation, then it can create an energy efficient and environment-friendly living environment (Berthold et al., 2011).

In this technology, the innovative concept of vehicle-to-neighbor (V2N) is included. In V2N a residential neighborhood management system is formulated where the concepts of V2H at the local level, V2N at the level of urbanization, and V2G at a global level are carried out. In this manner, sharing energy between neighbors at a lower cost at certain moments is achieved (Pal and Kumar, 2018).

3.5.4 Challenges and issues in vehicle-to-grid technology

The benefits of the implementation of V2G technology are significant, however the interaction of a million V2G-driven EVs poses some challenges that should be addressed. These issues are associated with charging and discharging strategy as well as with bidirectional charging and are attributed to harmonic pollution and load fluctuation (Ma et al., 2016). The communication system and infrastructure also are of paramount significance for the successful implementation of any V2G technology and for safeguarding the privacy preservation in V2G EVs.

Other issues that need to be addressed include inter alia the following:
- V2G communication security and reliability,
- V2G modeling objectives,
- architecture, and
- integration software.

Additionally, technical aspect challenges in V2G-driven EVs include:
- physical layer,
- MAC layer,
- V2G communication requirement,
- security threats and authentication protocol,
- routing protocols, and
- wireless charging.

3.6 Case studies—worldwide projects

During the past decade, a number of projects regarding the deployment of smart grids and smart charging have been implemented around the world. Table 3.5 summarizes the characteristics of some of these projects, the majority of which mainly address issues regarding the impact on the grid, the driving and charging behavior of users, and the technical and economic integration of EVs. Some of the leading smart grid projects include the Smart Grid Smart City in Australia (https://data.gov.au, 2020), Ontario Smart Metering Initiative in Canada (Smart Metering

Table 3.5 Smart charging projects around the world.

Type of charging	Case studies found in
Uncontrolled Time-of-use tariffs	China, Germany, Japan, the United Kingdom, the United States
Basic control	Pepco, Maryland, United States: 200 households
	Consolidated Edison, New York, United States: off-bill incentive for managed charging
	Xcel Energy, Minnesota, United States: 100 households
Unidirectional control (V1G)	Green eMotion, the EU project (2015): reduction of grid reinforcement cost by 50%
	Sacramento Municipal Utility, California, United States: reduction of grid upgrade expense of over 70%
Bidirectional vehicle-to-grid (V2G)	eVgo and University of Delaware project in the United States with transmission system operator PJM, led by Nuvve; Interconnection—commercial operation
	Nuvve, Nissan, Enel, in England and Wales with transmission system operator National Grid—operating precommercially
	Nuvve, DTU, Nissan, PSA, Enel project in Denmark, with TSO energinet.dk ("Parker Project")—operating trialJeju, Republic of Korea project developing fast and slow V2G; Toyota city project with 3100 EVs
	Renault, ElaadNL and Lombo Xnet, project in Utrecht, the Netherlands—AC V2G
Bidirectional vehicle-to-X (e.g., V2H)	ElaadNL and Renault in Utrecht, the Netherlands: 1000 public solar-powered smart charging stations with battery storage around the region in the largest smart charging demonstration to date. Increase in self-consumption from 49% to 62%—87% and decrease in peak of 27%—67%
	DENSO and Toyota intelligent V2H (HEMS and V2G integrated model), Nissan (V2H)—all of Japan (7000 households, commercial operation)
Dynamic pricing with EVs (controlled)	Nord-Trøndelag Elektrisitetsverk Nett in Norway
	San Diego Gas & Electric in California: trialing prices posted 1 day ahead

Initiative, 2016), Low Carbon London in Great Britain (https://innova-tion.ukpowernetworks.co.uk), Yokohama Smart City Project in Japan (www.collaborative.city), and Juju Smart Grid System in South Korea (Smart Grid on Jeju Island). Moreover, Box 3.5 presents a number of smart grid projects that were adopted under the concept of smart city in EU. These include roadmaps, route maps, national strategies, etc.

In addition, as many projects with regard to the deployment of smart grids and smart charging within the concept of the smart city are currently running, an indicative list is presented here:

• *ARENA Distributed Energy Resources Programme (Australia)*: This is an ongoing project (2019—22), which aims to investigate and trial novel approaches to increasing network hosting capacity with the objective

BOX 3.5 National/regional smart grid roadmaps and platforms in the EU

Several EU Member States have adopted smart grid projects under the concept of the smart city. These can be encountered under different names (roadmap, route map, strategy, etc.) and are assigned either to national authorities or to private organizations. Here a number of relative initiatives are listed:

In Germany a roadmap was drafted by the federal association of the energy and water industry, BDEW (BDEW Bundesverband der Energie- und Wasserwirtschaft e.V., 2013).

In the United Kingdom, the smart grid vision and route map was adopted in 2014 by the Department of Energy and Climate Change (Department of Energy and Climate Change, 2014).

In Denmark, a smart grid strategy was adopted in 2013 by the Danish Ministry of Climate, Energy, and Building (Danish Ministry of Climate, Energy and Building, 2013).

In France, it was the environment and energy management agency which adopted a strategy in 2013 (French Environment & Energy Management Agency (ADEME), 2013).

In Austria, a technology roadmap was developed during the Smart grids 2.0 strategy process on behalf of the federal ministry for transport, innovation and technology (Smart Grids Austria, 2015).

In Sweden, an action plan was adopted in 2014 by the Swedish coordination council for smart grids, which was appointed by the Swedish government in 2012 (Coordination Council and National Knowledge Platform for Smart Grids, 2014).

In Ireland, a smart grid roadmap to 2050 was adopted by the Sustainable Energy Authority of Ireland in 2011 (Sustainable Energy Authority of Ireland, 2011).

Smart grid platforms are networks of different smart grid stakeholders who get together to foster the transition to smarter grids, to promote the development of joint initiatives, and to disseminate best practices and lessons learned. Smart grid platforms have been set up in many European countries, that is, in Spain, Austria (SmartGrid Austria, 2008), Czech Republic (Česká technologická platforma Smart Grid, 2009), Ireland (Sustainable Energy Authority of Ireland, 2009), Norway (The Norwegian Smart grid Centre, 2010), Denmark (Smart Energy Network RD&D, 2013), Italy (Smart Grid Italia, 2014), France (Think Smart Grids, 2015), etc.

of allowing the system to operate securely whilst maximizing the ability of distributed energy, such as solar PV, to provide energy to the grid in Australia (https://arena.gov.au/knowledge-innovation/distributed-energy-integration-program/).

- *Charge the North (Canada)*: This is an ongoing demonstration project (2017—ongoing), which aims to collect EV data from 1000 EV owners across Canada to better understand their behavior and habits. Fleet Carma (the contractor) aims to influence better grid planning in addition to supporting optimal EV charging deployment and demonstrating charging solutions for workplaces and multiunit dwellings (https:// www.fleetcarma.com/charge-the-north-summary/). The demonstration project is divided into three sections:
- FleetCarma will monitor and capture data on driving and charging habits from 1000 EVs in Canada. The analysis will provide an overview of the EV drivers' behavior, as well as aid the optimal planning of new EV charging station installations across the country.
- Alectra Utilities, a distribution company, will analyze real-world data from smart-chargers installed in the workplace to minimize EV and grid integration issues. The smart-charger controls the power rate at which EVs are charged to support efficient grid operation, while ensuring EVs are fully charged as specified by the owner. This smart system will include integration of solar power and energy storage in the workplace's building management system.
- A new charge reimbursement system will be tested in multiunit dwellings that is more cost efficient and does not require installing a submeter.
- *Fundamental Theory of Planning and Operation for Power Systems With High Share of Renewable Energy Generations (China)*: The project (2016—20) aims to study the basic theory and method of future planning and operation of high-proportion renewable energy power systems in China and to provide a standardized system for high-proportion renewable energy scenarios. The project aims to throw light on the following key scientific issues: (1) power system planning and operation under a high penetration of uncertainty; and (2) stability mechanism of a power system under a high share of power electronic devices.

  The project proposes an efficient panoramic operation simulation method for an AC—DC hybrid complex power system with high renewable penetration. A new power system flexibility theory is proposed and used in the evolution planning of energy—electricity—grid coordination (Liu et al., 2018).
- *Smart Otaniemi (Finland)*: Smart Otaniemi in Finland constitutes an innovation ecosystem that connects experts, organizations, technologies and pilot projects. It brings the building blocks of a smart energy

future together. The testing platform is being built around Nokia's 5G network (https://smartotaniemi.fi/). Smart Otaniemi is an ecosystem of more than 50 partners, working on seven concrete pilots, developing new ideas and creating new business. The ecosystem is open for new partners with new pilot ideas, ranging from quick testing of new solutions, to more research-oriented topics in the energy field. The identified topics for substance roadmaps are energy storage, flexibility market, Power-to-X, autonomous driving, and future city structures. The idea is to be able to experiment new solutions on a system level, whilst also utilizing the simulation and virtual modeling potential that the research partners in Otaniemi can provide—creating next-generation energy solutions for different region.

- *Grid-Scale Energy Storage System (India)*: The objective of this project, which was inaugurated on February 13, 2019, is the provision of grid stabilization, enhanced peak load management, added system flexibility, and increased reliability for approximately 2 million consumers. It is worth mentioning that this is India's first grid-scale battery-based storage system, which will address key challenges such as peak load management, system flexibility, frequency regulation, and reliability of the network (Smart- energy.com, 2019).

- *Synchro Phasor-Based Automatic Real-Time Control (SPARC) (Norway)*: The objective of this project (2018—22) is to develop new knowledge, methods, and tools for automatic control and protection of transmission systems based on phasor measurement unit (PMU) data, in order to improve system stability and robustness to contingencies, and by this contribute to the future stable and secure operation of the Nordic power system. In this context, this project will contribute to the development of methods and tools for automatic control and wide area protection in transmission systems (www.sintef.no).

- *WiseGRID—Wide Scale Demonstration of Integrated Solutions and Business Models for European Smart GRID (EU)*: The project's (2016—20) main objective is to provide a set of solutions and technologies to increase the smartness, stability, and security of an open, consumer-centric European energy grid. The project is coordinated by Etra Investigacion y Desarrollo SA (Spain). Furthermore, the project will combine an enhanced use of storage technologies, a highly increased share of RES and the integration of charging infrastructure to favor the large-scale deployment of EVs. It will place citizens at the center of the transformation of the grid (www.wisegrid.eu).

- *FLEXITRANSTORE—An Integrated Platform for Increased FLEXIbility in smart TRANSmission grids with STORage Entities and large penetration of Renewable Energy Sources (EU)*: The objectives of this project (2017−21), which is coordinated by European Dynamics Belgium S.A. (Belgium), are (http://www.flexitranstore.eu):
- to assist the evolution toward a pan-European transmission network with high flexibility and interconnection levels and
- to ensure that the management of the technologies developed with the Flexible Energy Grid demonstrates flexible resource applications that mitigate the effects of RES variability on the network.
- *TILOS—Technology Innovation for the Local Scale, Optimum Integration of Battery Energy Storage (EU)*: The TILOS project (2015−19) is testing the integration of an innovative local-scale, molten-salt battery ($NaNiCl_2$) energy storage system in the real grid environment on the island of Tilos (Greece). It is planned to test smart grid control system and provision of multiple services, ranging from microgrid energy management, maximization of RES penetration and grid stability, to the export of guaranteed energy amounts and the provision of ancillary services to the main grid. The battery system is used to support both stand-alone and grid-connected operations, while ensuring its interoperability with the rest of microgrid components and DSM (https://www.tiloshorizon.eu).

Strong differences exist between the ongoing projects, including the overall level and pace of investment. Several country-specific circumstances have a significant impact on the activity of a country, such as its size, population, and electricity consumption. Moreover, the promotion of initiatives at national level can support the growth of national organizations and accelerate smart grid investment. Companies that succeed in strengthening their expertise and experience at the national level can start pursuing emerging business opportunities in other countries. Besides strengthening the national export potential, a favorable national policy and regulatory framework is also important to make the country attractive for foreign smart grid investment. In particular, the adoption of smart grid roadmaps is a clear sign that smart grids are high on the national agenda, thus attracting foreign investors to seek partnerships with local stakeholders to enter the national market. The creation also of national and regional smart grid platforms can also promote the development of smart grid projects. Finally, another factor which affects the promotion of smart grid projects is the adoption of national and regional smart specialization strategies.

3.6.1 Smart charging in island systems

The majority of islands worldwide depend on fossil fuel; thus affecting the island's energy security as well as its economy and environment. As a matter of fact, islands have to cope with the common challenges of high energy costs, local CO_2 emissions, supply security, and system stability with the additional issue of a strong seasonality of energy loads. The islands not connected to the national grid are particularly sensible to those issues. Actually, island energy systems are mostly based on fossil fuels that have to be imported from the mainland, making them vulnerable both to oil price fluctuations and weather conditions that may leave islands isolated for weeks. For this reason, the implementation of advanced distributed energy resource applications is of paramount significance for the sustainability of islands. While each isolated system is different in terms of weather, population, and economic activity, the response to power system shocks in island regions is generally "tighter"—that is, the loss of a few electricity supply units has a bigger impact than in interconnected systems, and the effects of voltage drops are more significant. In this regard, balancing the grid is more difficult, the risk of load shedding and blackouts is higher, and more reserves are required (Ramírez Díaz et al., 2015).

One of the major challenges for the adoption of renewable energy solutions is how to combine different RES (i.e., wind, solar), which are intermittent, into a single hybrid energy system (Lund et al., 2014). This issue together with the characteristic small-size energy systems of islands are key barriers for the penetration of renewable energy solutions in an island's energy system. In this direction, a number of studies and relative projects have been carried out in order to showcase the synergies that have been developed with the aim to provide efficient solutions for isolated areas. These include:

Island of Barbados: An EV scenario for 2030 with solar and wind supply covering 64% of demand and more than 26,000 EVs in the system demonstrated a five times lower production cost with the most efficient smart charging strategy compared to uncontrolled charging. Even uncontrolled charging would lead to higher level of curtailment, even if lower than the reference scenario without EVs (Taibi and Fernández, 2017).

Tenerife (Canary Islands, Spain): The impact of 50,000 EVs would increase the renewable share in the island's electricity mix up to 30%, reduce CO_2 emissions by 27%, reduce the total cost of electric generation by 6%, and reduce the oil internal market by 16% (Ramírez Díaz et al., 2015).

São Miguel (Azores archipelago—Portugal): EVs could help increase renewable energy production (Camus and Farias, 2012).

Samsø Island (Denmark): 100% renewable energy generation by using EVs as well as zero-emission vehicles (Pascale-Louise Blyth, 2011).

3.6.1.1 Smart energy management for autonomous isolated areas—the case study of Greek islands (implementation of hybrid energy systems)

Isolated electricity systems are characterized by several peculiarities that complicate and raise the costs of electricity generation. More specifically, generation units installed in isolated systems cannot be of too high nominal capacity as the loss of one generator would affect the overall system. As a result, the technical management of the network with regard to the frequency and voltage control is far more complicated and economies of scale cannot be adequately exploited, certainly not at the same level as in large electricity systems. In these circumstances, the introduction and development of RES provide a valuable alternative to conventional production based on fossil fuels, both from a social and economic point of view. Arguably, RES in autonomous systems can provide a solid instrument for meeting most objectives of the European energy policy: economic efficiency, environmental friendliness, and security and diversification of supply. In this direction, a simulation is performed, to a representative, medium-sized island of the Aegean Sea.

Data of the presented case study come from the study of Nanaki and Xydis (2018), who investigated the benefits of the implementation of hybrid energy system as a smart energy strategy for autonomous isolated areas. The case study refers to a typical Greek island, located in the group of Cyclades islands, with a total area of 109 km^2. It is noted that this strategy can be implemented to islands of similar characteristics. The island's population, is approximately 2000 inhabitants; however, this number changes significantly during the summer months due to the intense tourist season. Despite the fact that in the entire island complex wind and solar potential is dominating, the current use of RES on the island is rather limited. As a matter of fact, the wind resource potential is in the order of 8 m/s, which encourages investigation for wind-based energy solutions.

Fig. 3.5 presents the proposed configuration, which comprises a wind farm coupled with storage (lead—acid batteries are currently considered), supported also by the minimum contribution of the local autonomous power stations for the island under study. The proposed configuration also employs PV panels. A fleet of EVs, operated by an aggregator is also

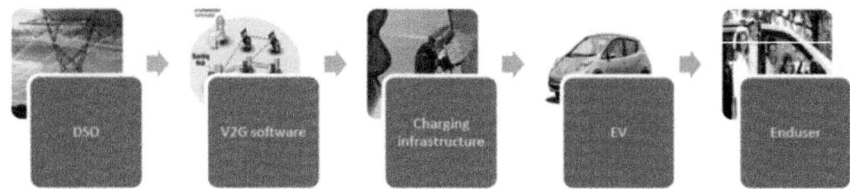

Figure 3.5 Energy value chain in a V2G setup.

being employed in this study. It is noted that the hybrid system (HS) is not extended to replace the diesel generator, but to minimize the diesel usage and use instead RES. In an autonomous system, the voltage and frequency fluctuations are more prominent due to the dynamic changes in the load by the intermittent RES.

The microgrid and distributed generation system is performed with the optimization tool—HOMER (Lambert et al., 2006). The system under consideration aims at a reliably power supply, while minimizing the system costs. The primary load demand of the island during summer months peaks daily between 10:00−12:00 and 18:00−21:00 which reaches 3 MW during the summer months. In the winter time the demand fluctuates between 0.6 and 1.5 MW.

The simulation model takes into consideration thermal electricity generators; the first one, 500 kW Genset, simulates diesel units up to 500 kW, whereas the second one, 2000 kW Genset, simulates diesel plants up to 2500 kW. Based on the regulation, a Mandatory Pool system was introduced for power generation and supply in the wholesale market for the interconnected system. All suppliers are liable to buy electricity from the Pool and all units can be operated only if selected by the market operator based on their bid offers to the Pool. For the simulation, the initial capital, replacement, and O&M costs for 500 kW Genset were taken as €0, €200,000, and €195,000, respectively with a 15,000 hours lifetime, whereas the initial capital costs, O&M, and replacement costs for 2500 kW Genset are €0, €1,150,000, and €195,000, respectively, with a 15,000 hours lifetime.

The renewable energy potential of the island for the year of 2018 is based on the available meteorological data (Hellenic National Meteorological Service, 2018). Following the meteorological investigation, one of the most demanding problems associated with the design of the system is the optimization of various associated subsystems with regard to the overall system performance and the energy cost. Under the smart grid paradigm, coordinated charging and fleet participation should be implemented by an EV aggregator acting as a load-serving operator, bidding in the day-ahead energy and in the ancillary services markets on behalf of the EV owners, aiming at minimizing charging costs. In this study an aggregator of 33.6 kWh V2G, managing a fleet of EVs equipped with NiMH batteries and with max. discharge rate of 80% is considered. The main costs that the aggregator should take into account in order to be able to participate in the regulation market are the installation costs of a concrete and reliable infrastructure with bidirectional transfer of data between the aggregator and the system operator and between the EV charging stations and the aggregator's data center. The cost of batteries is still high, however as innovation is tested and applied via new applications, costs are slowly decreasing. While the initial capital and replacement costs are taken as €6000 kW^{-1} and €4900 kW^{-1} respectively, the O&M cost is 300 and the lifetime is 8 years. Finally, a DC−AC unit converter is also used in the system for investigating an interval of 2000 kW. While its initial capital and replacement cost is considered to be €10,000 kW^{-1}, the O&M costs and the lifetime are 0 and 15 years, respectively. Fig. 3.6 depicts the energy system under study (Fig. 3.7).

Based on various runs it is suggested that 590 V2G batteries is the optimal solution for a large V2G system that could replace the existing generators setup. The optimum HES produces approximately 15,000 MWh/year total energy. While the wind turbines produce 56% of the total energy, the PV array generates 37% and the thermoelectric generators 8%. The system has 32.8% electricity excess. The ratio can be

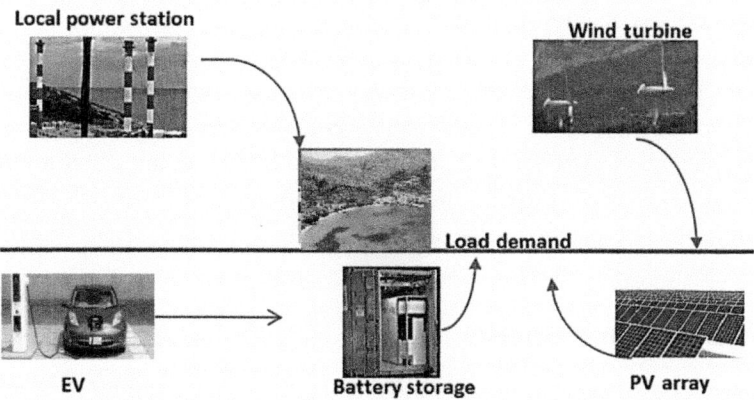

Figure 3.6 Suggested hybrid energy system.

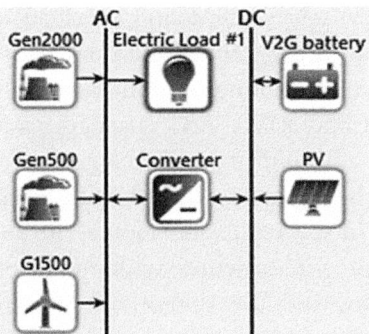

Figure 3.7 Energy system under study.

reduced by choosing smaller turbines, however, the NPC is an important factor at this point. Actually, the surplus of electricity production should not occur due to the control system (Torreglosa et al., 2016).

Energy storage is an important technological issue especially for the islands' renewable energy system. Storage technologies, using normal batteries for low demands that are not economically viable at a large scale should be considered. However, the batteries continue to have a major role on this type of systems, especially on the real life applications, as batteries are capable of providing energy in case of resource unavailability, but also contribute to the quality control supply. Finally, the benefits of the optimum energy system for the island under study are not only economical, but also environmental, as the hybrid energy system reduces significantly the emitted air emissions.

It is noted that the implementation of smart energy regions with the use of hybrid energy systems may be beneficial both in terms of environmental and economic viabilities. Furthermore, the use of hybrid energy systems supports the sustainability of the energy supply system. In this context, the environmental impacts, the system's capacity to meet requirements set by the consumers (both in terms of installed power and availability), and the capacity to use different primary sources, indigenous and imported, are taken into consideration. This study provides policy makers with useful general guidelines and suggests some practical implications for an energy autonomous system.

3.7 Concluding remarks

This chapter provided a comprehensive review of smart charging mechanisms within the concept of the smart city. The concept, framework, advantages, challenges, and optimization strategies of V2G, as well as an overview of different strategies, smart charging schemes, and relative benefits are also presented. Case studies from all over the world are also employed, in order to throw light on successful practices and potential barriers with regard to the end-user's motivation to use such smart charging systems.

It is shown that in addition to the economic benefits, the implementation of smart charging technology in a smart grid can bring numerous possible services, which are advantageous to the grid operation. It is important to mention that the implementation of V2G technology in the smart grid system facilitates the integration of renewable distributed generation, while EV charging from renewable distributed generation will be more environmentally friendly. Based on the above, smart charging, such as V2G, can be an important factor in accelerating the energy transition to low-carbon energy systems. Nonetheless, the energy transition to a low-carbon transportation system requires a holistic approach, engaging all levels of stakeholders, including communities, regions, governments, and representatives both of the public and private sectors.

The process of "smartening" the electricity grid, involves significant additional upfront investment, although it is expected to reduce the overall electricity supply cost to end users in the long term. Smart grid technologies, including V2G, are evolving rapidly and will be deployed at different rates around the world, depending on the local commercial attractiveness, their interoperability with existing technologies, regulatory developments, and investment frameworks.

References

Alternatives Fuel Data-AFD, 2020. <https://afdc.energy.gov/fuels/electricity_infrastructure.html> (accessed 15.05.20.).
Ancillotti, E., Bruno, R., Conti, M., 2013. The role of communication systems in smart grids: architectures, technical solutions and research challenges. Comput. Commun. 36 (17−18), 1665−1697.
ARENA Distributed Energy Resources Programme, <https://arena.gov.au/knowledge-innovation/distributed-energy-integration-program/> (accessed 2.06.20.).
Barnes, G., 2019. Electric vehicle-grid integration pilot program ("power your drive") fifth semi-annual report (corrected) of San Diego Gas & Electric Company (U902-e). Available from: <https://www.sdge.com/sites/default/files/regulatory/FINAL%20September%202018%20Power%20Your%20Drive%20Semi-Annual%20Rpt_0.pdf>.
Batty, M., Axhausen, K.W., Giannotti, F., Pozdnoukhov, A., Bazzani, A., Wachowicz, M., et al., 2012. Smart cities of the future. Eur. Phys. J. 214, 481−518.
Berthold, F., Blunier, B., Bouquain, D., Williamson, S., Miraoui, A., 2011. PHEV control strategy including vehicle to home (V2H) and home to vehicle (H2V) functionalities. In: Proceedings of the IEEE VPPC 2011: Vehicle Power and Propulsion Conference, September 6−9, 2011, pp. 1−6.

Bessa, R.J., Matos, M.A., 2012. Economic and technical management of an aggregation agent for electric vehicles: a literature survey. Eur. Trans. Electr. Power 22 (2012), 334−350.

Bhatt, J., Shah, V., Jani, O., 2014. An instrumentation engineer's review on smart grid: critical applications and parameters. Renew. Sustain. Energy Rev. 40 (2014), 1217−1239.

Boynuegri, A.R., Uzunoglu, M., Erdinc, O., Gokalp, E., 2014. A new perspective in grid connection of electric vehicles: different operating modes for elimination of energy quality problems. Appl. Energy 132, 435−451.

Broussely, M., 2010. Battery requirements for HEVs, PHEVs, and EVs: an overview, Electric and Hybrid Vehicles: Power Sources, Models, Sustainability, Infrastructure Mark, 2010. Elsevier B.V, pp. 305−345.

Camus, C., Farias, T., 2012. The electric vehicles as a mean to reduce CO_2 emissions and energy cost in isolated regions. The São Miguel (Azores) case study. Energy Policy vol. 43, 153−165.

Česká technologická platforma Smart Grid, 2009. <http://automa.cz/Aton/FileRepository/pdf_articles/40773.pdf>.

CHAdeMO, 2018a. CHAdeMO releases the latest version of the protocol enabling up to 400 kW. <www.chademo.com/chademo-releases-the-latest-version-of-the-protocol-enabling-up-to-400kw/>.

CHAdeMO, 2018b. CHAdeMO to jointly develop next-gen Ultra-Fast Charging Standard with China. <www.chademo.com/chademo-to-jointly-develop-next-gen-ultra-fast-charging-standard-withchina/>.

Charge the North, <https://www.fleetcarma.com/charge-the-north-summary/>.

CharIN, 2019. Singapore confirmed CCS − the Combined Charging System − as the charging standard in the ASEAN city state. <www.charinev.org/news/news-detail-2018/news/singapore-confirmed-ccsthe-combined-charging-system-as-the-charging-standard-in-the-asean-city/>.

Chunlin, G., Dequan, H., Qinbo, Y., Zhou, M., 2017. Dynamic sorting intelligent charging control strategy of electric vehicles based on time-of-use price. In: Proceedings of the 2017 China International Electrical and Energy Conference (CIEEC), October 25−27, 2017, Beijing, China, pp. 199−204.

Clint, J., Gamboa, B., Henzie, B., Karasawa, A., (Alternative Energy Systems Consulting, Incorporated). 2015. Considerations for Corridor Direct Current Fast Charging Infrastructure in California. California Energy Commission. CEC-600-2015-015.

Coordination Council and National Knowledge Platform for Smart Grids, 2014. <https://smartcitysweden.com/focus-areas/climate-energy-environment/smart-grids/>.

Daina, N., Sivakumar, A., Polak, J.W., 2017. Electric vehicle charging choices: modelling and implications for smart charging services. Transp. Res. Part Emerg. Technol. 81, 36−56.

Danish Ministry of Climate, Energy and Building, 2013. Smart Grid Strategy. <https://d346xxcyottdqx.cloudfront.net/wp-content/uploads/2013/11/Denmark_Smart_Grid_Strategy.pdf>.

Department of Energy and Climate Change, 2014. Smart grid vision and routemap. <https://assets.publishing.service.gov.uk/government/uploads/system/uploads/attachment_data/file/285417/Smart_Grid_Vision_and_RoutemapFINAL.pdf>.

Druitt, J., Früh, W.-G., 2012. Simulation of demand management and grid balancing with electric vehicles. J. Power Sources 216, 104−116.

EC, 2014. Directive 2014/94/EU of the European Parliament and of the Council of 22 October 2014 on the deployment of alternative fuels infrastructure. <https://publications.europa.eu/en/publicationdetail/-/publication/d414289b-5e6b-11e4-9cbe-01aa75ed71a1/language-en>.

ElaadNL, 2018. Sneller volle accu door flexibele laadsnelheid (Faster full battery due to flexible charging speed). <www.elaad.nl/news/sneller-volle-accu-door-flexibele-laadsnelheid/>.

Electrek, 2018. Tesla confirms Model 3 is getting a CCS plug in Europe, adapter coming for Model S and Model X. <https://electrek.co/2018/11/14/tesla-model-3-ccs-2-plug-europe-adapter-model-s-modelx/>.

Fazelpour, F., Vafaeipour, M., Rahbari, O., Rosen, M.A., 2014. Intelligent optimization to integrate a plug-in hybrid electric vehicle smart parking lot with renewable energy resources and enhance grid characteristics. Energy Convers. Manag. 77, 250–261.

Figenbaum, E., 2017. Perspectives on Norway's supercharged electric vehicle policy. Environ. Innov. Soc. Trans. 25, 14–34.

FLEXITRANSTORE, An integrated platform for increased FLEXIbility in smart TRANSmission grids with STORage Entities and large penetration of renewable energy sources. <http://www.flexitranstore.eu/sites/default/files/publications/FLEXITRANSTORE%20-%20Global%20Presentation.pdf>.

French Environment & Energy Management Agency-ADEME, 2013. <https://www.ademe.fr/en/research-and-innovation-0>.

Gallardo-Lozano, M.I., Milanés-Montero, M.A., Guerrero-Martínez, E., Romero-Cadaval, 2012. Electric vehicle battery charger for smart grids. Electr. Power Syst. Res. 90, 18–29.

García-Villalobos, I., Zamora, J.I., San Martín, F.J., Asensio, V., Aperribay, 2014. Plug-in electric vehicles in electric distribution networks: a review of smart charging approaches. Renew. Sustain. Energy Rev. 38, 717–731.

Giffinger, R., Fertner, C., Kramar, R., Kalasek, N., Pichler-Milanović, E.M., 2007. Ranking of European medium-sized cities. Centre of Regional Science, Vienna UT, October <http://www.smart-cities.eu/download/smart_cities_final_report.pdf>.

Goncalves, R.L., Saraiva, J.T., Sousa, J.C., Mendes, V.T., 2013. Impact of electric vehicles on the electricity prices and on the load curves of the Iberian electricity market. In: Proceedings of the EEM 2013: 10th International Conference on the European Energy Market, May 27–31, pp. 1–8.

Government of India, 2018. Charging infrastructure for electric vehicles - guidelines and standards. <https://powermin.nic.in/sites/default/files/webform/notices/scan0016%20%281%29.pdf>.

Han, S., Han, S., Sezaki, K., 2010. Development of an optimal vehicle-to-grid aggregator for frequency regulation. TSG 2010 (1), 65–72.

Harris, C.B., Webber, M.E., 2014. The sensitivity of vehicle-to-grid revenues to plug-in electric vehicle battery size and EVSE power rating. In: Proceedings of the 2014 IEEE PES General Meeting (PESGM), July 27–31, 2014, National Harbor, MD.

Hellenic National Meteorological Service, 2018. Available from: <www.hnms.gr>.

Hu, J., You, S., Lind, M., Ostergaard, J., 2014. Coordinated charging of electric vehicles for congestion prevention in the distribution grid. IEEE Trans. Smart Grid 5 (2), 703–711.

I. T. C. 69, 2010. IEC 61851-1 electric vehicle conductive charging system – part 1: General requirements. Technical Report.

IEEE (Institute of Electrical and Electronics Engineers), 2018. China and Japan push for a global charging standard for EVs, <https://spectrum.ieee.org/energywise/transportation/efficiency/a-globalcharging-standard-for-ev>.

International Electrotechnical Commission – IEC, 2011. IEC 62196-2 plugs, socket-outlets. vehicle connectors and vehicle inlets – conductive charging of electric vehicles – part 2: Dimensional compatibility and interchangeability requirements for A.C. pin and contact-tube accessories.

International Electrotechnical Commission-IEC, 2014. IEC 62196-1 plugs, socket-outlets. Vehicle connectors and vehicle inlets – conductive charging of electric vehicles – part 1: General requirements.

International Electrotechnical Commission-IEC, 2017. Electric vehicle conductive charging system: Part 1: general requirements. <https://webstore.iec.ch/publication/33644>.

International Energy Agency-IEA, 2019. Outlook to Electric Mobility. Paris, France.

Jiang, B., Fei, Y., 2013. Decentralized scheduling of PEV on-street parking and charging for smart grid reactive power compensation. In: Proceedings of the IEEE PES ISGT 2013: innovative smart grid technologies, February 24–27, 2013, pp. 1–6.

Jiang, W., Xu, S., Li, N., 2016. Contactless power charger for light electric vehicles featuring active load matching. J. Power Electron 16 (1), 102–110. Available from: https://doi.org/10.6113/JPE.2016.16.1.102.

Kaur, K., Kumar, N., Singh, M., 2018. Coordinated power control of electric vehicles for grid frequency support: MILP-based hierarchical control design. TSG 10, 3364–3373.

Kettles, D., Raustad, R., 2017. Electric vehicle charging technologies analysis and standards. Electric Vehicle Transportation Center, University of Central Florida. <http://fsec.ucf.edu/en/publications/pdf/FSEC-CR-2057-17.pdf>.

Lam, A.Y., Leung, K.-C., Li, V.O., 2012. Capacity management of vehicle-to-grid system for power regulation services. In: Proceedings of the 2012 IEEE Third International Conference on Smart Grid Communications (SmartGridComm).

Lambert T, Gilman P, Lilienthal P., 2006. Micropower system modeling with HOMER. Integration of Alternative Sources of Energy, Wiley Publications, p. 1.

Li, Z., Liang, Q., Cheng, X., 2014. Emerging WiFi direct technique in home area networks for smart grid: power consumption and outage performance. Ad Hoc Netw. 22, 61–68.

Li, Z., Chowdhury, M., Bhavsar, P., He, Y., 2015. Optimizing the performance of vehicle-to-grid (V2G) enabled battery electric vehicles through a smart charge scheduling model. Int. J. Automot. Technol. 16, 827–837.

Liu, J., 2012. Electric vehicle charging infrastructure assignment and power grid impacts assessment in Beijing. Energy Policy 51, 544–557.

Liu Y., Hui F., Xu R., Chen T., Li J., 2011. Investigation on the construction mode of the charging station and battery exchange station. Asia-Pacific Power and Energy Engineering Conference (APPEEC), pp.1–2.

Liu, H., Hu, Z., Song, Y., Lin, J., 2013. Decentralized vehicle-to-grid control for primary frequency regulation considering charging demands. TPWRS 28, 3480–3489.

Liu, J., Zhang, N., Kang, C., Kirschen, D.S., Xia, q, 2018. Decision-making models for the participants in cloud energy storage. IEEE Trans. Smart Grid 9 (6), 5512–5521.

Lopes, J.A.P., Soares, F.J., Almeida, P.M.R., 2011. Integration of electric vehicles in the electric power system. Proc. IEEE 99, 168–183.

López, G., Moreno, J.I., Amarís, H., Salazar, F., 2014. Paving the road toward smart grids through large-scale advanced metering infrastructures. Electr. Power Syst. Res.

Low Carbon London, <https://innovation.ukpowernetworks.co.uk/projects/low-carbon-london/> (accessed 01.06.20.).

Lund, H., Mathiesen, B.V., Liu, W., Zhang, X., Clark, W.W., 2014. Chapter 7 - Analysis: 100 percent renewable energy systems. Renew. Energy Syst. 185–238. Available from: https://doi.org/10.1016/B978-0-12-410423-5.00007-9.

Luo, X., Xia, S., Chan, K.W., 2014. A decentralized charging control strategy for plug-in electric vehicles to mitigate wind farm intermittency and enhance frequency regulation. J. Power Sources 248, 604–614.

Ma, Y., Bin, Z., Xuesong, Z., Zhiqiang, G., Yanjuan, W., Jinliang, Y., et al., 2016. An overview on V2G strategies to impacts from EV integration into power system. In: Proceedings of Control and Decision Conference (CCDC), IEEE, Chinese, pp. 2895–900.

Meissner, E., Richter, G., 2003. Battery monitoring and electrical energy management: precondition for future vehicle electric power systems. J. Power Sources 116 (1), 79–98.

Metha, S., 2010. Electric plug-in vehicle/electric vehicle status report. Electr. Eng. 2010, 1–15.

Muratori, M., 2018. Impact of uncoordinated plug-in electric vehicle charging on residential power demand. Nat. Energy 3, 193–201.

Mwasilu, J.J., Justo, E.K., Kim, T.D., Do, J.W., Jung, 2014. Electric vehicles and smart grid interaction: a review on vehicle to grid and renewable energy sources integration. Renew. Sustain. Energy Rev. 34, 501–516.

Nanaki, E., Koroneos, C., 2016. Climate change mitigation and deployment of electric vehicles in urban areas. J. Renew. Energy, 99, 1153–1160.

Nanaki, E.A., Xydis, G., 2018. Deployment of renewable energy systems: barriers, challenges, and opportunities. Advances in Renewable Energies and Power Technologies. Elsevier.

Nanaki, E., Xydis, C., 2019. Exergetic Aspects of Renewable Energy Systems — Insights to Transportation and Energy Sector for Intelligent Communities. Taylor and Francis, ISBN: 9781138088580.

Nguyen, D.T., Le, L.B., 2014. Joint optimization of electric vehicle and home energy scheduling considering user comfort preference. IEEE Trans. Smart Grid 5 (1), 188–199.

NREL (US National Renewable Energy Laboratory), 2017. Enabling fast charging: a technology gap assessment. <www.energy.gov/sites/prod/files/2017/10/f38/XFC%20Technology%20Gap%20Assessment%20Report_FINAL_10202017.pdf>.

Pacific Gas & Electric, 2017. PG&E & Clean Energy Programs.

Pal, S., Kumar, R., 2018. Electric vehicle scheduling strategy in residential demand response programs with neighbor connection. TII 2018 (14), 980–988.

Pascale-Louise Blyth, S., 2011. Electric cars on the 100% renewable energy island of Samsø. Master's thesis. Aalborg University. <https://projekter.aau.dk/projekter/files/52872570/SEPM4_2011_8.pdf>.

Paschero M., Anniballi, L., Del Vescovo, G., et al., 2013. Design and implementation of a fast recharge station for electric vehicles. In: Industrial Electronics (ISIE), 2013 IEEE International Symposium on, IEEE, pp. 1–6.

Pavić, I., Capuder, T., Kuzle, I., 2015. Value of flexible electric vehicles in providing spinning reserve services. Appl. Energy 157, 60–74.

Peng, C., Zou, J., Lian, L., 2017. Dispatching strategies of electric vehicles participating in frequency regulation on power grid: a review. Renew. Sustain. Energy Rev 68, 147–152.

Pillai, J.R., Bak-Jensen, B. 2010, Vehicle-to-grid systems for frequency regulation in an Islanded Danish distribution network. In: 2010 IEEE Vehicle Power and Propulsion Conference. IEEE, Lille, pp. 1–6.

Porsche, 2018. Mission E. <https://newsroom.porsche.com/en/products/porsche-taycan-mission-e-driveunit-battery-charging-electro-mobility-dossier-sportscar-production-christophorus-387-15827.html>.

Qi, W., Xu, Z., Shen, Z.J.M., Hu, Z., Song, Y., 2014. Hierarchical coordinated control of plug-in electric vehicles charging in multifamily dwellings. IEEE Trans. Smart Grid 5 (3), 1465–1474.

Rajakaruna, S., Shahnia, F., Ghosh, A., 2015. Plug in Electric Vehicles in Smart Grids, first ed. Springer Science and Business Media Singapore Pte Ltd.

Ramírez Díaz, A., et al., 2015. Impact of electric vehicles as distributed energy storage in isolated systems: the case of Tenerife. Sustainability Vol. 7 (11), 15152–15178.

Rauchfuss, L., Foulquier, J., Werner, R., 2014. Charging station as an active filter for harmonics compensation of smart grid. In: Proceedings of the IEEE ICHQP 2014: 16th International Conference on Harmonics and Quality of Power, May 25–28, 2014, pp. 181–184.

Rehman, U., Riaz, M., 2018. Real time controlling algorithm for vehicle to grid system under price uncertainties. In: Proceedings of the ICPESG, April 9–10, 2018, Mirpur Azad Kashmir, Pakistan, pp. 1–7.

Richardson, D.B., 2013. Electric vehicles and the electric grid: a review of modeling approaches, Impacts, and renewable energy integration. Renew. Sustain. Energy Rev. 19, 247–254.

Rotering, N., Ilic, M., 2011. Optimal charge control of plug-in hybrid electric vehicles in deregulated electricity markets. TPWRS 26, 1021–1029.

SAE International, 2018. Electric Vehicle Power Transfer System Using a Three-Phase Capable Coupler J3068_201804. SAE International, <www.sae.org/standards/content/j3068_201804/>.

Salisbury, M., Toor, W., 2016. How leading utilities are embracing electric vehicles. SWEEP (Southwest Energy Efficiency Project). <www.swenergy.org/data/sites/1/media/documents/publications/documents/How_Leading_Utilities_Are_Embracing_EVs_Feb-2016.pdf>.

Schey, S., 2013. Canadian EV infrastructure deployment. Available from: <https://www.bchydro.com/content/dam/BCHydro/customer-portal/documents/corporate/environment-sustainability/electric-vehicles/DC14-071%20Canadian%20EV%20Infrastructure%20Deployment%20Guidelines%202014_web.pdf>.

Shinde, P., Swarup, K.S., 2016. Optimal electric vehicle charging schedule for demand side management. In Proceedings of the 2016 First International Conference on Sustainable Green Buildings and Communities (SGBC), December 18–20, 2016, Chennai, India.

Siano, P., 2014. Demand response and smart grids — a survey. Renew. Sustain. Energy Rev. 30 (2014), 461–478.

Smart Energy Network RD&D, 2013. <http://www.smartenergynetworks.dk/>.

Smart-Energy.com, 2019. Tata Power inaugurates grid-scale battery storage system, February, 15, <https://www.smart-energy.com/industry-sectors/storage/india-announces-first-grid-scale-battery-storage-system/> (accessed 01.06.20.).

Smart Grid Austria, 2008. <https://www.smartgrids.at/english.html>.

Smart Grid Italia, 2014. <http://www.smartgrids-italia.com/>.

Smart Grids Austria, 2015. <https://www.smartgrids.at/english.html>.

Smart Grid in Australia, <https://data.gov.au/data/dataset/4e21dea3-9b87-4610-94c7-15a8a77907ef> (accessed 01.06.20.).

Smart Grid on Jeju Island, <https://www.youtube.com/watch?v = 2x4bpycRySI> (accessed 01.06.20.).

Smart Metering Initiative, Ministry of Environment, 2016. <https://www.auditor.on.ca/en/content/annualreports/arreports/en14/311en14.pdf> (accessed 01.06.20.).

Smart Otaniemi, <https://smartotaniemi.fi/>.

Southern California Edison, 2015. Electric car rate options—rate option 2: TOU-EV-4. <https://www.sce.com/wps/portal/home/business/rates/electric-car-business-rates>.

Sustainable Energy Authority of Ireland, 2009. Ireland — your smart grid opportunity. <https://www.smartgrid.gov/files/documents/Ireland_Your_Smart_Grid_Opportunity_201009.pdf>.

Sustainable Energy Authority of Ireland, 2011. Smart grid roadmap. <https://www.seai.ie/publications/Smartgrid-Roadmap.pdf>.

Synchro Phasor-based Automatic Real-time Control (SPARC). <https://www.sintef.no/en/projects/synchrophasor-based-automatic-real-time-control-sparc2/>.

Taibi, E., Fernández, C., 2017. The impact of electric vehicles deployment on production cost in a Caribbean Island country. IRENA Innovation and Technology Center (IITC), Bonn.

Tan, Z., Yang, P., Nehorai, A., 2014. An optimal and distributed demand response strategy with electric vehicles in the smart grid. IEEE Trans. Smart Grid 5 (2), 861–869.

Tesla, 2019, Introducing V3 Supercharging, Tesla, <www.tesla.com/blog/introducing-v3-supercharging>.

The Norwegian Smart grid Centre, 2010. <https://smartgrids.no/english/>.

Think Smart Grids, 2015. <https://www.thinksmartgrids.fr/wp-content/uploads/2015/10/THINKSMARTGRIDS-PRESS-KIT.pdf>.

TILOS—Technology Innovation for the Local Scale, Optimum integration of battery energy storage. <https://www.tiloshorizon.eu/>.

Torreglosa, J.P., García-Triviño, P., Fernández-Ramirez, L.M., Jurado, F., 2016. Control based on techno-economic optimization of renewable hybrid energy system for stand-alone applications. Expert Syst. Appl. 51, 59—75.

Wang, C.-S., Stielau, O.H., Covic, G.A., 2005. Design considerations for a contactless electric vehicle battery charger. IEEE Trans. Ind. Electron 52 (5), 1308—1314.

WISEGRID — Wide Scale demonstration of integrated solutions and business models for European Smart GRID. <https://www.wisegrid.eu> (accessed 02.06.20.).

Wu, D., Aliprantis, D.C., Ying, L., 2012. Load scheduling and dispatch for aggregators of plug-in electric vehicles. IEEE Trans. Smart Grid 3 (1), 368—376.

Yokohama, Smart city project. <https://www.collaborative.city/item/yokohama-smart-city-project/> (accessed 01.06.20.).

Zheng, Y., Dong, Z., Xu, Y., Meng, K., Zhao, J., Qiu, J., 2014. Electric vehicle battery charging/ swap stations in distribution systems: comparison study and optimal planning. IEEE Trans. Power Syst 29 (1), 221—229.

CHAPTER 4

Market introduction of electric vehicles to urban areas

4.1 Introduction

Energy is essential for the modern way of life. Nonetheless, the use of fossil fuels for energy purposes has resulted in excessive CO_2 emissions, environmental pollution, and oil dependency. The use of fossil fuels in the transportation sector contributes to global warming and climate change. Especially in urban areas such as cities, which are growing fast worldwide, the transport energy system needs to be able to provide innovative and more efficient ways to respond to the increasing demand for more sophisticated and complex services. In order to reduce significantly the use of fossil fuels in urban mobility, whilst improving air quality and increasing the accessibility and attractiveness of urban areas, it is necessary to increase the use of nonconventionally fueled vehicles for passenger and freight transport in urban areas. The introduction of electric vehicles (EV) is a promising option in order to achieve decarbonization objectives, energy security, improved urban air quality, and to increase energy efficiency. In particular, in the case of road transport, the substitution of internal combustion engine (ICE) vehicles cars with EV at a large scale is expected to improve the air quality (Nanaki et al., 2016). However, EVs penetration remains rather low except for only a few countries (e.g., Norway). The unattractiveness of EVs for the mainstream market in comparison to conventional vehicles can be mainly attributed to the expensive price and high uncertainties regarding battery upgrade, charging time, life expectancy, as well as the vehicles' driving range (Liao et al., 2017). It is noted that "range anxiety" and EV unfamiliarity may disappear as consumers are educated, but they remain strong initial obstacles to purchasing EVs (Nemry et al., 2009). Comparing the payback periods of several advanced vehicle powertrain options versus an advanced gasoline vehicle option, it is shown that only through significant cost reductions can EVs evolve to offer an interesting value proposition to consumers (Thiel et al., 2010).

In order to tackle all of these bottlenecks, supportive policies and integrated strategies aiming to accelerate the EV penetration in urban areas,

Electric Vehicles for Smart Cities
DOI: https://doi.org/10.1016/B978-0-12-815801-2.00004-6

such as cities, should be adopted. For instance, in order to meet the goals of the Paris agreement, transport emissions must be reduced by more than 90% by 2050 (United Nations, 2019). Such a radical change cannot be achieved through incremental improvements to existing vehicles, a shift to fossil gas, or through advanced biofuels and synthetic fuels that cannot be produced in the volumes needed to power all mobility. Future cars should be electric, chargeable in minutes with ranges of 500 km and powered from smart renewable grids.

In this direction, most attention has been given to improve the quality and reduce the production cost—through research and development—of the battery technology of EVs (Williander and Stålstad, 2013). Nonetheless, apart from research and innovation, focus should also be given to the implementation of business models for commercialization of EVs. Moreover, the deployment of EVs requires the integration of several new market actors such as vehicle producers, supply chain, charging infrastructure, providers, network operators, energy utilities, and service providers with new business models or innovative vehicle-to-grid (V2G) solutions (Zubaryeva et al., 2012).

This chapter aims to provide readers with a useful insight of market share and business models with regard to the deployment and the acceleration of electromobility in urban areas. Given the challenges to reaching targets for EV penetration in global markets, this chapter also investigates how business model innovation is helping companies to overcome barriers to adoption, enable value creation, and capture in the EV sector. In this direction, a diversity of new business models that have been implemented worldwide are presented as case studies. In addition, this chapter aims to contribute to the current discussion in the literature and among stakeholders on the effectiveness of policy measures in the diffusion of EVs. In this context, it aims to create an integrated approach for business model development taking into account the concepts of electrification and sustainability. The integrated approach of this model highlights the inefficient integration of EVs into the electricity sector; consumer perceptions about the adequacy of charging infrastructure; issues about equity of access to electricity; business models to enable the EV uptake that will adapt differently to different markets and regions; and the obstacles that the supply chain might face.

4.2 Business models

As per Osterwalder et al. (2005) a business model is a conceptual tool that contains a set of elements and their relationships and allows expressing the business logic of a specific firm. It is a description of the value a company offers to one or several segments of customers and of the architecture of the firm and its networks of partners for creating, marketing, and delivering this value and relationship capital, in order to generate profitable and sustainable revenue streams. Key parts of a business model are the value proposition, the customers, the necessary value creation structure, and the revenue structure, whereas the transformation of the individual components into real-world processes is the main function of a business model.

According to Osterwalder et al. (2005), business models can be classified in three different categories, based on their description by different authors:

- *Overarching business model concepts*: These include definitions of what a business model is and what belongs in it. For this reason, they are considered to be abstract concepts describing all real-world businesses. This category includes both definitions of what the concept of business model means as well as meta-models, which also define the elements included in it.
- *Taxonomies*: This category includes descriptions of different types or meta-model types that are generic but contain common characteristics. The types refer to simple categorization, whereas meta-model types refer to different models. Taxonomies may apply to specific industries instead of business in general.
- *Instance level*: This category includes real-world business models as well as conceptualizations, representations, and descriptions of them. They are employed to describe companies in case-based studies.

During the past decades, many frameworks have been developed, aiming to familiarize the concept of business models. These include inter alia the description of a business model with three simple "business model story elements": value creation, value delivery, and value capture (Kaplan, 2012). The value creation structure is divided into resources, partners, and activities. The value network determines the position of the focal firm and its partnerships within the value chain. Finally, value is captured by the focal firm and turned into profits through its cost and revenue models, as well as other sources such as government support (Fig. 4.1). All of the components are oriented toward the value proposition.

Table 4.1 summarizes nine elements of a business model framework, which can be used for business model development (Osterwalder and Pigneur, 2010; Osterwalder, 2004). The nine elements of the business model canvas framework are part of the following four areas: product, customer interface, infrastructure management, and financial aspects.

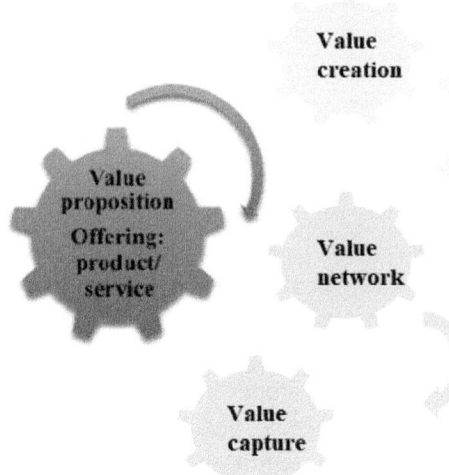

Figure 4.1 Basic definition of a business model.

Chesbrough and Rosenbloom (2002) highlight the business model's importance in taking technological innovations to market. They suggest six functions of a business model:

- Articulate the value proposition—the value created for users by the offering based on the technology.
- Identify a market segment and specify the revenue generation mechanism(s) for the firm.
- Define the structure of the value chain within the firm required to create and distribute the offering and determine the complementary assets needed to support the firm's position in this chain.
- Estimate the cost structure and profit potential of producing the offering.
- Describe the position of the firm within the value network linking suppliers and customers, including identification of potential complementors and competitors.
- Formulate the competitive strategy by which the firm will gain and hold advantage for rival.

Finally, Johnson et al. (2008) describe four elements of a business model to create and deliver value:

- *Customer value proposition*: Takes into consideration the target customer, job to be done, and offering that satisfies the job to be done.
- *Profit formula*: Defines how the company creates value for itself. It includes the revenue model, cost structure, margin model, and resource velocity.

Table 4.1 Business models elements and descriptions.

	Area		Business model element	Description
I.	Product	1	Value proposition	Overall view of a company's products and services that are of value to the customer
II.	Customer interface	2	Customer segment	Segments of customers a company wants to offer value to
		3	Channels	Getting in touch with the customer
		4	Customer relationship	The link a company establishes between itself and the customer
III.	Infrastructure management	5	Key resources	The arrangement of assets required to create value to the customer (the inputs in the value creation process and sources of capabilities)
		6	Key activities	Actions a company performs to do business and achieve its goals
		7	Key partners	Voluntarily initiated cooperative agreements for outsourcing activities and acquiring resources outside the enterprise
IV.	Financial aspects	8	Revenue streams	The way a company makes profit through a variety of revenue flows resulting from value propositions successfully offered to customers
		9	Cost structure	The representation in money of all the means employed in the business model elements

Source: Adapted from Osterwalder, A., Pigneur, Y., 2010. Business Model Generation: A Handbook for Visionaries, Game Changers, and Challengers. Hoboken: Wiley; Osterwalder, A., 2004. The Business Model Ontology: A Proposition in a Design Science Approach (Doctoral dissertation). University of Lausanne, Lausanne.

- *Key resources*: Resources required to deliver the customer value proposition, such as people, technology, equipment, channels, and partnerships.
- Four key processes together with key resources define how the value is delivered (including processes as well as rules, metrics, and norms).

4.2.1 Business models in the automotive industry: The shift to business innovation

The majority of automotive industries follow business models with a structured and linear approach for delivering a tangible product (e.g., vehicle) to the end user. Car manufacturers often have their own network of car dealers, leasing companies, and financing agencies. Apart from the primary business model of selling vehicles, car dealers offer personal leasing to consumers, trade secondhand cars, and earn additional revenues from maintenance services and replacement of car parts. Upstream suppliers to car manufacturers range from providers of computer chips and software to providers of components such as bumpers, engines, and upholstery. The upstream suppliers are deeply integrated into the supply chain.

Nonetheless, during the past decades the automotive industry has redesigned its approach, with regard to supply of products and services related to the development, design, manufacture, marketing, and sales of commercial vehicles. Both digital and nondigital transformative technologies have led many automotive industries to remodel their business from product to service-oriented enterprises (Lengton et al., 2015). Thus OEMs should adapt their strategies and should introduce new innovative business models aligned with novel technologies that place the customer needs at the forefront. In this way, actors collaborate to develop new mobility offerings in which possession of a car is less relevant than access to transportation means, and in which concerns about ecological impact are taken into consideration.

Various types of novel services, which provide a communication platform with other objects, are emerging in the automotive industry. These services provide an interaction between vehicles (e.g., collision–warning systems), between vehicles and road infrastructure (e.g., road information), and between vehicles and devices (e.g., smartphone integration) (Lengton et al., 2015; Papadimitratos et al., 2009). Auxiliary services include inter alia mobility management systems such as navigation systems, vehicle management systems that allow for services regarding better car usage, entertainment, safety (e.g., information regarding traffic jams), autonomous driving (e.g., automated parking), well-being, and home integration.

The above impel the design of new innovative business models, which are going to create products or offerings of value, able to compete with the offerings of new participants. Further to this, the need for decarbonization of the road transport sector, in conjunction with electromobility, as a potentially viable alternative to traditional petrol or diesel cars has been accompanied by an expectation that it will change the business models that vehicle manufacturers and others would need to access the market. Business model innovation has gained increasing attention since the early 2000s, and is considered a source of innovation that "complements the traditional subjects of process, product and organizational innovations" (Zott et al., 2011). In this direction, innovative sustainable technologies in the field of automotive industry are useful, in order to move toward the energy transition pathway to a low-carbon transport system. It is highlighted that innovative sustainable business models usually entail certain barriers for widespread market penetration, while current business models may be inadequate to address these barriers (Wells, 2004). For this reason, the implementation of prevailing business models is unlikely to achieve market success (Beaume and Midler, 2009). Finally, innovative business models may be a prerequisite for sustainable technologies to become commercially viable and fulfill their potential in tackling environmental problems (Christensen et al., 2012).

4.2.2 Business models for electric vehicles

The most common business model adopted for conventional vehicles is full purchase: acquiring ownership of the car by paying the full purchase price. Some alternative business models for car adoption are vehicle leasing and battery leasing [only for battery-electric vehicles (BEV)]. Nonetheless, in the case of EVs, this model faces some challenges, posing some questions about its suitability. In the first place, many potential consumers are concerned about the risks with regard to battery life, maintenance accessibility, rate of technology development, and residual value. In the second place, despite the fact that the total cost of ownership (TCO) of an EV throughout its lifetime may be around the same or is even lower than those for gasoline cars (Nanaki et al., 2015), the high purchase price which has to be paid at once creates a financial barrier for many potential customers.

Many studies have investigated some aspects of innovative business models for EVs. These include inter alia the studies of Wells (2013), who provided a brief overview of sustainable business models in the automotive industry; of Bohnsack et al. (2014), who investigated the impact of path dependencies of incumbents and startup firms in the EV industry; of Liao et al. (2019), who studied consumer preferences for battery lease, vehicle lease, and mobility guarantee; as well as of Nian et al. (2019), who developed a business model for EV without policy support. It is noted that some studies focus also on the business models for the infrastructure developer (Markkula et al., 2013), whereas other studies (Kley et al., 2011) employed a whole-system approach in developing business models taking into consideration the characteristics of vehicles, batteries, infrastructure, and system services (such as load shifting and backfeeding power) for various stakeholders. The role of enterprises and governments along the value chain of EV in the bus and taxi fleets has also been examined (Li et al., 2016), indicating that synergies between the private and public sector are beneficial to EV adoption. Business models on EV charging have also been examined, for instance Madina et al. (2016) indicated that access to private home charging is expected to be a strong driver for EV adoptions as long as owners can cover high annual mileages, charge their EVs at lower prices overnight, and benefit from subsidies for EV purchase. Furthermore, a study by Bessa and Matos (2012) highlighted the role of EV aggregators in supporting the V2G applications and business models.

Several studies have also analyzed business models with regard to the vehicle ownership cost. In this direction, a pricing model from the consumers' perspective taking into consideration the upfront purchase cost, operating costs, fuel cost, and other costs over the life cycle of vehicle ownership has been proposed. In addition, the role of factors such as subsidies, fuel economy, access to charging points, carbon emissions, and revenue preserving tax has also been investigated in different business models, indicating that subsidies for reducing the upfront purchase price of EVs play a crucial role in EV adoption.

Based on the above, it is obvious that novel business plans—aiming to lower the costs for the customer and improve customer acceptance by promising suitable benefits—are necessary for the energy transition to a low-carbon transportation system. For this reason, new mobility concepts and business models are necessary, in order to transform the technological advantages of EV into added value for the customers. The OECD (Oslo manual) distinguishes four types of innovation and suggests definitions that can be employed to different units (OECD, 2005):

1. *Product innovation*: It refers to the introduction of a good or service that is new or significantly improved with respect to its characteristics or intended uses. This includes significant improvements in technical specifications, components and materials, incorporated software, user friendliness, or other functional characteristics.
2. *Process innovation*: It refers to the implementation of a new or significantly improved production or delivery method. This includes significant changes in techniques, equipment and/or software.
3. *Marketing innovation*: It refers to the implementation of a new marketing method involving significant changes in product design or packaging, product placement, product promotion, or pricing.
4. *Organizational innovation*: It refers to the implementation of a new organizational method in the firm's business practices, workplace organization, or external relations.

Despite the fact that business model innovation plays a significant role in the long-term competitiveness of companies, its implementation constitutes a challenge for many established companies, mainly due to their complex structure (Schneider and Spieth, 2013). Especially in the case of electromobility, the lack of available methods of support cannot lead to clear results. In this direction, the adoption of an integrated approach—taking into consideration all stakeholders, including car and battery manufacturers, new mobility providers as well as policy makers and governments—will enable companies to pursue the most effective and profitable business model for EV. An integrated approach is expected to cope with the uncertainties of innovative business models for EV and will help to dismantle obstacles and thus promote the introduction of EV.

4.2.3 Business models for electric vehicles: An integrated approach

The findings from existing literature—as presented in Section 4.2.2—revealed the complex interactions between stakeholders, many of which are not part of the value chain of neither ICE vehicles nor electricity supply. In order to tackle the abovementioned key barriers, which hinder the EV market penetration and boosting of EV sales, many EV manufacturers have adopted novel business models by adjusting them to the traditional business model in two ways: providing additional services by altering the value proposition or reducing initial purchase cost by changing the revenue model (Kley et al., 2011). Nonetheless, despite its wide application and high relevance with actual purchase choice in reality, insight in the impact of EV business models on EV adoption is still lacking. For this reason, an integrated approach—taking into account all stakeholders—should be adopted for the development of alternative business models for the promotion of electromobility. Such an integrated approach can be used for policy makers and regulatory bodies to design the policy and regulatory framework to better promote electromobility.

In order to develop innovative business models and examine them systemically, it has to be investigated how these are differentiated from the classical business models. Especially in the case of promotion of EVs in urban areas, the suggested integrated business model (Fig. 4.2), should take into consideration all the identified drivers, which have been previously discussed in the literature. These include all the components that are influenced by electric mobility concepts (i.e., smart energy solutions; mobility services, and the vehicles) within the overall system. Fig. 4.2 presents the links between an integrated innovative strategy for the promotion of electromobility with relative organizational structures and processes. In this way, the objectives, the coordination of activities, the allocation of resources, as well as relative sources of revenue, cost structure, and make-or-buy options of the product are determined. It should be highlighted that EV cannot be deployed without parallel developments in charging infrastructure, taxation and incentive regimes, type approval processes, insurance policies, repair and maintenance facilities, and much

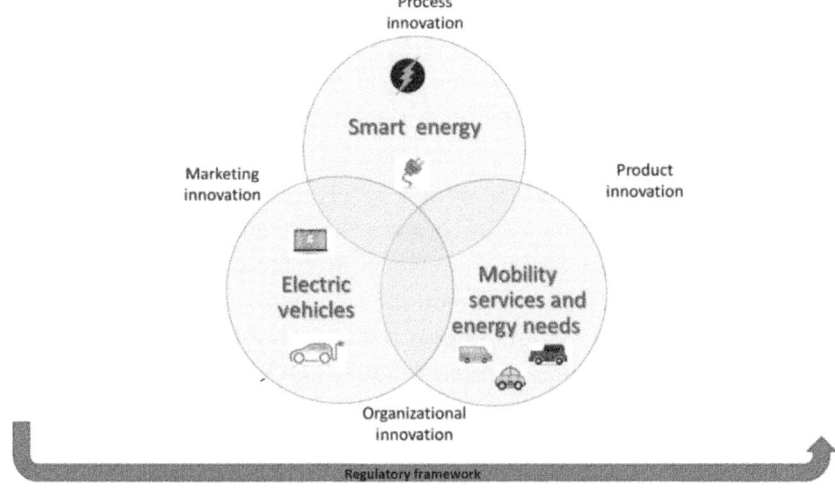

Figure 4.2 Basic concept for an integrated e-mobility business model.

more. This process challenges traditional vehicle manufacturer business models, whereas consumers (both retail and corporate) face new technological and financial risks.

4.2.3.1 Smart energy systems and digital technologies

As per EIP-SCC'S (2013) Strategic Implementation Plan the concept of smart cities can be summarized as: "Smart cities are regarded as systems of people interacting with and using flows of energy, materials, services and financing to catalyze sustainable economic development, resilience, and high quality of life; these flows and interactions become smart through making strategic use of Information and Communication Technologies (ICT) infrastructure and services in a process of transparent urban planning and management that is responsive to the social and economic needs of society." In this context, ICT are key drivers of business model innovation, as they enable new ways of creating and capturing value, new exchange mechanisms and transaction architectures, and new boundary-spanning organizational forms (Al-Debei and Avison, 2010). The concept of smart energy within the framework of smart cities, and especially through smart charging for EV holds the key to unleash synergies between clean transport and low-carbon electricity.

The charging infrastructure for supplying the EV with power is a key driver for the energy transition to a low-carbon transportation system in urban areas. Different alternatives, currently discussed include wired (conductive) and wireless charging points as well as battery swapping. The connections can be private, semipublic, or public. Semipublic connections refer to connections with restricted access—available only to authorized users (i.e., employees permitted to use companies' private car parks). The operator is responsible for installation, maintenance, and repair of the supply unit. Different schemes are available for paying the bill to the electricity provider: no fee, pay per use, or a fixed rate.

Furthermore, the power provided at the charging point plays a crucial role to the recharge of the vehicle. In Europe, domestic power connections range from 3.7 kW (one-phase) to about 11 kW (three-phase). Power connections above this usually are not used domestically and tend to be employed to public connections. Given that the voltage available across Europe is 230 V, high-voltage charging points can be realized using alternating current. However, in the United States and Japan, direct current is the norm due to the lower voltage level of 110 V. Similarly, three levels are used in North America to classify the different power

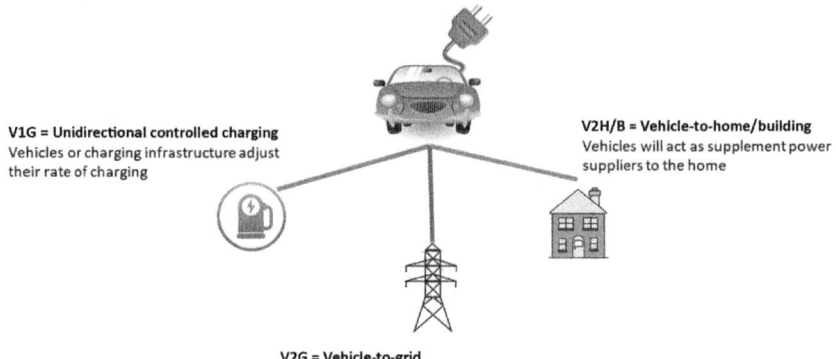

Figure 4.3 Novel forms of smart charging.

connections (Morrow et al., 2008). With regard to the type of connections, it is noted that unidirectional connections can only deliver power in one direction, while bidirectional connections transmit electricity in both directions. The use of potential system services such as backfeeding energy into the grid is dependent on this.

On the other hand, smart charging allows a certain level of control over the charging process. It includes different pricing and technical charging options. The simplest form of incentive—time-of-use pricing—encourages consumers to defer their charging from peak to off-peak periods. More advanced smart charging approaches, such as direct control mechanisms will be necessary as a long-term solution at higher penetration levels and for delivery of close-to-real-time balancing and ancillary services. The main forms of such charging include unidirectional power flow (V1G), V2G, vehicle-to-home (V2H), and vehicle-to-buildings (V2B) (Fig. 4.3). Each type of approach unlocks different options to increase the flexibility of power systems and to support the integration of renewable energy systems (RES), mainly wind and solar photovoltaics.

4.2.3.2 Mobility services and energy needs

Mobility-as-a-service (MaaS) is a concept that has been recognized in modern transport dialogues (Transport Systems Catapult, 2016). It is defined as "a transition from a paradigm under which mobility functionality is accessed through purchasing a product, to a paradigm where mobility functionality is the outcome of a service moving users from one location to another, disassociated from any requirement for asset ownership, and typically arranged on a journey-by-journey basis." Especially in the case of EV business models, there are two possibilities for the customer: (1) he can either buy the product in the form of a vehicle; or (2) buy the service. It should be noted that between these two alternatives, there are other ways to cover the mobility and energy needs of the final customer.

MaaS places users at the core of transport services, offering them tailor-made mobility solutions based on their individual needs (www.maas-alliance.com). The following characteristics comprise a MaaS:

- *Transport on demand.* MaaS satisfies users' needs for mobility by offering tailor-made transport on demand. A MaaS provider arranges the most suitable transport means, be it public transport, taxi or car rental, or even ride-, car-, or bike-sharing.
- *Subscription service.* Users have no need to buy travel tickets or sign up for separate transport accounts since a MaaS account provides the freedom to choose the mobility required, for an agreed period or pay-as-you-go subscription.
- *Potential to create new markets.* For transport providers MaaS can offer new sales channels, access to untapped customer demand, simplified user account and payment management, as well as richer data on travel demand patterns and dynamics.

The ecosystem of a MaaS consists of transport infrastructure, transportation services, transport information, and payment services (Hietanen, 2014). Within the ecosystem, actors such as local authorities or data management companies cooperate, so as to ensure the service's smooth operation and to improve their efficiency (Jittrapirom et al., 2017; Kawasaki, 2015).

Car sharing and carpooling as well as operating models such as Uber and Lyft are mobility services that lead to changes in societal and economic values; given that they change the habits of consumers. Such innovative operating models are beneficial for the promotion of EV in urban areas. In view of significant technological developments, such as big data, Artificial Intelligence (AI), the Internet of Things (IoT), and with the emergence of autonomous vehicles, the future of mobility is going to be affected. For this reason, an integrated business model is necessary in order to investigate the ways through which the energy needs for mobility services can be covered by the deployment of EVs. The integration of multiple forms of electric transportation modes—including public transport—and shared electric mobility services (e.g., e-car sharing, e-bike sharing, e-scooter sharing, e-bus, e-taxi) will give the chance to the user to travel in an eco-friendly and seamless way. Thus the concept of electric mobility as a service (e-MaaS) has emerged (www.emaas.eu). eMaaS refers to the integration of multiple forms of (electric) transportation modes and shared electric mobility services into a single mobility service, which is offered through a single customer-centered interface and also involves the prearrangement of electric mobility technologies and infrastructure (Roberto Reyes García et al., 2019). Finally, with regard to the eMaaS ecosystem, it is noted that this consists of the combination of MaaS, electric mobility systems (EMS) and shared electric mobility services (SEMS). Within the eMaaS ecosystem all three modules (MaaS, EMS, and SEMS) are complementary. This means that, even when each of the modules offers mobility options for the user, eMaaS cannot be achieved by means of only one or two modules (Roberto Reyes García et al., 2019).

4.2.3.3 Electric vehicles

The stakeholders in this category of business model, include not only the OEMs, car dealers, the bank, and the customer (classical vehicle purchase model), but also battery producers and energy suppliers. It is noted, that in many business models the characteristics of an electric vehicle, that is, energy storage (battery) and energy consumption (vehicle), are regarded separately (Andersen et al., 2009). When considering novel mobility concepts, battery and vehicle do not necessarily have the same owner—resulting in numerous ownership combinations. For instance, under exchange systems, the batteries can be used for more than one customer; a vehicle can also be made available to several customers in a car sharing scheme.

The battery cost can be paid via the selling price (pay for equipment). A fixed rate is also conceivable, either independent of use or dependent on it (pay per use). The type of billing depends on the mobility concept offered as well as on the ownership relations. The traction battery is mainly determined by its storage capacity. Moreover, charging stations enable a controllable charging of EV, which advances the interplay between the customer's system and the power grid. It is determined by its load speed. A component that plays a significant role through the entire life cycle of battery and vehicle is the second-life storage application. An alternative to recycling used EV batteries is reconditioning them and reusing them in stationary applications. Second-life battery solutions could also provide energy storage services. An EV battery needs to be replaced when the capacity declines to 70%−80%—that is, when it is no longer sufficient for daily mileage but is still in good condition to be used as an energy storage system. This offers a lifetime extension of up to 10 years for the battery, at a compelling price already today, believed to be around €150 (US$180) per kWh (Reid and Julve, 2016).

Further to this, innovative battery concepts include the resale of recycled batteries. Offering stationary storage allows auto companies with large battery manufacturing capacity to reduce exposure to fluctuating EV sales, reduce inventory, increase manufacturing utilization rates, and monetize the battery after the initial use. Several products for residential customers (smart home optimization) based on second-life batteries are already commercially available, while more advanced applications are in demonstration phases (Holder, 2018).

4.3 Integrated innovative business models for EVs (e-IIBMs): Implementation of a novel concept

Innovative business models will play a significant role in e-mobility transitions. Without novel business models the e-mobility transition may struggle to reach enough citizens to make meaningful contributions to air quality improvements and greenhouse gas reductions from transport. This section—based on the findings of Sections 4.2.2 and 4.2.3—presents an integrated innovative business model taking into account EV, energy demands, and mobility needs within urban areas, such as cities. The business model, as presented in Fig. 4.4, fulfills different stakeholders' needs in different ways and with various levels of complexity. From new mobility as a service offering, to ancillary energy market services using aggregated EV batteries, new value pools are emerging.

The suggested integrated innovative business model (Fig. 4.4) can help city governments to cover their particular mobility and energy needs, as it

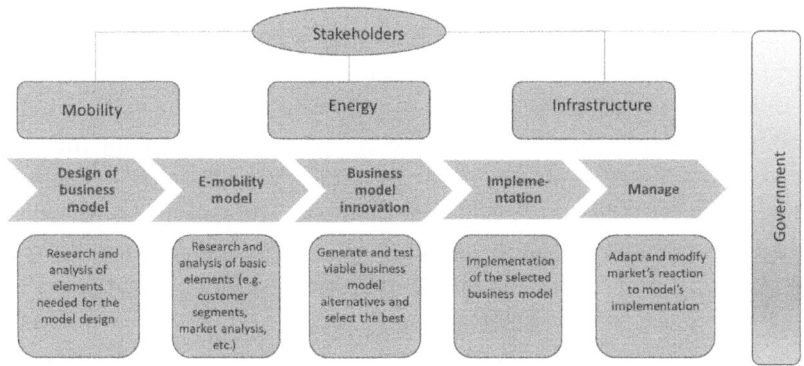

Figure 4.4 Suggested integrated business model for electric vehicles.

takes a multistakeholder perspective at a mobility, energy, and infrastructure level. This enables better monitoring and management, while at the same time it creates considerable opportunities for added value in any city, as it improves efficiency, enhances economic potential, attracts new businesses, and improves the living conditions of their citizens. The interlinkage between areas concerning energy production, distribution, and use; mobility and transport; and ICT offer new interdisciplinary opportunities to improve a city's mobility needs. This requires reconsideration of the value proposition, value creation, value network as well as relative revenue model. In this way, new sources of value are generated from business model innovation, which itself is a competitive advantage for the deployment of EV in urban areas.

The steps that are followed in order to implement an innovative e-mobility model include research and analysis of required elements for the model design, such as the investigation of disruptive technologies necessary for system-wide deployment to yield the most benefits and demand changes in existing processes. The following step includes research and analysis of basic elements for the deployment of electromobility, such as investigation of customer's needs, the capacity of the battery, the capacity of the traction battery of the electric vehicle, the maximum loading speed of the charging station, and the traction current consumption. In this step, also the charging strategies have to be elaborated accurately. The design of the technical system makes it possible to determine when it is necessary to exchange electricity with the energy provider. The selection of the most suitable business model as well as its implementation and management phases are the following steps.

The successful deployment of the above steps requires the collaboration between multiple actors in the value chain. The deployment of electromobility in cities needs also to overcome a possible reluctance on the part of city authorities to deploy untested but innovative products and services. Their integration involves a large number of coordinated actors and stakeholders, which have positive effects on securing financing mechanisms as well as on building the necessary critical mass in terms of ideas and thematic areas to address. Finally, it should be highlighted that the role of the state at national and international level is of great significance in regulatory framing, and in steering all manner of developments that are critical to the success or failure of EV business models. Hence it is only through active engagement and interaction between the state and business that innovative business models will be able to deliver low-carbon mobility.

4.4 Electric vehicles market overview

In 2018 (Fig. 4.5) the global sales of plug-in electric vehicles (PEVs) were more than 2 million (representing a 63% increase compared to 2017), 69% of which were BEVs. On average, EV sales grew rapidly during the period 2012−17, with a compound annual growth rate (CAGR) of 57%. However, the market is still in an incipient phase, with EVs representing only 1.3% of all light-duty vehicles sold in 2017 (MCKiNsEy, 2018). It is noted that all EV have gained 3% share in the mix since 2017, driven by growth in China, the arrival of the Tesla Model 3 and losses for PHEVs in Europe when the new fuel economy test procedure, the Worldwide Harmonized Light-Duty Vehicles Test Procedure (WLTP), became effective in September 2018.

China was for the second consecutive year the largest EV market in the world with a 55.5% of the global sales, selling approximately 1.1 million EV (75% being BEVs and 25% PHEVs) and recording a 63.5% year on year market growth, while Europe was the second largest market with 215,000 EVs sold (28.5% of the global market). Europe's growth was more moderate at 34%, held back by tight inventories, long waiting lists for popular BEVs, and the running-out of high-selling PHEVs. The United States sold 160,000 EVs in 2018. It is highlighted that the market share of PHEVs sold is increased in comparison to the BEVs in the EU and United States, while China is on the contrary oriented toward BEVs.

With regard to Europe's EV market, Norway has achieved the highest EV market penetration, amounting to 46%, implementing a national strategy to exploit the benefits of the green and cheap electricity of the already decarbonized energy sector (99% of the total electricity generation is hydropower). Iceland comes second with 17.5% and Sweden third with a percentage of 8% (IEA, 2019). In big markets, such as the United Kingdom and France, EV market penetration amounted to approximately

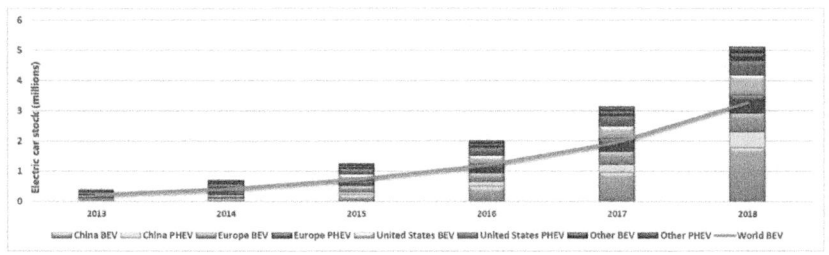

Figure 4.5 Number of passenger electric vehicles in main markets for the period of 2013−18 (International Energy Agency—IEA, 2019).

1.5%. It is noted that the share of the PEVs for the European light vehicle market was 2.3% in 2018 and reached 3.5% in December (highest ever for a single month). In terms of volume, September and the fourth quarter were affected by the WLTP introduction and the dwindling supply of popular PEV models (www.ev-volumes.com, EV volumes, 2019).

Electric two/three-wheelers on the road exceeded 300 million by the end of 2018, with the vast majority in China. In 2018 electric buses continued to witness dynamic developments, with more than 460,000 vehicles on the world's road, almost 100,000 more than in 2017. The market for e-buses is concentrated mainly in Asia Pacific, where a market penetration of 27.6% was reached in 2016. Since 2014 there has been a large uptake of e-buses in China, which is now responsible for 99% of the worldwide sales and fleet. Market penetration in North America and Western Europe is around 0.6%. Whereas China reached 340,000 e-buses in 2017, the largest fleet of e-buses in Europe is in the United Kingdom and accounts for only 344 units (BNEF, 2018).

In addition, low-speed electric vehicles (LSEVs) in 2018 were estimated at 5 million units, up almost 700,000 units from 2017. All LSEVs were located in China. Shared "free-floating" electric foot scooters flourished very rapidly in 2018 and early 2019 in major cities around the world. These foot scooter schemes now operate in around 129 cities in the United States, 30 in Europe, seven in Asia, and six in Australia and New Zealand. In freight transport, EVs were mostly deployed as light-commercial vehicles (LCVs), which reached 250,000 units in 2018, up 80,000 from 2017. Medium truck sales were in the range of 1000−2000 in 2018, mostly concentrated in China (IEA, 2019).

In 2018 Tesla emerged as the market leader with the launch of Model 3. Tesla sold the highest number of vehicles, reaching 11.8% (231,850 units) of the total market, closely followed by BYD with 11.3% (222,743) market share. In 2018, 207 models (143 BEVs and 64 PHEVs) were available for sale—compared to 165 (109 BEVs and 56 PHEVs) in 2017. In 2019, 45 models were added to the list (37 BEVs and 8 PHEVs). In third place comes BAIC with 165,000 units, and BMW comes in fourth with 129,000 units (The Beam Magazine, 2019). BMW became the first automaker to offer inductive charging on its BMW 530e iPerformance model at an additional cost of $3700 including taxes ($1000 for the module on the vehicle and $2700 for mounting the control box).

Finally, the global EV stock in 2018 was served by 5.2 million light-duty vehicle (LDV) chargers (540,000 of which are publicly accessible), complemented by 157,000 fast chargers for buses. The number of EV chargers continued to rise in 2018 to an estimated 5.2 million worldwide for LDVs (IEA, 2019). The majority of them are slow chargers (levels 1 and 2 at homes and workplaces), complemented by almost 540,000 publicly accessible chargers (including 150,000 fast chargers, 78% of which are in China). With the 156,000 fast chargers for buses, by the end of 2018 there were about 300,000 fast chargers installed globally. With regard to energy consumption, it is mentioned that the global EV fleet consumed an estimated 58 terawatt-hours (TWh) of electricity in 2018. Two-wheelers continued to account for the largest share (55%) of EV energy demand, while LDVs witnessed the strongest growth of all transport modes in 2017−18. China accounted for 80% of world electricity demand for EVs in 2018. The global EV stock in 2018 emitted about 38 million tonnes of carbon dioxide equivalent (Mt CO_2-eq) on a well-to-wheel basis. This compares to 78 Mt CO_2-eq emissions that an equivalent ICE fleet would have emitted, leading to net savings from EV deployment of 40 Mt CO_2-eq in 2018.

4.5 Factors influencing the adoption of electric vehicles in urban areas

The deployment of EVs in cities is affected by technological, regulatory, and socioeconomic factors. Therefore issues such as cost, model availability, charging infrastructure, as well as consumer understanding and awareness play significant roles in the successful electric vehicle adoption in urban areas.

Technology: Technological factors are related to the degree of required investments (i.e., charging infrastructure, etc.) as well as to developments in the auto industry and related level of technological readiness that will lead to lower purchase price. Immature technology has been a huge obstacle to the development of EV. This problem is reflected in high purchase price, short cruise range, and long charging time. It is highlighted that increased diversity of electric vehicle models is going to create more alternatives across all market segments. Manufacturers are increasingly offering all-electric or plug-in hybrid models across most vehicle classes to more broadly meet consumer demands. EV with increased electric range are entering the market. Next-generation vehicle models with at least 300 km of electric range could accelerate the trend toward a mass-market electric vehicle fleet.

On the other hand, limited driving range, long charging time, and EV's high purchase prices hinder EV adoption and diffusion (Barth et al., 2016;

Lee et al., 2017). For this reason, it is imperative to invest in charging points, so as to create a positive consumer perception about the adequacy of charging infrastructure as well as relative capacity. It has been indicated that EV sales are strongly correlated to the number of public charging points per million residents—as the higher the number of EVs on the road, the higher the demand for charging, which increases the amount of charging infrastructure, which in turn reinforces the confidence of prospective EV buyers in their decision to purchase EVs (Hall et al., 2017). Moreover, other technology factors, such as battery life, trunk space, and top speed, are regarded as some of the technical barriers for limiting consumer adoption (Li et al., 2017).

Regulatory: Regulatory factors refer to the adoption of policy measures and relative incentives, in order to create the initial market and to promote full-scale diffusion of EVs. Thus many countries that promote EV are providing policy support such as purchase subsidies, public expenditure, tax reduction, tax exemption, EV deployment target, free charging, and parking permissions. These factors, as they are of great significance to the implementation of e-business models, are going to be analytically discussed in Section 4.5.1.

Socioeconomic: These factors refer to socioeconomic factors, such as fuel prices, consumer characteristics, availability of charging stations, etc., that influence consumers' choices. Apart from the vehicle characteristics and regulatory framework, individual differences play a significant role in the adoption of electromobility in urban areas. As a matter of fact, it has been shown that consumer characteristics, such as income, education, gender, and level of environmentalism, significantly affect the purchase of EVs (Hidrue et al., 2011). In addition, levels of income and environmentalism are supposed to be positive factors on the willingness to purchase (Carley et al., 2013). Fuel prices seem to be the strongest predictors of HEV adoption and would similarly affect EV adoption depending on the relative price of electricity (Coffman et al., 2015).

4.5.1 Policy drivers for the implementation of electric vehicle business models in urban areas

Transitioning from internal combustion engine vehicles (ICEVs) to innovative technologies, such as EVs, constitutes a structural component of the global strategy for climate change mitigation. Nonetheless, EVs cannot yet compete in economic terms with ICE vehicles, at least at this stage of their development. EV introduction has been policy driven and is also subject to further global policy imposition until the technology, the manufacturing methods, and the supporting infrastructure technology matures to form economies of scale, achieving a significant decline in the value of EV acquisition and ownership cost (Nanaki et al., 2016). In this direction, and in order to address barriers—such as lack of infrastructure, affordability, and anxiety range—for electrically chargeable cars many incentives, policies, targets, mandates, and regulations have been used by many countries. These include national targets, mandates and regulations, financial Incentives, policies aiming in increasing the value proposition of EVs, public fleet procurement, etc. Table 4.2 summarizes some of the abovementioned policies and relative actions in different cities all over the world.

Targets, mandates, and regulations: Targets are an important tool for the policy-making process as they move the focus from the policy selection debate toward the policy implementation and its assessment. Mandates and regulations build on the definition of regulatory targets to provide a clear signal to manufacturers and customers as they set a medium- to long-term vision for defining the evolution of vehicle characteristics. Most significant measures in this category include zero-emission vehicle (ZEV) mandates and fuel economy regulations.

Financial incentives: The financial incentives directed at EV users and customers are essential for reducing the acquisition cost, mainly dictated by the high battery cost, and the TCO, in order for EVs to compete with ICE vehicles in the open market. The role of the financial incentives is to support the consumers and EV users financially in order to make EVs fictitiously an attractive option in the automotive market. Therefore their goal is to initiate and reinforce a positive feedback loop, which based on sales increase will drive the production scale-ups and the technology learning to further reduce the cost of EV batteries and other components making EV ultimately a viable market option. EV incentives can take the form of (1) direct rebates, (2) tax breaks or (3) exemptions, and can be framed in (4) technology-neutral, differentiated taxation that favors low-emission vehicles according to their GHG and pollutant emission performance and penalizes vehicles with high environmental costs.

For instance, the Netherlands, Norway, and Germany have implemented tax increases associated with the use of ICE vehicles and have provided tax benefits or exemptions to EVs. France, Germany, and the United Kingdom have introduced one-time subsidies for EV purchases (European Commission, 2017). France has relied on a bonus-malus system that offers a grant for purchase of a low-polluting vehicle and has placed a

Table 4.2 Indicative policies and measures in cities around the world for the promotion of EVs.

Category	Strategy	City	Policy	Implementation in other cities
Charging infrastructure	City charging strategy	Beijing	Target of 435,000 charge points by 2020, cooperation between private partners and state grid	New York, Oslo, Shenzhen, Shanghai, Tianjin, Guangzhou, Zhengzhou, Qingdao, Chongqing, Wuhan, Hangzhou, Changsha, London, Seattle, Tokyo
	On-demand public charging	Amsterdam	Demand-based allocation of curbside charging fulfilled by utility	Oslo, Paris, Beijing, Shanghai, Shenzhen, Guangzhou, Tianjin, Hangzhou, Zhengzhou, Qingdao, Wuhan, Chongqing, Changsha
	Charging infrastructure incentives	Tokyo	Incentives for charging stations at public and multiunit dwellings	Qingdao, London, Shanghai, Tianjin, Chongqing, Guangzhou, Los Angeles, San Francisco, San Jose, Shenzhen, Zhengzhou, Oslo
	Building and parking requirement	Beijing	100% of new residential parking spots and 20% of new commercial parking spots must have chargers	Amsterdam, Los Angeles, New York, Beijing, Shanghai, Shenzhen, Tianjin, Hangzhou
	Utility partnerships	Guangzhou	Utility construction of smart charging stations	Amsterdam, London, Oslo, Beijing, Tianjin, Guangzhou
Public fleets	Taxis	Shenzhen	All new taxis must be electric as of 2017	San Francisco, San Diego, Seattle, Shenzhen
	Electric ride-hailing	London	Only electric ride-hailing by 2025; Uber providing incentives	Chongqing, Shenzhen, Beijing, Hangzhou, Guangzhou, Zhengzhou, Oslo, Amsterdam, Los Angeles
	Car sharing fleet	Shanghai	Thousands of vehicles in multiple popular all-electric car sharing fleets	Guangzhou, Tianjin, Changsha, Zhengzhou, Amsterdam
	Buses	Shenzhen	Complete conversion of 16,500 buses	New York, Seattle, Beijing, Shenzhen, Zhengzhou, Shanghai, Tianjin, Oslo
	City fleet	Stockholm	Complete conversion of city car fleet	
Supporting actions	Purchase incentives	Zhengzhou	Offering large upfront subsidies to electric vehicles (as much as 26,400 yuan in 2017)	Beijing, Shanghai, Shenzhen, Guangzhou, Hangzhou, Tokyo
	Planned zero-emission zones	London	Zero-emission town centers by 2020 and city center by 2025	Los Angeles, Oslo, Paris, Seattle
	Parking benefits	San Jose	Free parking on street and at municipal garages	Amsterdam, Bergen, Paris, Shenzhen, Tianjin, Oslo
	Lane access	Bergen	Access to bus lanes	Los Angeles, Oslo, San Francisco, San Jose, San Diego
	Preferential registration	Shanghai	Electric vehicle drivers receive free license plate, avoiding auction system for conventional vehicles	Beijing, Tianjin, Shenzhen, Guangzhou, Hangzhou

Source: Adapted from Hall, D., Moultak, M., Lutsey, N. 2017. Electric Vehicle Capitals of the World: Demonstrating the Path to Electric Drive. ICCT, Washington DC. <http://www.theicct.org/EV-capitals-of-the-world>.

penalty on the purchase of a high-polluting vehicle since 2008. The subsidy covered 27% of the purchase price or up to €6300 for a BEV, and 20% or up to €4000 for a PHEV. The incentive proved to be effective as the number of sales increased year on year. In April 2015 EV sales in France surged and surpassed the 1% market penetration rate. This was the result of the introduction of a scrappage scheme of €3700 on top of the bonus-malus system. As of April 2015 users scrapping a diesel car and purchasing an EV could benefit from a fiscal incentive of €10,000 for a BEV and €7700 for a PHEV (Lévay et al., 2017). In addition, Ireland implemented in 2018 a new measure aiming to support the government's goal of 30% penetration of ZEV sales in the automotive market by 2030. Under this measure, electric car owners can claim a grant of up to €600 to cover the purchase and installation of residential charging points (Gallagher, 2018).

China has also offered substantial funding to support the purchase of EVs under the Electric Vehicle Subsidy Scheme (EVSS), which was launched in 2009. At first, the subsidies were available only for public procurement, but an extension in 2010 made private customers eligible for the grants as well. The scheme covered a wide range of vehicle types: buses, freight trucks, and passenger cars. For the latest category, China's initial EVSS lasted until the end of 2012 and provided up to CNY 50,000 for a PHEV and CNY 60,000 for a BEV depending on the rated power, electric range, and battery energy density. The scheme was renewed for the period 2013−15 with an updated subsidies amount of CNY 35,000 for a PHEV and between CNY 35,000 and CNY 60,000 for a BEV. In 2016 the scheme was extended again for the period 2016−20, and the phase-out of the subsidy program was set for 2021. To complement the one-time subsidies, in 2014 the Chinese government announced the exemption of EVs from the 10% purchase tax (Hao et al., 2014; ICCT, 2017; Perkowski, 2017).

Policies aiming to increase the value proposition of EVs: EV deployment can be supported by increasing the appeal of EVs over competing alternatives, providing advantages in terms of reduced fees, privileged access, free charging, emissions test exemption, as well as driving and parking facilitation. These policies focus on the support of EV ownership and use, and consequently must be developed at a municipal level and adapted to the unique local conditions of each urban area. For instance, countries such as the United States (Xingping et al., 2014) and Norway allow EVs to use carpool lanes or bus lanes so that consumers can avoid traffic jams. The creation of low-emission zones to provide preferential access to low-emitting vehicles, as in some German cities and in the United Kingdom, is also an increasingly popular and powerful tool for cities to promote e-mobility.

In this direction, in 2015 Germany—under the federal electric mobility regulation—allowed municipalities to grant special benefits to low-emission or EV. Privileges include free or preferential parking, access to high-occupancy vehicle lanes, and access to restricted traffic zones. The regulation applies to the whole country, however, it gives municipalities the responsibility to design and implement the incentives. Stuttgart, for example, provides free parking for EVs in public parking spaces (ICCT, 2016). In Amsterdam EV drivers have priority access to parking permits and also have reserved parking slots near charging stations (ICCT, 2016). In Norway BEVs drivers have free access to toll roads, benefit from reduced ferry rates, are allowed to circulate in bus lanes, and can charge and park their vehicles for free at public premises. EVs are also labeled with a special registration plate (ICCT, 2016).

Public fleet procurement: The public authorities as well as the private sector can contribute significantly to the deployment of EVs by providing the market with demand signals, while exploiting their societal role; thus they could act as advocates of EV promotion through their staff and customers. By the end of 2018 the global electric bus fleet numbered 460,000 electric buses, adding 92,000 new vehicles during the course of the year. Although global electric bus sales fell by 12% in comparison to 2017, the electrification of the vehicles segment progressed significantly. The world market for electric buses is mainly driven by China, which accounts for 99% of the market, Europe follows with a small but consistent increase in sales, while noteworthy electric bus deployment has been reported in India and Latin America (IEA, 2019).

Significant developments in policies, targets, and regulatory framework adopted in 2018 could accelerate the global market for electric buses, most notably the adoption of the Clean Vehicles Directive by the European Union, which provides for public procurement of electric buses; the announcement by India of the second phase of "Faster Adoption and Manufacturing of Electric Vehicles in India" (FAME) scheme, which aims to reduce the purchase price of hybrid and EV, with a focus on vehicles used for public or shared transportation; and the announcement by Chile of a national goal for 100% electrification of public transport by 2040. OEMs also move in the technological development of the segment and toward increased deployment in the major markets. More specifically Chinese manufacturers, such as BYD and Yutong, have been active in Europe and Latin America to deploy electric buses, and European manufacturers, such as Scania, Solaris, VDL, Volvo, and others, and North American companies (Proterra, New Flyer) have been following suit. According to BNEF, buses, which are already highly electrified globally, could reach an even higher electrification rate in the near future, with the global bus fleet comprising 30% by EVs by 2025, while the share of EVs in the segment is expected to exceed 40% by 2030. Furthermore, the referenced research forecasts that the electrification of the global bus fleet will exceed 65% by 2040, potentially displacing more than 10 MMbd of oil in comparison to 2019.

Policy influence on EV deployment: The deployment of EVs in such a premature EV market stage is policy driven. In this stage market sales are volatile and directly influenced by the annual developments of financial support policies applied in local markets. Policy strategies are also uncertain, as policy makers try to identify the transition to higher market maturity and consequently higher financial sustainability. Miscalculation in this identification might lead to local EV market crashes derived from the neutralization of vital for the market support policies and incentives. On the other hand, market experience showed that more fiscal incentives can revitalize an unresponsive market.

4.6 Case studies of business models used for the deployment of electromobility in urban areas

Various business models have been developed globally, either individually or in collaboration with municipalities, local agencies, OEMs, and different stakeholders, aiming to accelerate EV uptake in urban areas. During the past decades, many key industry players have developed EV projects regarding the uptake of electric cars, including BEVs and PHEVs. Table 4.3 provides a brief insight into industry and firm perceptions and offers a description of associated business models as well as relative strategies. It is highlighted that the current EV value chain is emphasizing *battery* (battery cell manufacturing and battery packing), *vehicle* (EV design, assembling and sales), and *infrastructure* enabling grid connection (infrastructure manufacturing and infrastructure network deployment). Furthermore, the EV industry involves new modules and components as a result of battery-based electric mobility concepts, such as recharging infrastructure

Table 4.3 Business models and strategies of different OEMs.

Firm/cars	Value proposition (content and segment)	Value network (production and sales process)	Revenue and cost model	Business model dependency	Business model evolution
General Motors Volt	*Product/service content* • Chevrolet Volt is an EV with a range extender • Considered renting the battery • In 2010 apps become an addition to the value proposition, allowing remote access to see charging percentage, next charging spot, etc. *Target segment* • Economy, multipurpose car (sedan) under Chevrolet brand	*Development and production* • Initially outsourced development and production of batteries, whereas later built own battery plant • Sought to keep costs low by reducing parts (Volt has 10% of the moving parts of an ICE) • Assembled Volt at existing Hamtramck plant in Detroit *Sales process and after-sales service* • Sales at GM Dealer • Service at GM Dealer; dealers need to meet certain requirements, need to purchase Volt tools, install two charging stations and have a demonstrator car at the dealership; special training is provided through web-based courses	*Pricing* • Initially considered to rent the battery • Plan to sell the car globally • Later offered selling or leasing of car including battery • Lease in the United States for $350 after $2500 down payment (36 month) • Gives 8 year/100,000 mile warranty on battery to increase residual value *Government support (United States)* • Loan from the US government through bailout plan • Integrated $7500 tax credits in offering	*Dominant business logic* • World's largest car producer for most of its history • Globally active focus on economic cars *Complementary assets* • Has production facilities • Has EV1, patents, battery management knowledge • Also developed hybrid technology	*Value proposition* • Initially designed the Volt to accommodate different low-emission vehicle technologies • Later only designed for plug-in hybrid *Value network* • Initially outsourced development and production • Consecutively added production facilities for EV core components *Revenue and cost model* • Initially considered to rent battery separately, but then decided to integrate the costs in the lease • After Nissan gave $350 lease for Leaf, GM also offered a $350 lease

	Product/service content	Target segment	Development and production	Sales process and after-sales service	Pricing	Government support	Dominant business logic	Complementary assets	Value proposition	Value network
Mitsubishi iMiev	• iMiev is a full EV • Initially planned with in-wheel EV motors • Later with central EV engine • Planned to look futuristic *Target segment* • Economic multipurpose • In 2009 targeted fleet customers in Japan • Intended to target urban delivery services • - In 2010 was offered to the wider public		• Refitted car based on Mitsubishi "i" car • Produced batteries in joint venture with GS Yuasa • Assembled in Mizushima plant, Japan	• Via Mitsubishi dealers	• In 2008 cost $45,000 before incentives of $25,000 in Japan • Price was reduced when Nissan announced its price ($40,700) for the Leaf from $48,800 to $42,130 ($30,700 after subsidies) in Japan • Offered for $30,000 in the United States	• Integrated government incentives in sales price in Japan	• Economy car producer	• Relatively small car producer • Production plant and commercialization network in place • Comparatively little previous knowledge of low-emission vehicles	• First targeted fleet market and subsequently the wider public *Value network* • n/a	
Tesla Roadster	• Full EV *Target segment* • Initially luxury sports car • Later planned to enter economic multipurpose segment		• Refitted roadster based on Lotus Elise • Mainly bought components • Developed its own battery management system • Bought abandoned Fremont plant to produce EV		• Selling and leasing • Started selling for $109,000		• Founder Elon Musk was Silicon Valley entrepreneur, co-founded and sold PayPal		• Initially started refitting Lotus Elise sports cars. Planned from the beginning to add a mid-sized car (which became the Model S) and an economic car	

(Continued)

Table 4.3 (Continued)

Firm/cars	Value proposition (content and segment)	Value network (production and sales process)	Revenue and cost model	Business model dependency	Business model evolution
		Sales process and after-sales service • Intended Internet sales and flagship store approach to control marketing expenses and quality, was not allowed in all states • Stores were designed by Apple store designer • After-sales service at customer through "Ranger" • Expected less income from after-sales	*Government support* • Received US government loan for development and production of the new Tesla Model S *Additional income* • Refitted Daimler's Smart EVs with their innovative battery management system • Was trading EV credits earned in the California ZEV program to other car producers • Provided Toyota with powertrain	*Complementary assets* • In 2009 received funding (estimated $50 million) from Daimler for a 10% stake • In 2010 Toyota invested $50 million in Tesla • Tesla bought Fremont plant from Toyota to produce new model S for $42 million	*Value network* • After buying the Fremont plant and obtaining money from the US Department of Energy, Tesla had the resources to develop and produce the Model S *Revenue and cost model* • –

Source: Adapted from Bohnsack, R., Pinkse, J., Kolk, A., 2014. Business models for sustainable technologies: exploring business model evolution in the case of electric vehicles. Res. Pol. 43 (2), 284–300.

and related services. This section provides an overview of prevailing business models with regard to the uptake of EVs, taking into consideration the aforementioned characteristics.

4.6.1 Business to consumer leasing

This business model refers to fleet management firms or car dealerships offering contractual leasing services of vehicles to other firms or to private customers, providing the benefits of car ownership without its burdens (Lovelock and Gummesson, 2004). The idea with this business model is to let a lease company own the car and lease it out to a chain of customers until its end-of-life (EOL). The potentially lower TCO can be shared between the lease company and its customers, and the residual value risk is significantly reduced. The offer, operational lease, is also in line with a general trend of lower interest in car ownership among younger generations.

It can also be seen as an alternative to financing a purchase by credit. Car leasing customers acquire permanent use of a car over a long period (from 6 months to several years), thus they perceive the car as their own property (i.e., psychological ownership; Peck and Shu, 2018), while legal ownership remains with the leasing firm. Leasing services are considered to be business to customer (B2C) solutions based on product service system (PSS).

4.6.2 Business to consumer sales or leasing with battery swapping

This business model shares some of the characteristics of the previous business model (i.e., vehicles are either sold by car dealerships or leased by fleet management firms or car dealerships), except that it takes into consideration battery charging—via battery swapping. In this way, the risk of early aging batteries and technological leaps (Christensen et al., 2012) as well as long charging times can be reduced. The concept of the battery swapping station (BSS) has been introduced as a viable way to handle the long charging. The BSS is based on the fact that the depleted EV battery can be replaced quickly with a full-charged one. Battery swapping requires a compatible interface between electric vehicle and swapping station. For this reason, the battery swapping provider has a contract with the customer, which contains the automated swapping of discharged to charged batteries for the electric vehicle. The BSS concept can be implemented in a microgrid or a network of microgrids instead of distribution networks. It is pointed out that the gathered depleted batteries will be charged at off-peak time periods (Xiaoqi et al., 2018), so as to decrease the stress on the network in the peak periods caused by the EVs charging power. Additionally, charging via BSS eliminates the uncertainty in the time of the EVs' charging—taking into consideration the fact that the batteries are charged at a predetermined time period.

4.6.3 Electric vehicles car sharing

The concept of car sharing refers to sharing vehicles that can be reserved and accessed by individuals at car sharing stations at any time of night or day. As the term is broad [ranging from free-floating to one-way and peer-to-peer (P2P) car sharing] a differentiation with reference to the distinct business models is necessary. In one-way car sharing, the user picks up the vehicle from a station or some other location and drops it off at their destination. This often means that vehicles end up in locations where they are not needed (Boldrini and Bruno, 2017). In free-floating car sharing systems, cars can be picked up and dropped off at any location. In most cases, users locate available vehicles via a smartphone app. It is noted that the first free-floating car sharing system was launched by Daimler in 2009 in the city of Ulm, Germany, and offered a mixed fleet of electric and gasoline vehicles (Finkorn and Müller, 2011). In P2P existing car users make their cars available for rent for short periods of time. An operator charges commission on transactions but does not have the overheads of vehicle acquisition, maintenance, etc. that standard car sharing operators have. Currently, car sharing operators offer also combined services that provide both free-floating and station-based trips within one tariff. For instance, Zipcar offers a wider variety of trip types, such as round-trip, one-way with and without parking, the option to travel between cities, etc. Some providers (e.g., Stadtmobil in Germany) offer both free-floating and stationary models.

The combination of the business model of car sharing and e-mobility Electric vehicles car sharing (EVCS) is a promising mode of individual inner-city transportation, as it is beneficial to decrease transportation emissions. Car sharing is considered to be a perfect application for EVs—on the basis of significant benefits for the customer's point of view (Fairley, 2013). The evaluation of drivers for the successful deployment of EVCS reveals that the customer satisfaction and appropriate planning of EVCS are of great importance (Xu et al., 2017). Furthermore, consumers' readiness and their unwillingness to pay for EVCS—compared to conventional powertrains—are significant success factors (Yoon et al., 2017). External factors, such as government subsidies or fuel and electricity prices also are of crucial importance for the promotion of ECVS (Plötz et al., 2015).

Despite significant technological progress, the following issues constitute challenging problems for the successful employment of EVCS schemes. These include inter alia:

- Operating range and long charge times; despite technological progress leading to increased range, their performance under real-world conditions remains limited (Zhang et al., 2017).
- Battery deterioration resulting in limited battery lifetime leads to a low resale value (Pelletier et al., 2017).
- Psychological factors associated with the driving of an EV (Kim et al., 2015).
- Varying market penetration of EVCS as well as e-mobility services in different regions.
- Issues regarding charging practices as well the operation of charging stations, including time of charging (preferably when not in use) and the approach of collection and drop off of vehicles. It is highlighted, that one-way car sharing systems in most of the cases, install a charging point in each one of their reserved parking spots or in popular locations where people want mostly to pick up or drop off vehicles. Nonetheless, this approach is not efficient, as charging stations are not utilized because no vehicle is parked. In addition, the charging points are normally available to any electric vehicle, meaning that they may be in use by noncar club members when they are required.

4.6.3.1 Electric vehicles car sharing projects and schemes around the world

There are many electric vehicle car sharing schemes and projects around the world. An indicative list is presented here:

- *CIVITAS, DYN@MO project*: This is an electric municipal car sharing scheme, which was developed and launched in 2016 for the city of Koprivnica, Croatia, its municipality, and its municipal companies, which used small and mid-sized gasoline-powered personal and delivery vehicles. The fleet was replaced by electric-powered vehicles (CIVITAS, 2019). A web-based application was developed, allowing end users—employees of the City of Koprivnica and connected institutions—the use of the purchased EV. The car sharing scheme has three sharing locations.

- *WeShare*: An all-electric car (consisting of 1500 Golf compact EVs) sharing service, called WeShare, was launched in July (2019), in Berlin by Volkswagen (VW) (www.we-share.io). They are to be followed by 500 additional e-up! vehicles at the beginning of 2020 and the first units of Volkswagen's new full-electric ID.3 when it is introduced in mid-2020. WeShare is a "free-floating" system without rental stations and is operated digitally via a mobile application, covering an area of around $150 \, km^2$. An expansion of WeShare, initially to Prague, together with ŠKODA, and then to Hamburg, is planned for 2020. Customers can use the mobile app and credit card to rent one of WeShare's EVs, which can be picked up and dropped off anywhere in the Berlin operating area. At launch, use of a car will cost €0.19 ($0.22) per minute, and will increase to €0.29 ($0.33) per minute in September 2019. The recharge is going to be made via the public charging network in Berlin, which includes newly created charging points at 70 branches of food retailers.

- *Car2Go*: This is a German one-way car rental company, a subsidiary of Daimler AG, providing car sharing services in urban areas in Europe, North America, and China. As of July 2017, car2go is the largest car sharing company in the world with 2,500,000 registered members and a fleet of nearly 14,000 vehicles in 26 locations in North America, Europe, and Asia (www.car2go.com). In most cities, car2go offers only two-passenger vehicles, namely two types of Smart Fortwo "car2go edition" vehicles: gasoline-powered, and electric-powered. Electric models are currently available in several markets, have a range of 84 miles (135 km). The user accesses the vehicles via a download-able smartphone app wherever they are parked. The car2go business model is similar in all markets, although rates vary by location. The rates are all-inclusive and cover rental, gas, insurance, parking (in authorized areas), and maintenance; a low fixed annual fee is sometimes also charged. In most markets, car2go vehicles can park in either specially designated parking spots, or in standard parking areas, with a special permit from the local municipality. Users have the option of refueling cars with a supplied charge card, customers receive bonus minutes for performing this service.

- *Chefenxiang*: This project refers to the first EV-Car sharing project in China, which was launched in 2011 and was operated by Hangzhou

EVnet Intelligent Technology Co., Ltd. (Xiaoyuan et al., 2015), which adopted the business model of American car sharing Zipcar and provided car sharing services both for ICEVs and EVs. Since then EV car sharing has begun commercial operation, in more than 15 cities. The EVCS scheme in China is a fixed station type (users are required to pick up and return EVs at the same station) and has the following characteristics: EVs are purchased by operating companies or obtained from OEMs or car rental companies with legal rights to operate; the most common rental distance is 5−10 km one-way and lease time is 30−60 minutes; the user needs to be registered via an application, so as to be a member and then following steps include reservation, pickup and usage, return of EV, and payment. The business model mostly used is O2O (Online to Offline), and in order to improve the efficiency of EV use and increase revenue, most operating companies will take a mode combining short-time and long-term lease. Business types include B2G (Business to Government), B2B (Business to Business), and B2C.

4.6.4 Electric vehicle grid nexus business models

Energy transition to electromobility and relative EV acceleration requires novel business models to develop electric vehicle supply equipment (EVSE). These business models refer to the current strategic positioning of actors in e-mobility, with a focus on the infrastructure. In this regard, two business models are going to be presented: vehicle grid integration (VGI) and V2G. VGI refers to the process by which EV batteries can be aggregated and integrated with the energy system, in order to provide a service to the electricity system. VGI models are based on unidirectional operation and are able to stop, start, and modulate the level of charging.

The V2G technologies are based on bidirectional operation and when necessary they can provide power to the grid. The EVs are supported by a battery storage pack and they operate like distributed energy resources in the electrical grids (Mehrjerdi et al., 2019). V2G models can additionally discharge energy from the EV battery to the grid. In this business model, battery owners can be remunerated (i.e., through a monthly fixed payment or sharing a portion of the revenues earned from the market, or credits allocated toward the purchase of charging services) while the electric vehicle is connected to the grid. These models depend on the use of algorithms to ensure that although customers effectively "give up" a level

of control over their EV charging, they are offered commercial proposi-
tions that remain convenient and do not require any substantial deviation
from their preferred habits or lifestyles. Such models are currently in operation or being piloted in several countries around the world including the
United States (California) and Europe. In this way, the V2G can be properly utilized in home energy management as a storage unit in order to
reduce the energy cost (Wu et al., 2016). Grid operators can purchase battery capacities for regulating short-term load peaks and storing renewable
energy (Weiller and Neely, 2014). In most of the cases, an aggregator,
who bundles the connected capacities of the vehicles to one megawatt
units for the grid operator, is necessary. Both business models entail the
aggregation of EVs (acting as batteries or storage units), which provide
"flexibility" services to the electricity system by modulating the amount
and the times of EV charging, so as to relieve "stress points" and enable
an efficient management of the electricity system.

With regard to V2G operation, the communication and charging protocol are of crucial importance, as they define whether signals can be sent
from an aggregator to the charging infrastructure and further to the vehicle, allowing the battery to discharge. Currently, four different communication and charging protocols are being used in the market for EVs:

- CCS—IEN 15 118 (DC fast charging mainly used by American and
  European producers)
- CHAdeMO (DC fast charging mainly used by Japanese producers)
- AC Fast Charging (used only by Renault)
- Tesla Superchargers (used only by Tesla)

It is highlighted that as with the EVs, the EVSE needs to comply with
the charging protocol and also be constructed in a way that allows for
bidirectional current to flow.

However, V2G models should be profitable and competitive; therefore it is necessary to develop and deploy viable business models, that take
into consideration factors such as minimum bid size, participating capacity,
state-of-charge (SOC), etc. (Peng et al., 2017). For this reason, service
providers should create value for the three main stakeholders: grid, aggregator, and EV owner.

4.6.4.1 Frequency regulation business model

A shallow charge/discharge cycling instead of deep depth of discharge
(DoD) is more suitable for V2G-enabled BEVs, as it can prevent fast battery degradation. This business model is beneficial to the battery cycle

lifetime without compromising the potential economic benefits that can be generated by engaging in frequency regulation (Li et al., 2015). In most of the cases a frequency regulation strategy comprises the aggregator, who dispatches the bidirectional charging according to the grid frequency deviation (Peng et al., 2017). Such a model is already in operation and the major payment for servicing this market is granted for availability and not supply of the actual service. Furthermore, this type of business model is in favor of the EV owner as it minimizes the risk of insufficient SOC. Services connected with this type of business model are beneficial to all stakeholders; nonetheless for the aggregator the challenge is forecasting when the service will be needed and when capacity will be available.

4.6.4.2 Reduction of peak load business model

Large-scale deployment of EVs into the energy grid could cause significant increase of load, leading to system overload during peak periods. Based on the above, a business model where V2G operators could dispatch intelligent signals that regulate when different EVs charge to reduce peak load is of great significance (Peng et al., 2017). This business model is economically viable as it has the potential to reduce the dimension of the energy distribution network. However, this model faces the following challenge: as there are no previous cases of selling such a service to distribution system operators (DSO), there is no pricing indication for this type of service, resulting in potential market uncertainty. Services connected with reduction of peak load have the potential to create a benefit for the DSO as an alternative to creating long-term investments in grid infrastructure, and for the aggregator there will be a higher predictability as the energy consumption patterns are of a well-defined size.

4.6.4.3 Synergetic smart energy business models

This category includes business models that have emerged from synergies among different actors in different segments, including collaboration between providers/enablers of aggregated EV services and auto manufacturers, utilities, and energy companies looking for new revenue streams. For instance, the virtual power plant operator Next Kraftwerke, and Jedlix, an EV aggregator and smart charging platform provider, have launched an international pilot project, which uses EV batteries to deliver secondary control reserve to the transmission system operator in the Netherlands (TennET). By connecting the EV to the

> **BOX 4.1 The case study of Enel**
>
> Enel, apart from providing charging infrastructure and bundled offers for home and public charging, has developed an accessible DC V2X home charging station able to charge and discharge at 10 kW. Enel has participated in various pilot projects, such as with Nissan in the United Kingdom, where they played the role of electricity supplier at the charging point, charging software provider, and aggregator (www.enel.com). In this pilot, EV clients received compensation in the form of a reduction in their electricity bill in exchange for the provision of grid services, and, thanks to smart energy service, they locally optimized their consumption by increasing self-consumption of their locally generated solar energy and saving on the network charges. Enel integrated the purchased V2G power into its larger aggregated ancillary services portfolio, thus creating a "buffer" for uncertainties due to possible deviations in the schedules of individual vehicles, without directly controlling them. Enel is paid by the transmission operators and DSOs and shares the value with the client.

platform, Jedlix is able to coordinate user charging preferences and establish a live connection with the EV. Depending on the charging preference, each EV can provide either positive or negative control reserves. Jedlix can combine user preferences, car data, and charging station information to provide a continuous forecast of the available capacity. This is then used by Next Kraftwerke in the bidding process of TenneT for procuring grid services (NextKraftwerke, 2018). The current VGI is based largely on the provision of charging management software from developers of proprietary solutions, such as AutoGrid or Nuvve, to utilities and fleets, sometimes operated by OEMs. The energy services platform provider model is no longer B2B but integrates the software and provides a spectrum of B2C services. The case study of Enel (Box 4.1) points out the need for the deployment and development of synergistic models.

4.6.4.4 Battery second use business model

This type of business model involves the reconditioning and reusing of second used batteries in stationary applications. Used batteries are removed from the EV when their maximum capacity has degraded to 70%—80% of the original capacity (Strickland et al., 2014). Second-life batteries, may still work well in a stationary application which is less restrictive in terms of space and weight than motive applications. Table 4.4 summarizes some

Table 4.4 Business models and applications of B2U.

Automaker	B2U partner/service provider	EV model	Capacity	B2U application	Country	References
Daimler	GETEC, The Mobility House, Remondis	Smart	13 MWh	Renewable energy	Germany	Daimler (2016)
Nissan	Eaton	Leaf	4.2 kWh	Residential energy storage	United Kingdom	Nissan Xstorage (2017)
Nissan	Eaton and The Mobility House	Leaf	4 MWh/4 MW	Peak shaving, backup power	The Netherlands	Nissan (2016)
Nissan	Sumitomo	Leaf	400 kWh/600 kW	Renewable energy	Japan	St. John (2015)
BMW	Vattenfall and Bosch	ActiveE and i3	2.8 MWh/2 MW	Renewable energy	Germany	Lambert (2016)
Tesla Roadster Renault	Connected Energy	Zoe	50 kWh/50 kW	Fast charging	United Kingdom	Renault (2017)

of the ongoing demonstration projects and commercial ventures. This offers a lifetime extension of up to 10 years for the battery, at a compelling price already today, believed to be around €150 (US$180) per kWh (Reid and Julve, 2016). Depending on the application, it can be used either for grid-to-battery (G2B) precharging during low price periods or battery-to-grid (B2G) discharging during high price periods.

Based on the findings of Section 4.4, as the EV market share is expected to increase globally, it is evident that a large number of retired EV batteries will become available at low cost price, providing services to stationary energy storage systems (ESS). Therefore EOL EV batteries can be regarded as a disruptive technology able to cause changes to the current picture of the automotive and energy industries. Potential B2U strategies and relative new market opportunities depend on many factors, especially on the interests of the different stakeholders involved, such as OEMs but also for new market participants such as electricity producers, grid operators, recycling companies, service providers, and final customers.

4.7 Concluding remarks

EV are a necessity for the energy transition to a zero-carbon energy future. In order to achieve global targets and mandates, it is imperative for current business models to change and to adapt, so as to achieve a sustainable competitive advantage, since innovative business models are often much more difficult to imitate compared to products and services. For this reason, business models need to extend beyond the boundaries of the business itself, and beyond the boundaries of a particular point in time. Business models should take a full value chain perspective, extending into wider networks, and also they should include a consideration of context and environment. Based on the above, it is obvious that business models aiming to accelerate the EV uptake will adapt differently to different markets and different regions. Consumer purchase choices differ in developed and developing markets (i.e., Europe and the United States vs China and India). The EVs market penetration could be supported or hindered by various governmental requirements. Actual and forecasted fuel and electricity costs, general transportation price levels, as well as subsidies and legislative changes are of crucial importance. Besides the costs for the vehicle itself, the cost for setting up an adequate charging infrastructure has also to be taken into consideration.

It should also be highlighted that EV business models are still emerging; they are by no means fully formed and should be considered dynamic entities.

From new mobility as a service offering, to ancillary energy market services using aggregated EV batteries, new value pools are emerging. Especially with technological progress and the emergence of connected and automated vehicles, shared mobility, V2G, wireless charging, etc., business models that embrace innovation, taking into consideration policy, regulatory, and commercial stakeholders will be important to e-mobility transitions. Without novel business models the e-mobility transition may struggle to reach enough citizens to make meaningful contributions to air quality improvements and greenhouse gas reductions from transport. An integrated approach, taking into consideration vehicle, energy, and mobility needs of urban areas such as cities, has been presented (innovative business models for EVs—e-IIBMs). This type of business model can be useful in increasing the market share of EVs, as it accounts for the needs of all stakeholders. Policy makers should embrace comprehensive policy frameworks aiming to support innovative business models as well as to implement financial purchase incentives and policies focusing on technical R&D.

References

Al-Debei, M., Avison, D., 2010. Developing a unified framework of the business model concept. Eur. J. Inf. Syst. 19, 359–376.

Andersen, P.H., Mathews, J.A., Rask, M., 2009. Integrating private transport into renewable energy policy: the strategy of creating intelligent recharging grids for electric vehicles. Energy Policy 37 (7), 2481–2486.

Barth, M., Jugert, P., Fritsche, I., 2016. Still underdetected – social norms and collective efficacy predict the acceptance of electric vehicles in Germany. Transp. Res. Part. F: Traffic Psychol. Behav. 37, 64–77.

Beaume, R., Midler, C., 2009. From technology competition to reinventing individual ecomobility: new design strategies for electric vehicles. Int. J. Automot. Technol. Manag. 9 (2), 174–186.

Bessa, R.J., Matos, M.A., 2012. Economic and technical management of an aggregation agent for electric vehicles: a literature survey. Eur. Trans. Electr. Power 22 (2012), 334–350.

BNEF, 2018. Electric Buses in Cities, Global Edition. Bloomberg New Energy Finance, London.

Bohnsack, R., Pinkse, J., Kolk, A., 2014. Business models for sustainable technologies: exploring business model evolution in the case of electric vehicles. Res. Pol. 43 (2), 284–300.

Boldrini, C., Bruno, R., 2017. Stackable vs autonomous cars for shared mobility systems: a preliminary performance evaluation. Proc. IEEE 20th Int. Conf. Intell. Transport. Syst. pp. 232–237.

Carley, S., Krause, R.M., Lane, B.W., Graham, J.D., 2013. Intent to purchase a plug-in electric vehicle: a survey of early impressions in large us cites. Transp. Res. Part. D, Transp. Environ. 18 (1), 39–45.

Chesbrough, H., Rosenbloom, R.S., 2002. The role of the business model in capturing value from innovation: evidence from Xerox Corporation's technology spin-off companies. Ind. Corp. Change 11 (3), 529–555.

Christensen, B.T., Wells, P., Cipcigan, L., 2012. Can innovative business models overcome resistance to electric vehicles? Better Place and battery electric cars in Denmark. Energy Pol. 48, 498–505.

CIVITAS, 2019. Electric municipal car-sharing scheme. <https://civitas.eu/es/measure/electric-municipal-car-sharing-scheme> (accessed 07.19.).

Coffman, M., Bernstein, P., Wee, S., 2015. Factors affecting EV adoption: a literature review and EV forecast for Hawaii. Electr. Veh. Transp. Cent. 2015.

Daimler, 2016. World's largest 2nd-use battery storage is starting up. <http://media.daimler.com/marsMediaSite/en/instance/ko/Worlds-largest-2nd-use-battery-storage-is-starting-up.xhtml?oid = 13634457>.

Electric mobility as a service, <http://www.emaas.eu/> (accessed 06.19.).

European Commission, 2017. EU Directive 2014/94/EU. National plans for alternative fuel infrastructure. Member States fiches. European Commission, Brussels.

European Innovation Partnership on Smart Cities and Communities, 2013. Strategic implementation plan. <https://smartcities.at/assets/Uploads/sip-final-en.pdf>.

EV Volumes, 2019. Global EV Sales for 2018 — Final Results. <http://www.ev-volumes.com/country/total-world-plug-in-vehicle-volumes/#>.

Fairley, P., 2013. Car sharing could be the EV's killer app. Inst. Electr. Electron. Eng. Spectr. 50 (9), 14—15.

Finkorn, J., Müller, M., 2011. What will be the environmental effects of new free-floating car-sharing systems? case car2go Ulm. Ecol. Econ. 70 (8), 1519—1528.

Gallagher, C., 2018. New government grant for electric car owners available. The Irish Times. Available from: <www.irishtimes.com/news/environment/new-governmentgrant-for-electric-car-owners-available-1.3342126> (accessed 06.18.).

Hall, D., Moultak, M., Lutsey, N. 2017. Electric Vehicle Capitals of the World: Demonstrating the Path to Electric Drive. ICCT, Washington DC. <http://www.theicct.org/EV-capitals-of-the-world>.

Hao, H., et al., 2014. China's electric vehicle subsidy scheme: rationale and impacts. Energy Policy 73, 722—732.

Hidrue, M., Parsons, G., Kempton, W., Gardner, M., 2011. Willingness to pay for electric vehicles and their attributes. Energy Econ. 33, 686—705.

Hietanen, S., 2014. 'Mobility as a Service' — the new transport model? Eurotransport 12 (2), 2—4/26—28.

Holder, M., 2018. Amsterdam Arena switches on giant Nissan LEAF battery storage system. Bus. Green. Available from: www.businessgreen.com/bg/news/3035094/amsterdamarena-switches-on-nissan-leaf-battery-storagesystem.

International Council on Clean Transportation — ICCT, 2016. Comparison of leading electric vehicle policy and development in Europe, Berlin. Available from: <www.theicct.org/sites/default/files/publications/ICCT_EVpolicies-Europe-201605.pdf>.

International Council on Clean Transportation — ICCT, 2017. Emerging best practices for electric vehicle charging infrastructure. Berlin. Available from: www.theicct.org/sites/default/files/publications/EV-charging-best-practices_ICCT-white-paper_04102017_vF.pdf.

International Energy Agency—IEA, 2019: Global EV Outlook 2019. https://www.iea.org/publications/reports/globalevoutlook2019/.

Jittrapirom, P., Caiati, V., Feneri, A.-M., Ebrahimigharehbaghi, S., González, M.J.A., Narayan, J., 2017. Mobility as a service: a critical review of definitions, assessments of schemes, and key challenges. Urban. Plan. 2 (2), 13—25.

Johnson, M.W., Christensen, C.M., Kagermann, H., 2008. Reinventing your business model. Harv. Bus. Rev. 86 (12), 50—60.

Kaplan, S., 2012. The Business Model Innovation Factory: How to Stay Relevant When the World Is Changing. Wiley, Hoboken, NJ.

Kawasaki, A., 2015. Fujitsu's approach to smart mobility. FUJITSU Sci. Tech. J. 51 (4), 3—7.

Kim, D., Ko, J., Park, Y., 2015. Factors affecting electric vehicle sharing program participants' attitudes about car ownership and program participation. Transp. Res. Part. D: Transp. Environ. 36, 96—106.

Kley, F., Lerch, C., Dallinger, D., 2011. New business models for electric cars—a holistic approach. Energy Policy 39 (6), 3392—3403.

Lambert, F., 2016. BMW and Bosch open new 2.8 MWh energy storage facility built from batteries from over 100 electric cars. https://electrek.co/2016/09/22/bmw-bosch-energy-storage-facility-built-from-batteries-from-over-100-electric-cars.

Lee, H.S., Won, J.P., Lim, T.K., Jeon, H.B., Cho, K.C., Park, Y.C., Kim, Y.C., 2017. Experimental study on performance characteristics of the triple fluids heat exchanger with two kinds of coolants in electric-driven air conditioning system for fuel cell electric vehicles. Energy Procedia 113, 209—216.

Lengton, M., Verzijl, D., Dervojeda, K., Netherlands, P., Probst, L., Frideres, L., 2015. Internet of things connected cars. Bus. Innov. Observatory Contract No. 190.

Lévay, P.Z., Drossinos, Y., Thiel, C., 2017. The effect of fiscal incentives on market penetration of electric vehicles: a pairwise comparison of total cost of ownership. Energy Policy 105, 524—533.

Li, Z., Chowdhury, M., Bhavsar, P., He, Y., 2015. Optimizing the performance of vehicle-to-grid (V2G) enabled battery electric vehicles through a smart charge scheduling model. Int. J. Automot. Technol. 16, 827—837.

Li, Y., Zhan, C.J., De Jong, M., Lukszo, Z., 2016. Business innovation and government regulation for the promotion of electric vehicle use: lessons from Shenzhen, China. J. Clean. Prod. 134, 371—383.

Li, W., Long, R., Chen, H., Geng, J., 2017. A review of factors influencing consumer intentions to adopt battery electric vehicles. Renew. Sustain. Energy Rev. 78, 318—328.

Liao, F., Molin, E., van Wee, B., 2017. Consumer preferences for electric vehicles: a literature review. Transp. Rev. 37 (3), 252—275. https://www.tandfonline.com/doi/full/10.1080/01441647.2016.1230794.

Liao, F., Molin, E., Timmermans, H., Van Wee, B., 2019. Consumer preferences for business models in electric vehicle adoption. Transp. Policy 73, 12—24.

Lovelock, C., Gummesson, E., 2004. Whither services marketing? In search of a new paradigm and fresh perspectives. J. Serv. Res. 7 (1), 20—41.

Madina, C., Zamora, I., Zabala, E., 2016. Methodology for assessing electric vehicle charging infrastructure business models. Energy Policy 89, 284—293.

Markkula, J., Rautiainen, A., Järventausta, P., 2013. The business case of electric vehicle quick charging — no more chicken or egg problem. EVS27 Symposium. November 2013. Barcelona.

MCKiNsEy, 2018. Global Electric-Vehicle Market Is Amped Up and on the Rise. McKinsey & Company. Available from: www.mckinsey.com/industries/automotive-and-assembly/our-insights/the-global-electric-vehicle-market-is-amped-up-and-on-the-rise.

Mehrjerdi, H., Hemmati, R., Farrokhi, E., 2019. Nonlinear stochastic modeling for optimal dispatch of distributed energy resources in active distribution grids including reactive power. Simulat. Model. Pract. Theor. 94, 1—13.

Morrow, K., Karner, D., Francfort, J., 2008. Plug-in hybrid electric vehicle charging infrastructure review. https://wecanfigurethisout.org/ENERGY/Lecture_notes/Electrification_of_Tranportation_Supporting_Materials%20/INL%20-%20PHEV%20infrastructure%20review.pdf.

Nanaki, A.E., Xydis, G., Koroneos, C., 2015. Electric vehicle deployment in urban areas. Int. J. Indoor Built Environ. 25 (7), 1065—1074.

Nanaki, A.E., Xydis, G., Koroneos, C., 2016. Electric vehicle deployment in urban areas. SAGE J. Indoor Built Environ. 25 (7).

Nemry, F., Leduc, G., Munoz, A., 2009. Plug-in Hybrid and Battery—Electric Vehicles: State of the Research and Development and Comparative Analysis of Energy and Cost Efficiency. Institute for Prospective Technological Studies, European Commission Joint Research Centre, Luxembourg.

NextKraftwerke, 2018. Next Kraftwerke and Jedlix Launch Initiative to Use Electric Car Batteries for Grid Stability.

Nissan, 2016. Nissan, Eaton and the mobility house sign 10 year deal to make the world-famous Amsterdam Arena more energy efficient with battery storage. https://newsroom. nissan-europe.com/eu/en-gb/media/pressreleases/426164259/nissan-eaton-and-the-mobility-house-sign-10-year-deal-to-make-the-world-famous-amsterdam-arena-more?preview = true&t = fb709602-e6a7-42d7-828d-666cbd2978ea.

Nian, V., Hari, M.P., Yuan, J., 2019. A new business model for encouraging the adoption of electric vehicles in the absence of policy support. Appl. Energy 235, 1106—1117.

Nissan Xstorage, 2017. https://www.nissan.co.uk/experience-nissan/electric-vehicle-leadership/xstorage-by-nissan.html.

OECD, 2005. Oslo Manual: Guidelines for Collecting and Interpreting Innovation Data, third ed. Paris.

Osterwalder, A., 2004. The Business Model Ontology: A Proposition in a Design Science Approach (Doctoral dissertation). University of Lausanne, Lausanne.

Osterwalder, A., Pigneur, Y., 2010. Business Model Generation: A Handbook for Visionaries, Game Changers, and Challengers. Wiley, Hoboken, NJ.

Osterwalder, A., Pigneur, Y., Tucci, C.L., 2005. Clarifying business models: origins, present and future of the concept. Commun. Assoc. Inf. Syst. 16, 1—40.

Papadimitratos, P., De La Fortelle, A., Evenssen, K., Brignolo, R., Cosenza, S., 2009. Vehicular communication systems: enabling technologies, applications, and future outlook on intelligent transportation. IEEE Commun. Mag. 47 (11), 84—95.

Peck, J., Shu, S.B., 2018. Psychological Ownership and Consumer Behavior. Springer, Chicago, IL.

Pelletier, S., Jabali, O., Laporte, G., Veneroni, M., 2017. Battery degradation and behavior for electric vehicles: review and numerical analyses of several models. Trans. Res. Part. B: Methodol. 103, 158—187.

Peng, C., Zou, J., Lian, L., 2017. Dispatching strategies of electric vehicles participating in frequency regulation on power grid: a review. Renew. Sustain. Energy Rev. 68, 147—152.

Perkowski, J., 2017. How China is raising the bar with aggressive new electric vehicle rules. Forbes. Available from: www.forbes.com/sites/jackperkowski/2017/10/10/china-raises-the-bar-with-new-electric-vehicle-rules/#a92230977ac.

Plötz, P., Gnann, T., Wietschel, M., Ullrich, S., 2015. How to foster electric vehicle market penetration? A model based assessment of policy measures and external factors. European Council for an Energy Efficient Economy, Paris. pp. 843—853.

Reid, G., Julve, J., 2016. Second-life batteries as flexible storage for renewable energies. BundersverbErneuerbare Energ. e.V. Hann. Messe . Available from: <www.bee-ev.de/fileadmin/Publikationen/Studien/201604_Second_LifeBatterien_als_flexible_Speicher.pdf>.

Renault, 2017. Electric vehicle charging on highways with second-life batteries. <http://press.renault.co.uk/Corporate/3a483d7c-2680-4733-987f-1c6581a69492.aspx>.

Roberto Reyes García, J., Lenz, G., Haveman, S., Maarten Bonnema, G., 2019. State of the art of electric Mobility as a Service (eMaaS): an overview of ecosystems and system architectures, 32nd Electric Vehicle Symposium (EVS32), May 19—22, 2019, Lyon, France.

Schneider, S., Spieth, P., 2013. Business model innovation: toward an integrated future research agenda. Int. J. Innov. Manag. 17 (01), 1—34.

St. John, J., 2015. Nissan, Green Charge Networks turn 'second-life' EV batteries into grid storage business. <https://www.greentechmedia.com/articles/read/nissan-green-charge-networks-turn-second-life-ev-batteries-into-grid-storag>.

Strickland, D., Chittock, L., Stone, D.A., Foster, M.P., Price, B., 2014. Estimation of transportation battery second life for use in electricity grid systems. IEEE Trans. Sustain. Energy 5 (3), 795—803.

The Beam Magazine, 2019. The global PEV market. <https://medium.com/thebeammagazine/a-year-in-review-the-electric-vehicle-market-fab1172d4e9f>.

Thiel, C., Perujo, A., Mercier, A., 2010. Cost and CO_2 aspects of future vehicle options in Europe under new energy policy scenarios. Energy Policy 38, 7142.

Transport Systems Catapult, 2016. Mobility as a service, exploring the opportunity for mobility as a service in the EU. <https://ts.catapult.org.uk/wp-content/uploads/2016/07/Mobility-as-a-Service_Exploring-the-Opportunity-for-MaaS-in-the-UK-Web.pdf>.

United Nations Climate Change, <https://unfthccc.int/process-and-meetings/the-paris-agreement/d2hhdC1pcy> (accessed 08.06.19.).

Weiller, C., Neely, A., 2014. Using electric vehicles for energy services: industry perspectives. Energy (77), 194−200.

Wells, P., 2004. Creating sustainable business models: the case of the automotive industry. IIMB Manag. Rev. 16 (4), 15−24.

Wells, P., 2013. Sustainable business models and the automotive industry: a commentary. IIMB Manag. Rev. 25 (4), 228−239.

WeShare, 2019. <https://www.we-share.io/en/> (accessed 12.08.19.).

Williander, M., Stålstad, C., 2013. New business models for electric cars, EVS27 International Battery, Hybrid and Fuel Cell Electric Vehicle Symposium.

Wu, X., Hu, X., Moura, S., Yin, X., Pickert, V., 2016. Stochastic control of smart home energy management with plug-in electric vehicle battery energy storage and photovoltaic array. J. Power Sources 333 (2016), 203−212.

Available from: < www.maas-alliance.com> (accessed 17.06.19.).

Xiaoqi, T., et al., 2018. Asymptotic performance evaluation of battery swapping and charging station for electric vehicles. Perform. Eval. 119, 43−57.

Xiaoyuan, W., Xuying, Y., Huan, S., 2015. Innovative practice of EV-car sharing in China for urban E-mobility. World Electr. Veh. J. 7, ISSN:2032-6653.

Xingping, Z., Jian, X., Rao, R., Yanni, L., 2014. Policy incentives for the adoption of electric vehicles across countries. Sustainability 6, 8056−8078.

Xu, F., Liu, J., Lin, S., Yuan, J., 2017. A VIKOR-based approach for assessing the service performance of electric vehicle sharing programs: a case study in Beijing. J. Clean. Prod. 148, 254−267.

Yoon, T., Cherry, C.R., Jones, L.R., 2017. One-way and round-trip carsharing: a stated preference experiment in Beijing. Transp. Res. Part. D: Transp. Env. 53, 102−114.

Zhang, G., Ge, S., Yang, X.-G., Leng, Y., Marple, D., Wang, C.-Y., 2017. Rapid restoration of electric vehicle battery performance while driving at cold temperatures. J. Power Sources 371, 35−40.

Zott, C., Amit, R., Massa, L., 2011. The business model: recent developments and future research. J. Manag. 37 (4), 1019−1042.

Zubaryeva, A., Thiel, C., Barbone, E., Mercier, A., 2012. Assessing factors for the identification of potential lead markets for electrified vehicles in Europe: expert opinion elicitation. Technol. Forecast. Soc. Change 79, 1622.

CHAPTER 5

Climate change mitigation and electric vehicles

5.1 Introduction

The impact of climate change is evident in regions around the world. Box 5.1 summarizes the significant evidence of climate change. Global warming, which is caused by greenhouse gas (GHG) emissions dominated by CO_2 (90%), is affecting people's life and health. As a matter of fact, global warming has sounded an alarm to human beings. It was reported that the temperature in the Arctic Circle reached 32°C in the summer of 2018 and deaths caused by the extreme hot weather happened worldwide, including in Europe, Japan, and Canada. The recent IPCC Special Report on Global Warming of 1.5°C points out that it is urgent that decision-makers, consumers, and businesses take action in order to tackle climate change through the transformation of global energy use (IPCC, 2018).

The transportation sector is one of the major contributors to global energy consumption, GHG emissions, and air pollutants, such as sulfur dioxide (SO_2), nitrogen oxides (NOx), and particulate matter (PM) (Nanaki et al., 2015). To be more specific, according to the Intergovernmental Panel on Climate Change (IPPC, 2014), the transportation sector contributes to 14% of global GHG emissions. Especially, the road transport sector is responsible for 83% of total energy consumption in transports (Letnik et al., 2018). The World Health Organization (WHO, 2016) estimates that 3 million deaths and 85 millions of disability-adjusted life years can be associated with urban air quality. Taken into consideration the fact that the market for passenger cars is projected to double from around 1 billion today to 2 billion by 2040 (BP, 2018), it is evident that urban areas, such as cities, will face the challenges of energy security, climate change mitigation, and urban air quality.

The alleviation of the abovementioned challenges can be achieved through the energy transition to low and zero carbon energy carriers. The use of alternative, environment-friendly fuels and powertrains seems to be

BOX 5.1 Evidence of climate change

Throughout history, the Earth's climate has faced significant changes. During the past 650,000 years, seven cycles of glacial advance and retreat have been noted. About 7000 years ago the last ice age marked the beginning of the modern climate era—and of human civilization. Most of these climate changes are attributed to very small variations in the Earth's orbit, which change the amount of solar energy that Earth receives. The current warming trend is associated with human activity since the mid-20th century and proceeds at a rate that is unprecedented over decades to millennia (IPPC, 2014).

It is highlighted that in April 2018, the Mauna Loa Observatory in Hawaii recorded an average concentration of atmospheric carbon dioxide (CO_2) above 410 parts per million (ppm) (National Oceanic and Atmospheric Administration, 2018). This was the highest monthly average in recorded history, and according to ice core records it is the highest value in at least the last 400,000 years. Global averaged CO_2 atmospheric concentration reached 405 parts per million (ppm) in 2017 (Blunden, et al., 2018), up from 402.9 ppm in 2016. The global growth rate of CO_2 has nearly quadrupled since the early 1960s, with no sign of deceleration. Evidence of this warming trend can be summarized as below:

Global Temperature Rise: The planet's average surface temperature has risen about 1.62 degrees Fahrenheit (0.9°C) since the late 19th century, a change driven largely by increased carbon dioxide and other anthropogenic emissions into the atmosphere (www.nasa.gov, 2019). Most of the warming occurred during the past 35 years, with the five warmest years on record taking place since 2010. It is noted that 2016 was the warmest year on record (www.nasa.gov, 2017).

Warming Oceans: The oceans have absorbed the majority of the increased heat, with the top 700 meters of ocean showing warming of more than 0.4 degrees Fahrenheit since 1969 (Levitus et al., 2017).

Shrinking Ice Sheets: The Greenland and Antarctic ice sheets have decreased in mass. It is estimated that Greenland lost an average of 286 billion tons of ice per year during the period of 1993- 2016, while Antarctica lost about 127 billion tons of ice per year during the same time period (www.nasa.gov, 2018).

Glacial Retreat: Glaciers are retreating almost everywhere around the world—including in the Alps, Himalayas, Andes, Rockies, Alaska, and Africa (National Snow and Ice Data Center World Glacier Monitoring Service, 2019a).

Decreased Snow Cover: Satellite observations reveal that the amount of spring snow cover in the Northern Hemisphere has decreased over the past five decades and that the snow is melting earlier.

(Continued)

BOX 5.1 (Continued)

Sea Level Rise: During the last century the global sea level rose about 8 inches. The rate in the last two decades, however, is nearly double that of the last century and is accelerating slightly every year (Nerem et al., 2018).

Declining Arctic Sea Ice: During the past decades, both the extent and thickness of Arctic sea ice has declined rapidly (National Snow and Ice Data Center World Glacier Monitoring Service, 2019b).

Extreme Events: Extreme heat and cold waves are recorded around the world. For instance, since 1950, the record of high temperature events in the United States has been increasing. The United States. has also witnessed increasing numbers of intense rainfall events (USGCRP, 2017). In addition, a polar vortex triggered in 2019 the coldest arctic outbreak in the US Midwest (www.phys.org, 2019).

Ocean Acidification: Since the beginning of the industrial revolution, emissions from industrial and agricultural activities increased the amount of CO_2 in the atmosphere, resulting in a significant increase (about 30%) of the acidity of surface ocean waters (www.pmel.noaa.go, 2019). The amount of CO_2 absorbed by the upper layer of the oceans is increasing by about 2 billion tons per year (Copenhagen Diagnosis, 2011).

a key strategy for heading toward a sustainable transport system. Electric vehicles (EVs) are a promising option for future low–carbon transportation systems as they have the potential to contribute to a better life quality in cities as well as to the reduction of GHG emissions in the transport sector. In addition, the penetration of EVs in urban areas is beneficial to highly populated areas, in terms of carbon emissions (Nanaki and Koroneos, 2016).

During the past decades, various types of EVs have been developed and commercialized including battery electric vehicles (BEVs), hybrid electric vehicles (HEVs), and plug-in hybrid electric vehicles (PHEVs). In this direction—as was highlighted in Chapter 4, Market Introduction of Electric Vehicles to Urban Areas—a broad portfolio of different policy measures and different business strategies have been implemented at the national and local level all over the world, for example, Kyoto, Cancun (Tobin et al., 2018) and COP24 (Kuchler and Bridge, 2018), as well as in the EU [i.e., the European White paper (Schippl et al., 2016) and the Carbon Target Strategy for 2050], with the goal to support their market penetration. With regard to the European Commission, it is highlighted that the EC has adopted initiatives to build a Single European Transport Area for a competitive and resource efficient transport system. The White Paper includes proposals to reduce Europe's dependence on imported oil and to cut carbon emissions in transport by 60% by 2050 (EC, 2017).

Despite the fact that EVs are beneficial to the urban environment, as they have zero tailpipe emissions, their usage from a life cycle point of view is not synonymous with zero environmental impacts (Nanaki and Koroneos, 2013). The manufacturing of an EV entails a higher environmental impact than that of an internal combustion engine vehicles (ICEV), with battery production being one of the main contributors on the production phase GHG emissions (Patterson et al., 2011). Similarly, electricity consumed during the use phase for charging the EV mostly comes from the existing electricity grid, resulting (due to the additional load) in increased emissions from the electricity power system. This is highly dependent on the power mix (Nanaki and Koroneos, 2013).

In this direction, life cycle analysis (LCA) is a useful tool for the environmental impact assessment of alternative powertrains. A vehicle's LCA comprises two cycles: (1) vehicle life cycle that includes vehicle assembly, maintenance, dismantling, and recycling; and (2) fuel life cycle, which is also referred to as the well-to-wheels (WtWs) cycle, that includes the following steps: fuel extraction, processing, distribution, storage, and use. On that account, a number of studies have explored the environmental impacts of alternative powertrain technologies. These include, inter alia, the studies of Karaaslan et al. (2018); Bicer and Dincer (2018); Lombardi et al. (2017); Tagliaferri et al. (2016); Bauer et al. (2015); Bartolozzi et al. (2013); Nanaki and Koroneos (2013); Hawkins et al. (2012a); Hawkins et al. (2012b).

This chapter identifies the transportation sector as one of the main sectors contributing to climate change and assesses the benefits—in terms of climate change mitigation—of alternative powertrains, such as EVs. The importance of technical novelties that improve—in terms of sustainability—the urban transportation flow is also highlighted. Furthermore, this chapter analyzes the environmental impacts of road fleet electrification, in terms of life cycle emissions and points out the contribution to the reduction of current urban emissions and improvement of air quality. Basic guidelines for the conduction of comparative LCA of electric and conventional powertrains are presented. Finally, a case study is presented in order to provide useful insight to vehicle designers and manufacturers, fuel producers and distributors, as well as to policy makers, with regard to the environmental impacts of electromobility.

5.2 Transport as part of the energy system

The need to accelerate efforts to tackle climate change, coupled with increasing public concern for air quality necessitate an integrated systems approach, so as to overcome the associated challenges. Especially, for the transport sector to meet projected mobility and freight demand while reversing CO_2 emissions growth, specific measures need to be deployed to the maximum effect. In this direction, regulations and policies, in terms of CO_2 and pollutant emissions, set by public authorities worldwide, that aim to reduce the oil dependence and to accelerate the use of renewable energies and alternative powertrains in the transportation sector are of great significance. Fig. 5.1 illustrates the areas that are being taken into consideration, in order to facilitate the decarbonization and reduce emissions from the transportation sector.

The proposed system approach takes into account major changes in the policy and transportation environment including the efficiency and utility of alternative powertrains, such as EVs. Improving energy efficiency in conjunction with smart technology, storage and higher share of renewable fuels are a priority in the envisaged zero emission future; therefore their impact on the transportation energy system is of great significance. The reduction of CO_2 and pollutant emissions from the transport sector requires integrated

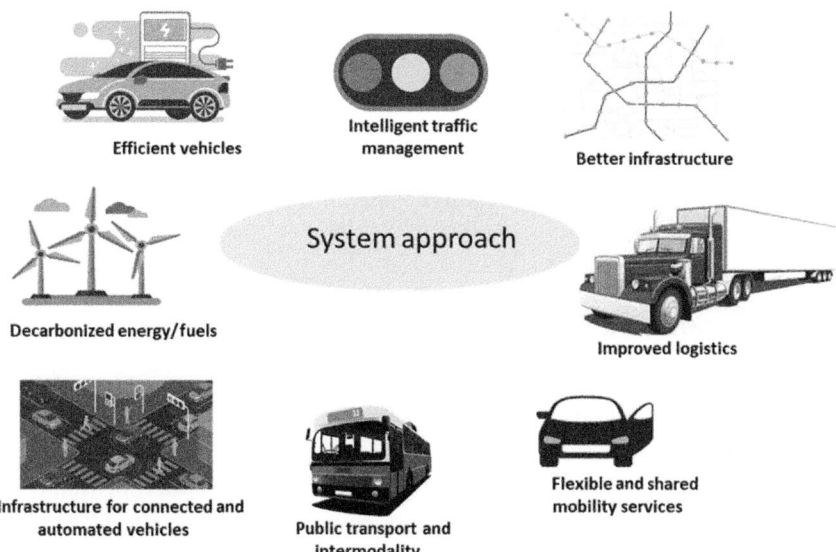

Figure 5.1 Integrated system approach.

policy efforts to enhance efficiency and the promotion of alternative powertrains. The system approach also takes into consideration the anticipation and management of demand by steering new mobility developments in cities and long-term technology and policy visions for the hard-to-abate aviation, shipping, and road freight subsectors.

Energy efficiency measures in transport can take many forms, including managing travel demand to reduce frequency and distance, as well as dependence on high-energy-intensity modes (e.g., car and air); shifting travel to the most efficient modes; system-level and operational efficiency measures; and deploying energy-efficient technologies for vehicles and the fuels that drive them [e.g., electrification enables the use of motors that are far more efficient than internal combustion engines (ICE)]. It is noteworthy that fuel quality is an essential factor in decreasing GHG emissions that emanate from transportation. In addition, this approach considers also areas that affect urban areas, such as cities. These include inter alia new interesting mobility offers for leasing or sharing EVs; the potential and impact of connectivity and automation; growing availability of charging infrastructure; intelligent traffic management; public transport and inter-modality as well as improved logistics.

Based on the above, for the design and implementation of a sustainable urban transportation system, it is vital to understand and analyze the interactions among factors that shape the transportation energy system. Analyzing and assessing the potential impacts of alternative powertrains, such as EVs, from a life cycle point of view will provide an integrated view with regard to the reduction of energy consumption and CO_2 emissions. Furthermore, the assessment of potential impacts can provide useful insight to policy makers, so as to enable effective policy intervention, reduce the environmental pressures, and implement a low- to zero-carbon transport policy.

5.3 Transport energy consumption

Worldwide, petroleum and other liquid fuels are the dominant source of the transportation sector. To be more specific, in 2016 world energy production was 13,764 Mtoe, representing a 0.3% reduction, compared to 2015 (IEA, 2018). Fossil fuels accounted for 81% of production (standing for 0.6% decrease compared to 2015). Growth in oil and natural gas was entirely offset by the coal production's sharp decline for the second year in a row (−5.9% in 2016, after −2.3% in 2015), after 15 years of continuous growth. Together the production of these three fossil fuels decreased by 1.1% in 2016.

Fig. 5.2 indicates that the OECD's increase in final energy consumption in 2016 was largely driven by a growth in transport (+19 Mtoe compared to 2015). Transport energy consumption increased consistently across the three OECD regions, and accounted for over a third of the OECD total final consumption. To be more specific, the transport sector was the largest consuming sector (34%), whereas the industry sector ranked second (31%) and the residential sector ranked third in 2016 (19%). It is also noted that the increase in transport was significant in road energy consumption in Mexico, Poland, Turkey, and the United States.

In 2017 the transportation sector of the United States consumed about 29% of the total energy (Bureau of Transportation Statistics, 2018), which came from fossil fuels. Energy consumption of the transportation sector in non–OECD Asia countries in 2016 relied mainly on oil (IEA, 2018). With regard to the European Union, in 2016 energy consumption in transport in the EU-28 was 29% higher than in 1990; whereas in the EEA-33, this figure reached 34%. In the EU-13, most of this growth occurred in road and maritime transport. In the EU-15, however, the growth occurred mainly in air transport, although the largest absolute increase in energy consumption occurred in road transport (EEA, 2018).

It is noted that in 2016 transport strongly relied on oil products (mainly gasoline and diesel, standing for 90%), whereas electricity accounted for 37% and 53% of total energy consumption in residential and commerce/services, respectively (IEA, 2018). Based on the above, it

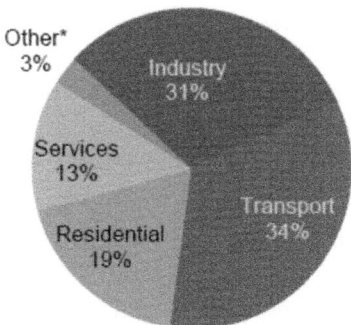

Figure 5.2 Organisation for Economic Cooperation and Development total final consumption in 2016 (IEA, 2018). *Other includes agriculture, forestry, fishing and non-specified.*

is evident that the large energy consumption of the transportation sector poses a great threat to urban air quality. In this direction, advanced fuels and vehicle technologies offer a potential pathway to address the adverse effects of GHG emissions and climate change.

5.4 Emissions from the transportation sector

The transportation sector is the second largest emission source of GHGs worldwide; its annual average carbon emissions account for one quarter of the world's total (IEA, 2018). The environmental pressure imposed by the transportation sector is triggering global climate change, influences human health, and ultimately impacts the sustainable development of human society. Global energy-related CO_2 emissions grew 1.7% in 2018 to reach an historic high of 33.1 Gt CO_2, with the transportation sector being responsible for 24% of direct CO_2 emissions from fuel combustion. Furthermore, road vehicles (including cars, trucks, buses, two- and three-wheelers) are responsible for nearly three-quarters of transport CO_2 emissions. Emissions from aviation and shipping continue to rise, indicating that these subsectors need an integrated approach, so as to abate relative emissions.

Emissions from oil for transport grew by 120 MtCO_2 in 2016, representing a 2% increase- compared to 2015 (IEA, 2018). Since 2013, emissions from oil have continued to increase, with a rate of $+4$%, especially in Asia and America—mostly linked to the raising demand for oil for transport. As per IEA's report, it is highlighted that in 2016 the Americas had the highest transport emission levels worldwide (IEA, 2018). It is pointed out that in the United States, the transportation sector is responsible for nearly 28.5% of emissions and is considered to be one of the fastest-growing emissions of any energy end-use sector (Bloomberg New Energy Finance, 2018). In 2016 Brazil reached a share of 8% after more than doubling its transport emissions since 1990. Asia—with annual growth rates five time larger than the Americas (4.5% versus 0.7%)—reached comparable levels in 2016 (around 2.5 GtCO_2), starting from less than half in 1990.

In 2016 transport emissions in China (0.8 GtCO_2) were half those of the United States, representing 35% of transport emissions in Asia; whereas India had a share of 11% and Japan 9% (15% lower compared to 1990 levels). In Europe, transport emissions in 2016 were 6% larger than in 1990, with 0.5% annual growth between 2012 and 2016. To be more specific, the European transportation sector is responsible for 25.8% of EU's (EU-28) total CO_2 emissions, with cars and vans representing more than two thirds of these (EEA, 2017). Transport is the only sector in which emissions have grown since 1990, contributing to the increase in the EU's overall emissions in 2015. Transport related emissions further increased in 2016 and in 2017 EU oil consumption increased at its fastest pace since 2001. Africa has almost tripled its transport emissions since 1990, although in 2016 levels were lower than 400 $MtCO_2$. Oceania in the same period increased by 60%, reaching 1015 $MtCO_2$.

During the period of 2000 and 2016, China had the largest increase in transport emissions; this could be linked to GDP growth, as the average annual growth of 9% in per capita GDP since 2000 was the main driver for the 600 $MtCO_2$ emissions growth. In the United States, while population (+15%) and GDP (+33%) increased, transport emissions stayed almost flat due to the improvements in intensity on GDP (−21%) and carbon intensity of the energy mix (−6%) mostly due to an increased share of biofuels (IEA, 2018).

With regard to the global transport sector, energy intensity (total energy consumption per unit of GDP) dropped by 2.1% in 2018 after falling an average 1.5% per year between 2000 and 2017. The combined effects of carbon intensity of the energy mix (−2%) and intensity of GDP (−7%) helped emissions remain flat despite growth in the economy and population. In 2016 global emissions per capita were 4.3 tCO_2, +14% compared to 2000 levels. China's per capita emissions more than doubled, reaching values similar to these of the European Union. While the population grew by less than 10%, total CO_2 emissions almost tripled (IEA, 2018). While between 2000 and 2016 India doubled the emissions, its per capita value was still one quarter of the European Union in 2016. Flat since 2000, Africa had the lowest per capita emissions among all regions, around one tenth of those of the United States. It is noteworthy that in order for Africa, Asia, and the Americas to reach comparable levels of emissions per capita as the European Union, an additional 13 Gt CO_2 (around two-fifths of global CO_2 emissions) would need to be emitted in 2016.

5.5 Electric vehicles and energy transition: major challenges to energy transition

A major objective—after the Paris agreement—of most countries' national transport policies was the increase of the penetration of EVs into existing vehicle mobility. For instance, the European Union plans to reduce CO_2 emissions by at least 40% below 1990 levels by 2030, by introducing steps toward achieving targets (2050) involving reducing its CO_2 footprint by 80%—95% (European Commission, 2019a, 2019b). The use of electricity instead of fossil fuels for vehicle propulsion is expected to achieve the targets, set by many regulatory measures regarding CO_2 emissions reduction. For this reason, the deployment of electromobility to urban areas can significantly reduce direct tailpipe emissions of CO_2 and air pollutants like nitrogen oxides (NOx), nonmethane hydrocarbons (NMHC), and PM from road transport. In terms of their utilization, EVs are beneficial in terms of acceleration, low noise, higher energy efficiency, and environmental performance. However, from the perspective of the entire life cycle, some studies have found that EVs may transfer environmental impacts from the utilization stage to the production and power supply stage (Notter et al., 2010, Nanaki and Koroneos, 2016). For this reason, in terms of sustainability the production of required electricity by various renewable and carbon-free energy sources is of great importance, as it can help reduce pollution, with a considerable decarbonization effect and improve resource efficiency (depending mainly on the level of infrastructure and on the demand for additional electricity).

A number of studies (OEKO, 2016; Mai et al., 2018) have explored the impacts of the additional electricity required to cover the extra demand arising from the increased percentage of EVs in 2050 (reaching approximately 80%). It is stated that the additional power production is a necessity in order to meet the electricity demand that will result from the high rates of EVs ownership. The latter is likely to have an enormous impact on the overall power system worldwide. Nonetheless, the avoided CO_2 emissions in the transport sector should outweigh the higher emissions from electricity generation. In countries with high shares of fossil fuel power plants, EV demand could, however, lead to higher CO_2 emissions (Nanaki and Koroneos, 2016).

Based on the aboveme, a broaden assessment—taking into consideration not only the direct tailpipe emissions, but also the upstream emissions and sustainability impacts of fuel/electricity production and distribution from a "well-to-wheels" approach—is of great significance for policy makers as well as for all stakeholders involved in creating a zero-energy transport future. This is especially useful in cases where policies extend beyond operations to vehicle production and disposal. LCA is a useful tool that can be employed in order to monitor the impacts of current regulatory frameworks that refer to the energy transition to a low-carbon transportation energy system. Furthermore, LCA can provide useful inputs to policy makers, to lessen the disparity between policy coverage and the actions needed to meet emissions reduction goals. It is noteworthy that the concept of life cycle thinking and relative results from LCA serve as the basis for decision-making to design more environment-friendly energy systems (Koroneos et al., 2013).

5.6 Life cycle assessment

Life cycle assessment constitutes a methodological framework for evaluating and quantifying the lifetime environmental impacts of products, processes, or activities (UNEP, 2011; ISO, 2006). *Life cycle thinking* is a way of thinking that includes the economic, environmental, and social consequences of a product or process over its entire life cycle. According to SETAC (SETAC, 1991): *"It is a process to evaluate the environmental burdens associated with a product, process or activity by identifying and quantifying energy and materials used and wastes released to the environment. The assessment includes the entire life cycle of product, process or activity, encompassing extracting and processing raw materials, manufacturing, transport and distribution; use, reuse, maintenance; recycling, and final disposal."*

Developed in 1994, the ISO 14040 (ISO, 1997) standard set the methodological basis for the quantification of environmental impacts of different processes. It was accompanied by the ISO 14044 (ISO, 2006). These two standards promote a harmonization of the methodology used, more robustness and reliability of the results, and a more formalized communication. According to ISO 14040, LCA is a *"compilation and evaluation of the inputs, outputs and potential environmental impacts of a product system during its life cycle."*

The methodology as per international standards ISO 14040 (ISO, 1997), ISO 14044 (ISO, 2006) consists of the following four successive steps (Fig. 5.3):

1. *Definition of the goal and scope of the project/ study.* During this stage, the intended application, the motivation for carrying out the study, and the intended audience have to be defined. This stage sets also other criteria, such as product functions, system boundaries and limits, calculation of rules applied, assumptions, as well as the functional unit. The functional unit is the unit of measure used to evaluate the service rendered by the product. It makes the analysis coherent and allows the results of the LCA (impacts) to be reduced to a common unit to compare two products.

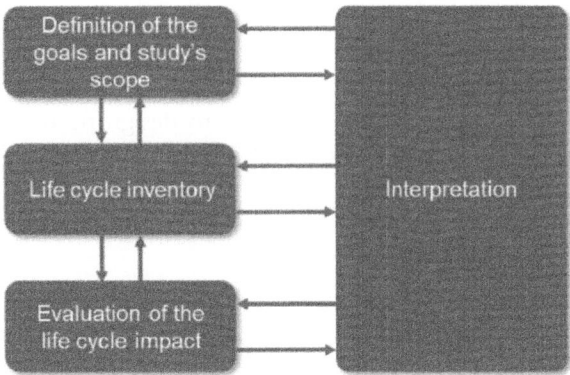

Figure 5.3 Life cycle assessment stages.

2. *Life Cycle Inventory (LCI)*. This stage entails the collection of all the information regarding the incoming and outgoing material and energy flows during the life cycle stages of the product or service or system.
3. *Life Cycle Impact Assessment (LCIA)*. Based on the LCI, the potential environmental impacts resulting from extracted resources and from emitted pollutants are quantified during this stage. Emissions are classified according to their contribution to the different impact categories; while their potential contribution is expressed in terms of impact equivalents (e.g., in CO_2-equivalents for climate change). This stage includes up to 16 impact categories (e.g., US EPA, 2013) including climate change, ozone depletion, acidification, eutrophication, human toxicity, ecotoxicity, land use, PM/respiratory inorganics, photochemical ozone formation, and resource depletion.
4. *Interpretation*. This stage verifies the results of the assessment taking into account completeness, sensitivity, and consistency checks; leading to general conclusions with limitations and recommendations.

Finally, it should also be noted that the concept of life cycle thinking is also complementary to key aspects of the concept of the circular economy (an alternative to the traditional linear economy, which focuses on make, use, and dispose)—taking into consideration that both concepts are assessing impacts and propose solutions to optimize the product or system under study. Taken into consideration the fact that in the context of the automotive industry, an integrated approach is required, so as to reach the emission reduction targets, it is imperative to evaluate and assess not only the emissions emitted during the vehicle use phase but also the environmental impacts induced during all phases of the vehicle's life cycle [manufacturing, logistics, use, maintenance, and end of life].

5.6.1 Life cycle assessment and electric vehicles

LCA studies regarding vehicles take into consideration usually all the processes throughout the life cycle of vehicles including: raw material extraction, production of components, assembly, transport, vehicle use, and the end-of-life (EoL) treatment. In the case of EVs BEV, HEV, plug-in hybrid (PHEV) the stages taken into consideration include also the raw material extraction and production of batteries as well as the raw material extraction and production of electricity (Fig. 5.4).

The environmental assessment of vehicle technologies can either follow a "well-to-wheel" (WTW) approach, covering only the life cycle of the energy carrier (i.e., fuels or electricity) used to power the vehicles, or a "complete LCA," which consists of the production and recycling of the vehicle and the WTW part. The WTT includes the production of fuel and electricity including its upstream processes such as fuel extraction, refinery, distribution and storage of the fuel, and production and distribution of electricity. TTW covers the tailpipe emissions and any other emissions during the use of the vehicle. The EoL treatment includes recycling, recovery, and disposal. Table 5.1 summarizes the abovementioned life cycle system boundaries and relative considerations.

The life cycle approach is of great importance as it allows comparison of different powertrains from a holistic system perspective, given that it compares not only the exhaust emissions but also the emissions from the

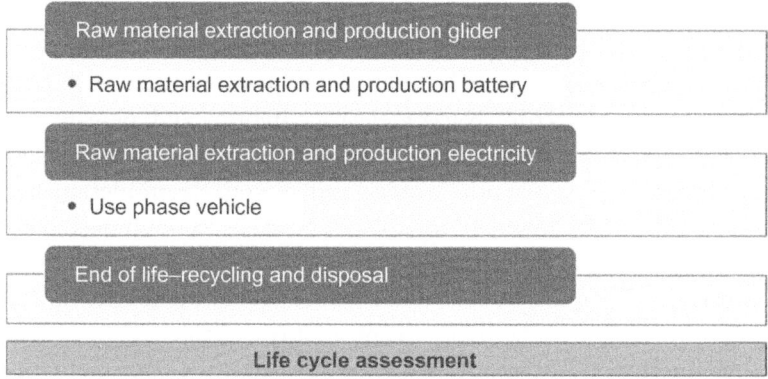

Figure 5.4 Overview of life cycle stages of battery electric vehicles.

Table 5.1 Life cycle assessment categorization and relative life cycle system boundaries.

Tailpipe only Well-to-wheel		• Considers vehicle point of use only • Considers the fuel or energy vector life cycle, from primary energy through to use in the vehicle• Frequency split into "well-to-tank" and "tank-to-wheels" (vehicle consumption during use)
Vehicle life cycle		• Considers the whole life cycle (cradle-to-grave) from material extraction, through production to use and end-of-life processes
Whole mobility system life cycle		• Considers impact of subject within the wider techno-, socio-, and eco-spheres. It includes changes to infrastructure or analyzing externalities
Cradle-to-gate		• Considers production phase of the vehicle of component, including material extraction• Analysis stops at end of production. Use and EoL stages are not included.

whole life cycle. For instance, when comparing a BEV with an ICEV running on diesel, the comparison only of exhaust emissions can lead to misleading results, given that the BEVs have no emissions during operation. However, their operation from a life cycle point of view is not beneficial to the environment as they are responsible for substantial amounts of emissions during the production processes of electricity and vehicle.

Several studies have analyzed and compared from a life cycle point of view the performance of vehicles with different propulsion technologies, such as ICE, pure electric, battery electric, hybrid, and plug-in hybrid cars. These include inter alia LCA studies that focus only on specific components of BEVs (i.e., traction battery and power electronics) (Majeau-Bettez et al., 2011; Ellingsen et al., 2014), as well as LCA studies that take into account the whole vehicle (Samaras and Meisterling, 2008; Nanaki and Koroneos, 2013; Casals et al., 2016). Samaras and Meisterling (2008) evaluated the emissions of hybrid vehicles from cradle to gate with an economic input—output model by LCA. Nanaki and Koroneos (2013) assessed the environmental impacts of a conventional, hybrid, and electric car. Casals et al. (2016) compared EVs with conventional vehicles running on gasoline with regard to global warming potential (GWP) in European countries by performing a Monte Carlo analysis. In some cases, LCA studies compare the different technologies at individual vehicle levels in one or more specific energy markets under the current or future conditions (Bauer et al., 2015; Cox et al., 2018; Tagliaferri et al., 2016). A detailed LCA with complete inventories on battery EV was performed by Notter et al. (2010) and Hawkins et al. (2013); nonetheless, the results of the recycling stage in both studies are based on the Ecoinvent database (Swiss Centre for Life Cycle Inventories, 2014). It is noted that the entire life cycle of vehicles, including the battery and the entire power system, has been analyzed in a limited number of studies.

The abovementioned LCA studies reveal the existence of significant environmental impacts, which depend on different EV powertrain technologies. For instance, BEVs should distinguish the vehicle glider, powertrain, and battery (Bauer et al., 2015, Tagliaferri et al., 2016). Despite the fact that BEVs have zero tailpipe emissions, the materials and production processes of the battery cells and packs increase their environmental impact (Cerdas et al., 2018; Held et al., 2016). With regard to the use stage, two factors influence the overall environmental impact of EVs: the *energy demand* and the *source of the energy carrier*. Especially in the case of BEVs, empirical studies suggest that external vehicle characteristics (i.e., mobility patterns, road and traffic conditions, etc.) as well as the technological performance affect the energy consumption (Helmers et al., 2017, Wu et al., 2015). Nonetheless, empirical studies indicate that the real-world values for all powertrain technologies can differ from the ones measured on standard driving cycles (Wang et al., 2015, Wu et al., 2015).

Finally, the contribution of the *stage of* EoL treatment (recycling, recovery, disposal) to the overall impact is minor; yet is still subject to considerable uncertainty (Hawkins et al., 2013). The recycling, recovery, and disposal of the glider is similar for the different powertrain technologies; nonetheless, in the case of BEVs, the larger the battery, the higher the environmental burden of recycling and disposal. A number of studies have thrown light on potential recycling processes for different Lithium-ion (Li-ion) battery technologies (Buchert and Sutter, 2015, Cerdas et al., 2018). It should be noted that first-hand data on energy and materials flows, which cause high uncertainty in the EoL treatment, are limited (Ellingsen et al., 2017).

Based on the above, it is evident that all vehicle stages (including energy production and emissions during operation, as well as burdens involved by raw materials extraction and production, components manufacturing, dismantling, and materials disposal) are of great importance for the assessment of different propulsion technologies. Also, another point that should be highlighted is the difficulty in the accuracy of inventory data regarding the production of vehicles.

5.6.2 Life cycle assessment principles

LCA studies can be categorized by their approach. In this contest, there are LCA studies that follow a *bottom-up approach*, which means that they start with each production step, mapping input and output flows, to build up to the final product; others follow a *top-down approach*, meaning that they start from known macro parameters describing the overall system, they gradually unravel the macro information into data describing the subprocesses of the production system. There is also a third category of LCA studies that follows an approach that combines bottom-up and top-down approaches to discern the life cycle system.

With regard to the modeling approach, this can be distinguished to *attributional* or *consequential*. An *attributional assessment* determines the environmental impacts resulting from activities that have contributed to the production, use, and disposal of the product. *Attributional modeling* is accounting based. It depicts the potential environmental impacts that can be attributed to a system along its supply chain, use, and EoL. The system is modeled as it is, was, or is forecast to be. It makes use of historical, fact-based, measurable data. It includes the processes that contributed to the system being studied. It uses cutoff rules and allocation to isolate the product system. A *consequential assessment* determines the environmental impacts resulting from activities that change due to the production, use, and disposal of the product. Consequential modeling is science based. It focuses on the physical and social unit processes that change as a consequence of a decision. Its purpose is decision support. Results do not represent the environmental impacts of the functional unit in itself, but the environmental exchanges resulting from adding or subtracting one functional unit compared to doing nothing.

5.6.3 Overview of a vehicle life cycle assessment stages

The stages that are taken into consideration when performing an LCA for both a conventional ICE and an EV are going to be presented in the following sections, so as to provide useful insight in the challenges arising at each step.

5.6.3.1 Functional unit

The scope of an LCA study should clearly specify the functions (performance characteristics) of the system studied (see ISO 14040 and ISO 14044). The functional unit provides the reference for normalizing input and output data. It should be clearly defined, measurable, and technology-neutral. The functional unit is used, in order to normalize the different units and scale of the analysis components to a consistent measure. The majority of passenger transportation LCAs use the kilometer driven (*per drive km*). This means that the environmental impacts are calculated over *the total life cycle and divided over the total km driven during the lifetime of the vehicle.* This allows fair comparisons among vehicles with differing expected lifetime mileages, as the functional unit is no longer the vehicle but the mobility service it provides. On the other hand, some other studies use as a functional unit the *person-km driven*, meaning that they divide the total environmental impact by the *total km driven during the lifetime of the vehicle multiplied with the average number of passengers in the car.* It is noted that in both cases the life span of the vehicle plays a significant role for the output of the analysis.

5.6.3.2 Production stage

The production stage of a vehicle takes into consideration the following processes and steps:

1. *Raw material extraction process* including emissions and resources used.
2. *Transport* of components and materials to the production facilities and transport to the assembly plant/plants.
3. *Emissions and inputs/outputs* in the production facilities.
4. *Transport of products and parts to dealers or directly to customer.*

It is noteworthy that the production and assembly processes of vehicles are a complex procedure involving many components and subsystems, sourced from different suppliers. Nonetheless, it is imperative to gather a complete list of materials, so as to be able to assess which components have the highest environmental impact. The scope of the study will define the level of detail required to get full material content. For instance, steel needs to be analyzed with regards to its complete content including alloys etc. Therefore as steel and other materials derive from many forms, their exact composition differs depending on the type that is utilized.

Compared to ICE vehicles, EVs have a different structure, such as traction batteries, electric motors, and in some cases a dedicated platform that has been adapted to electric drive instead of a traditional ICE. For this reason, the components that need to be taken into consideration and

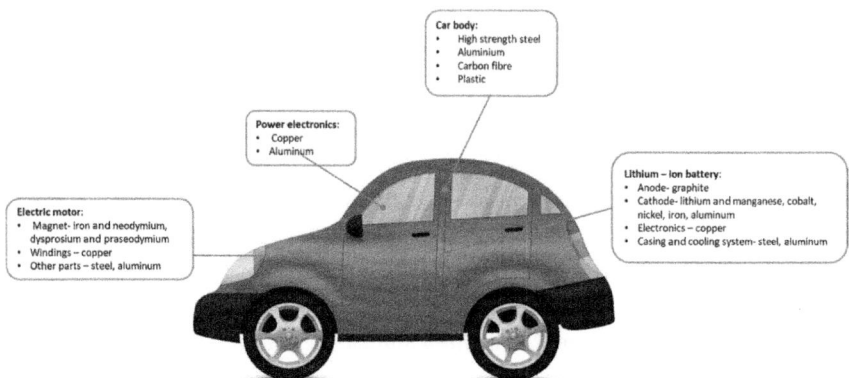

Figure 5.5 Major raw materials commonly used in battery electric vehicles. *Ccompiled from data in Hawkins, T.R., Singh, B., Majeau-Bettez, G., Strømman, A.H., 2012a. Comparative environmental life cycle assessment of conventional and electric vehicles. J. Ind. Ecol. 17 (1), 53–64; Mathieux, F., et al., 2017. Critical Raw Materials and the Circular Economy. European Commission Joint Research Centre, Ispra, Italy.*

need a detailed analysis are the following: electric machines; power electronics and control systems; batteries for traction, lithium batteries or other relevant types; components impacted by increased vehicle mass (i.e., tires). Taking into consideration the fact that electric machines in many cases contain rare earth elements (REEs) and other critical and scarce materials, a detailed analysis of their material content is of great significance. Also power electronics and control systems usually contain metals (i.e., copper, lead, etc.).

In the case of BEVs, the abovementioned components contain amounts of base metals such as aluminum, iron, and critical raw materials (CRM). CRMs, including REEs, are more abundant in EVs than in ICEVs (Mathieux et al., 2017). The extraction of these materials is an energy-intensive process, which also includes refining (Gradin et al., 2018). In many cases, the same materials and similar quantities are used both for ICEVs and BEVs. Fig. 5.5 illustrates a simplified picture of metals and raw materials required for BEV components.

The use of raw materials in EVs is associated with a number of environmental impacts, such as:

- *GHG and air pollutant emissions* from energy-intensive mining and refining processes (Ellingsen and Hung, 2017).
- *Health and ecosystem impacts* of air pollution from metallurgical processes; water and soil contamination from mining activities.

- *Impacts resulting from land use for mining*: mining processes enable the release of toxic emissions and leakages of toxic substances, which can have significant impact to eutrophication; acidification of water bodies and wetlands; soil contamination with heavy metals and soil erosion.
- *Depletion of CRMs and REEs*: the mining of REEs, such as dysprosium and neodymium, used in electric car magnets has been associated with pulmonary embolisms and damage to the liver with accumulated exposure (Rim et al., 2013).

5.6.3.3 Influencing factors of environmental impacts of electric vehicles production stage

The results of LCAs from the production stage depend on a variety of (uncertain) factors. These factors can be attributed either to different methodological approaches (i.e., assumptions made regarding vehicle lifetime; IEA, 2017a,b) or to differences in the vehicles and systems under examination (i.e., type of vehicle; Hawkins et al., 2013). The major factors affecting the environmental impacts of EV production can be summarized in Table 5.2.

In regards to battery types, it is highlighted that the majority of BEVs currently use one of the several types of Li–ion batteries, which provide high-energy densities (crucial for the vehicle range). The different types of Li-on batteries are distinguished by the cathode material used (Dunn et al., 2012):

- Lithium—nickel—manganese—cobalt oxide (LiNMC)
- Lithium—iron—phosphate (LiFePO4)
- Lithium—manganese oxide (LMO)
- Lithium—cobalt oxide (LCO)
- Lithium—nickel—cobalt—aluminum oxide (LiNCA).

It is argued that $LiFePO_4$ batteries have the potential for the lowest production impacts on a per unit of energy delivered basis, due to their long cycle life expectancy (Majeau-Bettez et al., 2011). Nonetheless their low energy density means that they cannot provide sufficient ranges for most BEVs and are mostly restricted to hybrid EVs (Ellingsen and Hung, 2017), with BEVs using mostly LiNMC batteries.

Finally, it is noted that the production locations of the vehicle and its many components may not be the same as its geographical region of use. Therefore the environmental impacts of the energy used during production and assembly may be different to the energy used during vehicle use. For instance, different parts of BEVs are manufactured in different

Table 5.2 Factors affecting the environmental impacts of electric vehicles production stage.

Factors	Reasoning
Vehicle and battery size	• The larger the electric vehicles the more energy is required during the manufacturing stage. Vehicle size also affects the energy consumption, which is discussed in Section 5.6.1.3. • Larger battery capacity to boost driving range significantly increases the environmental impacts of production (IEA, 2017a,b).
Lifetime mileage	• The longer the lifetime mileage of a vehicle, the lower the influence of production-related emissions on the total life cycle impacts, as use stage impacts become more dominant.
Battery type (chemistry and configuration)	• Higher specific energy density means that less material is needed to deliver a given vehicle range, thereby reducing environmental impacts on a per vehicle basis. • Higher life cycle expectancy can play a significant role in reducing the environmental impact of battery production (when assessed on a per unit of energy delivered or kilometer-driven basis).
Manufacturing energy efficiency	• When the full capacity of production plants is used for the production of batteries then the energy consumption per vehicle is reduced. • Maximizing the throughput of particularly energy-intensive processes (i.e., electrode drying) enables facilities to be used at full capacity (Dunn et al., 2012).
Electricity generation mix	• The generation mix available in the place and at the time of vehicle manufacture is responsible for greenhouse gas and air pollution emissions associated with electricity production. Therefore the decarbonization of the electricity grid has the potential to abate relative carbon emissions.

locations, whereas 90% of battery manufacture (the most energy-intensive step) occurs in China, South Korea, and Japan, where the carbon intensity of electricity production is relatively high (Ellingsen and Hung, 2018). In this direction, many vehicle OEMs are investigating opportunities for reducing the environmental footprint of their production facilities and supply chain, such as installing wind turbines or solar panels at factory sites. For this reason, the energy mix used in the factory may be different to the national average of the plant location.

5.6.3.4 Use stage

The use stage of a vehicle takes into consideration the following: the use (including the fuel or electricity), repair, and service of the vehicle. The energy consumption of a vehicle, during the operation stage, is influenced by a number of factors, such as the driving cycles, specific circumstances, driving behavior, auxiliary load, and climate. In this stage, LCA studies proceed with the calculation of energy consumption and then with the assessment of associated emissions linked to the fuel or electricity consumed. Finally, the impacts from repair and maintenance are also quantified. The goal and scope of the study specifies the choice of method to assess the environmental burdens produced by the use stage.

The calculation of a vehicle's energy consumption can either be made with the use of real data sources, which determine realistically the environmental impact of driving a specific vehicle on the road in a specific use case or by modeling of "real world" vehicle energy consumption, which describes the average driving behavior. Overall, the energy consumption of an EV is perceived as a combination of several subconsumptions:

- Basic consumption (driving from A to B, without the consumption of any device which is not directly needed for propulsion).
- Additional consumption due to heating and air conditioning of the passenger compartment.
- Additional consumption due to auxiliaries (light, radio, navigation etc.).
- Additional consumption due to internal battery losses in standstill.
- Additional consumption due to battery charging losses.

Technological and driver behavior factors affect the above subconsumptions. To be more specific, the type of vehicle (weight, shape, and tires), the driving patterns (acceleration and speed driven) as well as the ambient conditions, which play a crucial role in the additional energy consumption for heating and cooling, can affect the above subconsumptions. Consumption for heating and air conditioning per km also depends on average speed, since consumption relates both to the power of the devices and the length of time they are used. Energy consumption by auxiliaries also depends on the devices (efficiency, power), how long they are used, and at which average speed.

Attention should also be given to the system of regenerative braking and coasting, which is utilized in order to optimize energy consumption. As per Del Duce et al. (2016) the calculation of the mechanical energy of an EV along the NEDC trajectory can be made via the following equation (assuming driving on a flat road):

$$(t)\% = m_v(t) + 1/2 \times C_w \times \rho \times A \times v^2(t) + C_r \times m_v \times g \qquad (5.1)$$

where $F(t)\%$ is the force required for traction of vehicle; m_v is the mass of vehicle; $a(t)$ is the acceleration; $v(t)$ is the speed; C_w is the aerodynamics drag coefficient; ρ is the air density; A is the frontal area; C_r is the rolling resistance; g is the acceleration due to gravity.

Once the mechanical power required for moving the vehicle is known for each step of the trajectory, it is then possible to estimate how much electrical power needs to be taken from the battery in order for the drivetrain of the vehicle to sustain that motion. This can be done by backtracking how the power is dissipated within the drivetrain due to the efficiencies of the various components. The additional energy consumption for auxiliaries is then calculated. The standby and mean electrical power demand of each device (e.g., lighting, navigation, etc.) define its energy consumption. As exact data on the consumption of auxiliaries is lacking, this contribution to the vehicle's energy consumption can be estimated from the power demand and a use strategy for the devices. Standard default values are also provided in the Eco-Invent v3 database (Del Duce et al., 2016).

Finally, with regard to the ambient temperatures, it is highlighted that these affect the energy consumption of the vehicle, due to the energy needed to reach the ambient temperature for human comfort—around 20° C−23°C (ArGV3, 2011). Some drivers might switch the heating on when the passenger cabin is below 20°C while others might only use the heater if it is much cooler. The energy needed to reach the ambient temperature for human comfort depends on a number of factors such as ambient conditions of the vehicle, direct and diffuse radiation, vehicle insulation, etc. Air conditioning in current BEVs uses the same system found in conventional ICE vehicles. Compared to heating, the power demand of air conditioning is relatively low. Current systems require around 1 kW (standard ICE air-conditioning system driven by an electric motor). In addition to the comfort related operation of heating and air conditioning, some users activate the air conditioner for safety reasons (i.e., fogged windscreen). A special case of comfort device use is precooling or preheating the vehicle while plugged into the charging device. In this case, the vehicle's heating or air-conditioning system is not powered by the high voltage battery, but directly from the main grid. The maximum heating or cooling capacity is dependent on the maximum output of the power supply.

5.6.3.5 Electricity generation and associated emissions

The overall results of an LCA of an EV strongly depend on the specific electricity source or energy mix employed for the production of electricity (Hawkins, 2013). For instance, an energy mix largely based on coal power plants is going to lead to very different impacts when compared to one based on electricity coming from renewable energy systems (RES) (Nanaki and Koroneos, 2013). For instance, WTW GHG emissions of typical BEVs charged exclusively with coal-generated electricity are at least as high as for an equivalent ICEV, at between 139 and 175 $gCO_2e/$ km, whereas charging with other fossil fuel generation types results in slightly lower GHG emissions for BEVs than ICEVs (Nordelöf et al., 2014). In contrast, a BEV charged exclusively with wind power would have WTW GHG emissions of only $1-2$ gCO_2e/km. For this reason, OEMs are pursuing direct links between clean electricity and EVs. For example, Tesla's Gigafactory in the United States, which produces 35 gigawatt-hours (GWh) of lithium–ion batteries per year, runs completely on renewable energy, most of which is produced onsite (www.tesla.com).

In this direction, policies and legislations, aiming to abate climate change through the reduction of CO_2 emissions, are expected to lead to increases of the percentage of RES in different energy mixes. Nonetheless, if the mass penetration of EVs and the challenges of increased electricity capacity are considered, it can be deducted that the modeling of the electricity used for charging the EV should be consistent with the goal and scope of the study. When defining the electricity generation in LCA studies, the best approach is the one that best describes the electricity production technologies used for charging the battery in the geographical area and time frame defined by the goal and scope of the study.

A five-step procedure to assist in the assessment of the emissions produced from the electricity generation are presented in Dotzauer (2010):

- *Average electricity principle*: This approach uses emissions from the system's average electricity mix in assessments. This approach is useful for bookkeeping purposes, when the electricity mix has been determined (i.e., in an attributional LCA).
- *Marginal electricity principle*: This approach should be applied in short-term consequence analyses, when the electricity use is not part of the current system but will occur in a future system (i.e., in a consequential LCA). A change in electricity use requires a change in electricity generation, which will affect the marginal production unit. As electricity production units are taken into operation in merit order, based on

operating costs, the marginal production unit will either be the producing unit with the highest operational costs, or the unit to next be taken into operation.

- *Long-term development of the power system*: This approach can be applied in long-term consequential LCAs. This approach deals with the build margin. Depending on the future development of the electricity sector, different production units will constitute the margin.
- *Emission trading impact:* This approach states that with the cap on GHG emissions in the European Union Emission Trading System (EU ETS), increased electricity use cannot lead to increased emissions. Nonetheless this approach is not useful, given that emissions have been known to increase within the system (Agora Energiewende and Sandbag, 2018).
- *Contracted delivery*: This approach argues that if the customer buys a certain kind of electricity, e.g., hydropower, then the emissions from that kind or mix should be used in assessments.

With regard to *distribution networks* and *charging pattern*, it is pointed out that all the components used to realize the transmission and distribution network (electricity lines, transformers, switches, etc., differentiating between the specific voltage level in the network where these are used) should be part of the inventory. Data on electricity transmission and distribution infrastructure are typically also available from LCI data providers. It should further be considered that all these components have losses which accumulate along the line. Therefore losses from production site to plug have to be accounted for when quantifying the electricity generation. It has been argued that the *time of charging* does not have a high impact on the value of average emissions; whereas the amount of RES in the marginal mix was twice as high in a scenario where EV charging was controlled, enabling load-shifting, than its value in a scenario where charging was uncontrolled (Jochem et al., 2015). On the other hand, it has been indicated that GHG can be reduced by 12% if off-peak charging is used (Van Mierlo et al., 2017).

5.6.3.6 Maintenance

LCA should take into consideration, the materials or components replaced due to maintenance. The environmental impact and inputs/outputs of the maintenance stage can be modeled using the data that was obtained for the production of the vehicle. Service intervals can normally be obtained from service documentation. When it comes to replacement of unplanned parts it is more complicated to obtain detailed data. For EVs, the expected lifetime of the battery is of crucial importance, as it has a substantial influence on the final result of the study. The maintenance stage, usually takes into consideration oils, other fluids, and filters; brake parts; tires; batteries; and any other parts changed during service intervals. If exchange of batteries is included it is important to take into consideration the fact that the new battery will have a different environmental impact since battery development is advancing quickly.

5.6.3.7 End of Life stage

The treatment of waste and EoL products produces secondary (recycled) materials, energy resources (e.g., heat), and reconditioned parts for reuse. These outputs are used in subsequent products, where they replace primary production of material and/or change the energy mix. In this context, the product being recycled has its primary function (what it was made for), and a secondary function of providing resources for the subsequent life cycle of another product. In *closed loop recycling* the life cycle model loops the secondary material or energy back to an earlier process where it replaces primary input. In *open loop recycling* all or part of the secondary material is used in another product system. The recycled material can either have the same inherent properties as the primary material or it may undergo changes to its inherent properties during recycling. There are different methods that can be employed, in order to calculate associated burdens and benefits.

In the EoL stage, the disassembly of the vehicle, the required treatment steps, recycling processes, and waste disposal should be calculated in the LCI. Components belonging to the system include:

- *Battery*: recycling of the case material, battery management system, battery cells, critical materials (e.g., lithium).
- *Electric motor*: depending on type of motor (permanent magnet, induction, etc.), recycling of metals, recycling or reuse of magnets, recycling of scarce materials [e.g., rare earth metals (REMs)].
- *Electronics*: for example, power electronics, nonpropulsion electrical systems: recycling of cables, electronics, valuable materials.
- *Wheels and tires*: recycling of the wheels, recycling of the tires.
- *Shredding of residual car body*: shredding, separation, and treatment of the heavy and light fractions, respectively recovered material fractions and their intended material recycling processes

The recycling processes involve reconditioning, material recycling, and energy recovery. The produced materials are reusable parts, recycled materials, or recovered energy and can be categorized to so-called secondary goods.

In regards to EU, the End of Life Vehicles Directive (2000/53/EC) requires vehicle manufacturers to be responsible for their vehicles and components after use (Ramoni and Zhang, 2013). Under this responsibility vehicle manufacturers are financially or physically responsible for either taking back their products, with the end goal of reusing, recycling, or remanufacturing, or alternatively obliged to delegate the responsibility to a third party (Ellingsen and Hung, 2018). This mandatory process, involves inter alia the removal of all fluids and hazardous components, as well as the removal of substances and parts that require special treatment and a particular recycling or disposal process. Depending on further regional requirements and demands, additional parts or components for reuse or recycling are dismounted. Some components could serve as spare parts, others need selective collection for easier recycling (e.g., tires, plastic parts). The residual vehicle, which includes all components that do not require special treatment (e.g., wheels, SBSS), is shredded. The shredded material is separated using additional sorting processes in order to extract different material fractions, particularly the ferrous and nonferrous metal fractions. Only nonrecyclable remains are treated as waste. Subsequently, each material fraction, as well as special parts or components, are recycled in order to create secondary goods.

5.6.3.8 End of Life of batteries

EoL of traction batteries involves reuse, remanufacture, and refunctionalization as well as recycling. Battery reuse involves either direct reuse in EVs or cascaded use in alternative applications, such as energy storage. The reuse of batteries in EVs not only extends the lifetime of the batteries, but also delays the need for further EoL processes. Remanufacture and refunctionalization involves processing the materials into a useable form for either the same or a different function. Direct reuse of traction batteries in EVs, where there is remaining capacity in the battery, can be made in cases of early vehicle failure; vehicle crashes; life span mismatch (Richa et al., 2017). Cascaded use involves using batteries in different and less demanding stationary applications; in this way, there are significant economic advantages through the resale value of used batteries and avoiding the costs of purchasing a new battery (Neubauer et al., 2012). Box 5.2 illustrates a commercially available energy storage technology.

Remanufacturing of traction batteries (mainly Li-ion) is considered to be a new approach to EoL treatment and currently is not deployed on a large scale. This process involves the return of active cathode and anode materials to their original state for reuse in new Li-ion battery cells (Gaustad, 2018). This creates a closed loop in which high-value materials are remanufactured into new batteries, while the remaining materials are fed into recycling streams (Gaustad, 2018). This is considered to be the most environment-friendly EoL option (Ramoni and Zhang, 2013). Box 5.3 presents a case study of remanufacture of EV batteries.

BOX 5.2 Case study of cascaded battery reuse (Connected Energy, 2017)

E-STOR is a commercially available energy storage technology, which uses second-life EV batteries to store and supply energy. The batteries are recharged at low power, store the energy, and then release it at high power. Connect Energy and Renault have used E-STOR technology to provide quick charging stations for EVs on highways in Belgium and Germany. This is a very useful technology and within the concept of circular economy, as it plays a crucial role in reducing energy costs, improving energy resilience, and promoting the use of RES.

BOX 5.3 Case study of battery remanufacture (Nissannews, 2018)

Remanufacture of EV batteries for reuse in EV cars

In 2010 Nissan launched 4R Energy Corp., a joint venture with Sumitomo Corporation, which worked on the development and testing of using EV batteries as part of a stationary energy storage system. In March 2018 Nissan opened a plant in Namie, Japan, where recycled and refabricated batteries will be used to offer the world's first exchangeable refabricated battery for EVs, and will also be used in large-scale storage systems and electric forklifts. At the plant, used battery packs are disassembled and any modules that have lost more than 20% of their capacity are replaced from other batteries. The discarded modules are repurposed for cascaded reuse (e.g., energy storage systems). The remanufactured batteries will be sold at about half the price of a new replacement battery. The facility is capable of processing 2250 battery packs per year, although it will initially process only a few hundred.

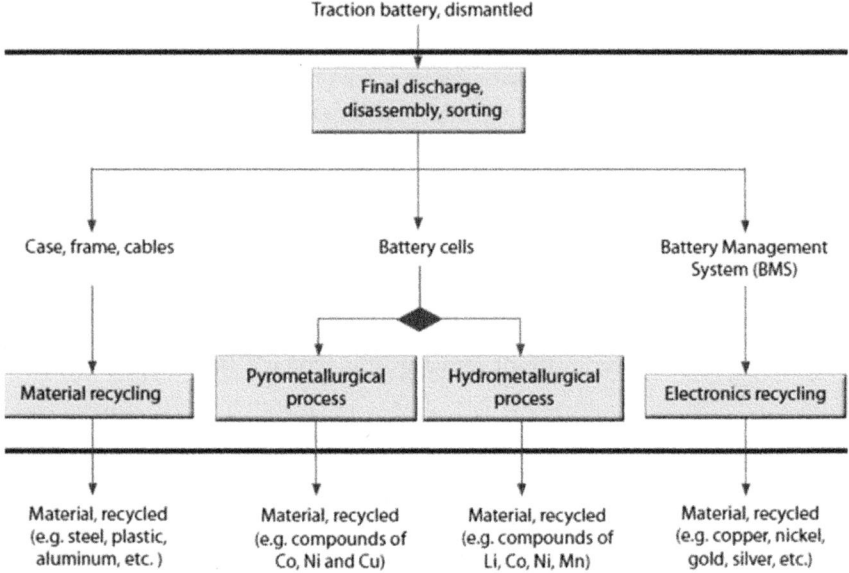

Figure 5.6 Different pathways for recycling of traction batteries.

Current industrial battery recycling processes usually combine different unit operations, including mechanical separation, pyrometallurgical treatment, and hydrometallurgical treatment (Diekmann et al., 2017). The various recycling pathways cover different materials, require different material and energy inputs, and achieve different yields. Recycling starts with *final discharge and disassembly* and the *cell recycling*. The battery is disassembled to its individual components, which (except for the battery cells) follow different recycling pathways (Fig. 5.6). The case, frame, and cables of the battery and its modules proceed to the corresponding material recovery processes. The battery management system follows the electronics recycling pathway (Fig. 5.6).

5.6.3.9 End of Life of electric motors
EVs use different types of electric motors; out of these, electric motors with permanent magnets are of particular interest as they achieve higher power density, compared to nonpermanent motors. Nonetheless, their EoL requires special treatment, given that they contain REMs, such as dysprosium, neodymium, etc. Accurate inputs−outputs in LCA studies at this stage are of crucial importance. Fig. 5.7 illustrates different recycling pathways, including reuse and material recycling for an electric motor

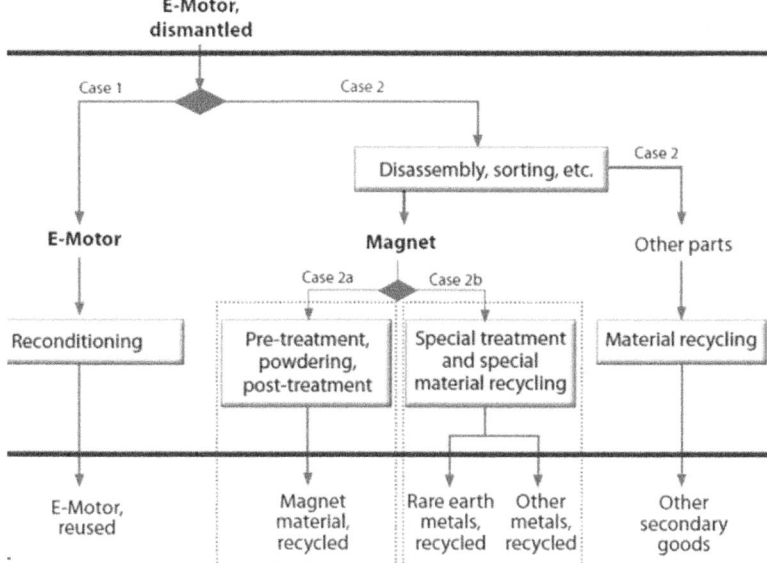

Figure 5.7 Different pathways for recycling of electric motors.

with permanent magnets. Usually, these depend on the condition of the magnet. For instance, in case of reuse (Fig. 5.7, Case 1) the expected lifetime and quality of the remanufactured electric motor has to be considered as it can be shorter than the first life cycle. Further to this, the recycling of the magnetic material (Fig. 5.7, Case 2a), which is going to be used in a new magnet, involves the removal of the magnet from the engine, pulverization, and relative mix, so as to be reformed into a new magnet. Depending on the quality of the new magnet, a value correction might be needed. It is also noted that different parts of permanent magnets (Fig. 5.7, Case 2b) can be separated and used in new applications. The same is applied to other components (Fig. 5.7, Case 2).

5.7 Comparative life cycle assessment of a battery electric vehicles and an internal combustion engine vehicle—the case study of European Union

Life cycle assessment is employed in this case study, in order to compare the environmental performance of different vehicle technologies. The objective of this case study is to evaluate the environmental behavior of BEVs and HEVs compared to ICEVs within the European region.

5.7.1 Goal and scope definition

The goal of the study is to compare the environmental impacts of a BEV and an ICE vehicle. The scope of this study, with respect to the fuel supply chain, the energy mix as well as the choice of vehicle technologies, is within the EU. The functional unit used in this study is the function of *1 km of driving distance* by the car. The system boundaries consist of the entire LC of the vehicle, including production, use, and EoL. The use stage takes into account the whole WTW impact, which covers the LC steps from energy resource extraction to the energy conversion in the vehicle (i.e., driving). Finally, the EoL is evaluated basied on the current state-of-the-art regarding disposal processes within the European automotive sector.

The small passenger car segment is chosen for the comparative assessment; with gasoline and diesel powered versions of the Volkswagen Golf representing the average conventional vehicle, and similar sized vehicles in the same category (e.g., Nissan Leaf, Toyota Prius Plug-in) are also considered. In regards to BEVs, a vehicle of lithium battery technology is taken into consideration. The vehicles are assumed to have an average life span of 14 years and an annual mileage of 14,865 km. The ReCiPe methodology is used to perform the impact assessment (Goedkoop and Huijbregts, 2012).

In regards to the impact assessment, the selection of the characterization methods was made considering the following impact categories:
- GWP
- Photochemical oxidant formation (POF)
- Particulate matter formation (PMF)
- Human toxicity potential (HT)

5.7.2 Life cycle inventory

A short description of the main parts of the LCI is summarized in this section. The inventory involves the collection and processing of all the necessary data required to assess the technologies under study. These constitute exchanges with the ecosphere that are triggered during the vehicle's propulsion, i.e., energy and raw materials, atmospheric emissions, waterborne emissions, solid wastes, and other releases attributed to car movement, are quantified and allocated to the defined functional unit.

The inventory is mainly based on secondary data, which are retrieved from Ecoivent database (Ecoivent, 2009). The production stage covers the entire construction process, from raw materials' extraction to the manufacturing of car components. The LCI data of the Volkswagen Golf

A4 vehicle (Schweimer and Levin 2000) were retrieved, in order to model the manufacturing stage of all the ICE vehicles with respect to their specific weights. The LCI takes into consideration all the materials of the converter and all the manufacturing processes (AEGPL, 2004). LCI data of traction batteries were collected (Matheys et al., 2007), whereas the ratio between the lifetime driven distance (208,110 km) and the cycle life of the lithium-ion battery (100,000 miles or 160,934 km) (teslamotors.com) has been used to calculate the number of batteries needed for the BEV.

The use stage of the vehicles is subdivided to *Well-to-Tank* (WTT) and *Tank-to-Wheel* (TTW). The WTT part covers the production and the distribution of the fuel, while the TTW phase covers the use of this fuel by the vehicle. In order to assess the environmental of EVs in Europe, the European electricity supply mix has been used. The LCI of the electricity supply mix includes the shares of electricity production per type of technology. With regard to diesel and gasoline, LCI takes into account all the processes in the refinery. TTW considers the tailpipe emissions and the fuel (or energy) consumption. The average CO_2 emissions (g/km) as well as the HC, SO_2, NOx, CO, PM, CH_4, and N_2O emissions (g/km) for each vehicle under study are taken into account. The fuel consumption and the emissions are modeled according to the New European Driving Cycle (NEDC) for all vehicles on the European market (www.ecoscore.be). With regard to the EoL treatment, an energy consumption of 66 kWh/t (Hischier, 2007) is considered for the shredding and the further separation processes for the body shell. Different recycling processes (hydrometallurgical, etc.) have also been considered according to the battery technology.

5.7.3 Results of comparative life cycle assessment

Fig. 5.8, which illustrates the GWP of the vehicles under study over their complete life cycle, illustrates that the BEV charged with the European electricity mix, has the lowest emissions, followed by the PHEV and HEV powertrain. Fossil fuel vehicles seem to impose the bigger environmental burdens, in terms of CO_2 emissions. On the other hand, CO_2 emissions from the manufacturing of BEV are higher than the diesel fuel vehicle, due mainly to the battery and associated electrical components. Nonetheless, a big share of the impact of the lithium battery is balanced by the benefit of the recycling.

Fig. 5.9 presents the POF potential of the vehicle technologies under study. POF expresses the ability of NOx and nonmethane volatile organic compounds (NMVOCs) to form ozone on the ground level and it is

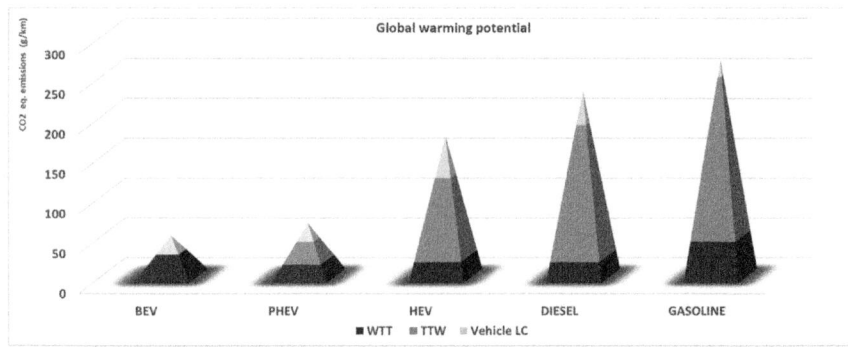

Figure 5.8 Global warming potential of different vehicle technologies.

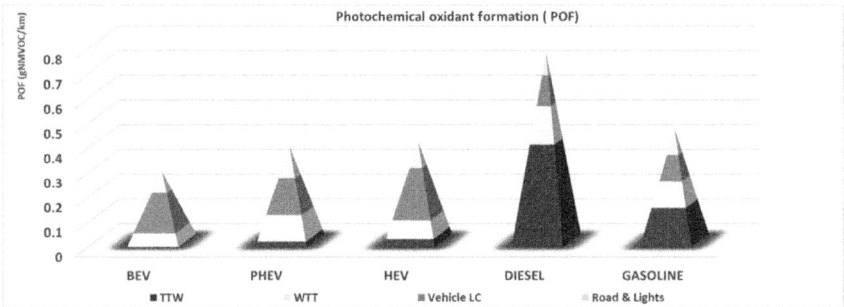

Figure 5.9 Photochemical oxidant formation potential for the vehicle technologies under study.

expressed as "kg NMVOC equivalent." It is evident that the BEV has the lowest overall score, followed by PHEV and HEV. The conventional vehicles have higher overall scores compared to EVs.

The impact category of PMF is indicative of pollution in European urban areas, such as cities. PMs (or fine dust particles) are emitted directly from the vehicles, as primary particles and also secondary particles that are created when SO_2, NOx, and NH_3 interact with the atmosphere. Fig. 5.10 illustrates the scores of the vehicles under study for PMF in terms of PM10 equivalent. The unit PM10 equivalent includes both primary and secondary PM emissions. The BEV has the lowest score among the compared vehicle technologies, as it has no tailpipe emissions. PM emissions are also produced by abrasion of tires, road, and brakes.

HT potential is a specific midpoint impact category that contributes to potential harm on human health. It takes into consideration both the inherent toxicity and general source-to-dose relationship of the polluting

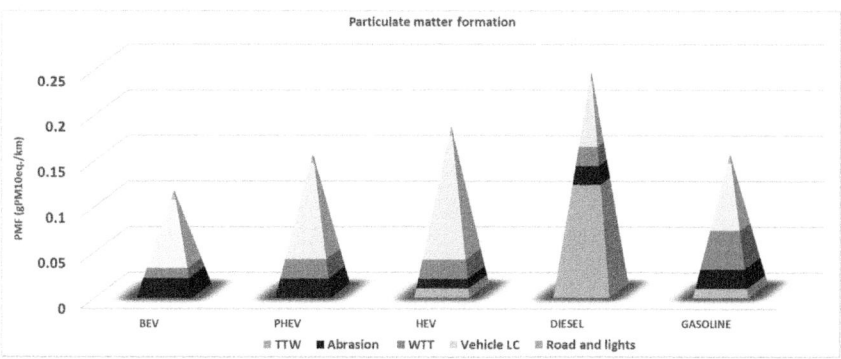

Figure 5.10 Particulate matter formation for the vehicle technologies under study.

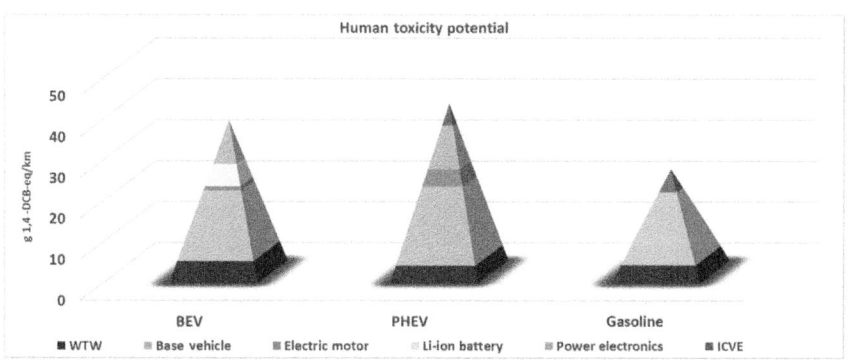

Figure 5.11 Human toxicity potential for the vehicle technologies under study.

substances. The toxicity potential can be evaluated in terms of carcinogenic and noncarcinogenic compounds (McKone and Hertwith, 2001). Fig. 5.11 summarizes the results for HT potential of three vehicle technologies. It is expressed in units of 1,4-dichlorobenzene (DCB) equivalents, a well-known pesticide. In all the vehicles, the largest fraction of toxic emissions originates from the mining of materials that are used in the base vehicle manufacturing (body shell and other common parts).

In the case of BEVs, the specific components, such as the Li-ion battery, electric motor, and power electronics, are responsible for a significant amount of the overall impact. Toxic substances are mostly discharged from the mining processes of raw materials, for vehicle manufacturing, and the energy carrier for electricity. The WTW stage of the BEV has higher emissions attributed to the mining of nuclear, coal, and other fossil fuels in the fuel supply stages of electricity production. The energy-intensive materials processing and tailing of mining wastes in nuclear and coal extraction contributes an important share to the human toxicity impact (Nordelöf et al. 2014). Intensive use of precious materials, such as copper and nickel in BEV applications, leads to the excessive disposal of mine tailings that contain sulfur and heavy metals. Improved waste management in the mining sites (e.g., copper mining sites in Chile, China, etc.), could affect these results and reduce the human toxicity score of the BEVs. Also, the integration of more renewable energy might lead to the reduction of toxic emissions in the WTW stage of BEVs. However, all these aspects regarding the minimization of HT potential of BEVs need further research.

5.8 Concluding remarks

This chapter has identified the importance of LCA methodology—following an integrated approach—in assessing different powertrains, aiming to abate the adverse effects of climate change in urban areas such as cities. The energy transition to a zero-carbon emission transport sector is crucial, so as to create sustainable and "livable" cities. This chapter has provided recommendations and guidelines with regard to the conducting of LCA for vehicles of different powertrains within a systems perspective. It has been indicated that data gathering and the interaction between transport and energy systems are of great importance and should be taken into consideration in an LCA. LCA studies regarding the impacts of EVs should continue to be updated and developed, so as to depict the different EV models that are increasingly available, as well as to throw light on the needs of emerging data on real-world use and EoL treatment of traction batteries.

The case study, revealed that conventional vehicles using fossil fuels have the largest impact on climate change. Hybridization has a positive effect on climate change. BEVs have the lowest impact on climate change and therefore offer opportunities to reduce both GHG emissions and air pollution. The energy source used to generate the electricity is also of crucial importance. On the other hand, areas where EVs could have potential negative impacts are also identified. For instance, the use stage of electric cars is not zero-impact; indeed, despite BEVs presenting no local emissions during operation, the production of electricity for battery charging is strongly energy intensive and it involves air emissions, thus causing a not negligible environmental burden. Finally, uncertainties and the need for further research in the stage of EoL treatment are also presented. Box 5.4 summarizes key impact questions that can be used by all stakeholders, when attempting to quantify the environmental impacts of different powertrains.

BOX 5.4 Impact questions for the performance of LCA studies of EVs

Key points in regards to the conduction of an LCA of EVs

- Are vehicles with lower tailpipe emissions cleaner?
- Does it make sense to look only to tailpipe emissions?
- Is it enough to combine fuel production and tailpipe emissions?
- Should their appropriate EoL treatment processes should also be taken into account in LCA studies?
- Which environmental impacts arise from the in-use stage of the BEV life cycle?
- Does the study include new data collected from the manufacturer or through research in the field (primary data)? Or, does the study rely on previous publications?
- What key assumptions have been made for the life cycle model?
- Is the vehicle fuel consumption (L/100 km or kWh/100 km) based on simulation, a laboratory test (e.g., WLTP), or "real world" results? What duty cycle has been considered?
- What generic life cycle inventory (LCI) data was used for materials, manufacturing processes, and other life cycle stages?
- What environmental impact factors have been considered?
- Is the study subject based on the current model year, historic model, or hypothetical future product?
- What has been assumed about the vehicle lifetime (years)? And what scenario has been presented about the vehicle's future EoL?
- Are the environmental impact factors for in-use fuel and energy consumption based on current energy mix, historic energy mix, or projected future energy mix? Has allowance been made for temporal effects?

References

AEGPL-Europe, 2004. Automotive LPG-Autogas: A Competitive Alternative Fuel for Improving Air Quality. AEGPL-Europe, Brussels, Belgium.

ArGV3, 2011. Wegleitung zur Verordnung 3 zum Arbeitsgesetz. Swiss State Secretariat for Economic Affair.

Bartolozzi, I., Rizzi, F., Frey, M., 2013. Comparison between hydrogen and electric vehicles by life cycle assessment: a case study in Tuscany, Italy. Appl. Energy 101, 103–111.

Bauer, C., Hofer, J., Althaus, H.J., Del Duce, A., Simons, A., 2015. The environmental performance of current and future passenger vehicles: life cycle assessment based on a novel scenario analysis framework. Appl. Energy 157, 871–883.

Bicer, Y., Dincer, I., 2018. Life cycle environmental impact assessments and comparisons of alternative fuels for clean vehicles. Resour. Conserv. Recycl. 132, 141–157.

Bloomberg New Energy Finance, 2018. New Energy Outlook 2018.

Blunden, J., Arndt, D.S., Hartfield, G., 2018. State of the climate in 2017. Bulletin of the American Meteorological Society 99 (8), p. Special Supplemen.

BP, 2018. BP Energy Outlook – 2018 Edition. London, Great Britain. Available from: <http://webcast.bp.com/economics/energyoutlook/07/registration/?utm_source = WebGlobalTeaser1>.

Buchert, M., Sutter, J., 2015. Ökobilanzen zum Recyclingverfahren EcoBatRec für Lithium-Ionen-Batterien. Berlin, Darmstadt.

Bureau of Transportation Statistics U.S. Energy consumption by the transportation sector, 2018. <https://www.bts.gov/content/us-energy-consumption-transportation-sector>.

Casals, L.C., Martinez-Laserna, E., García, B.A., Nieto, N., 2016. Sustainability analysis of the electric vehicle use in Europe for CO2 emissions reduction. J. Clean. Product. 127, 425–437.

Cerdas, F., Egede, P., Herrmann, C. 2018. LCA of electromobility. In: Hauschild, M.Z. Rosenbaum, R.K., Olsen, S.I. (Eds.), Life Cycle Assessment, Springer International Publishing AG, pp. 669–694, 10.1111/jiec.12157

Connected Energy, 2017. Global first as highway motorists benefit from rapid charging capability using 2nd life Renault batteries. <https://www.c-e-int.com/resources/news-events/renault-global-first>.

Cox, B., Mutel, C.L., Bauer, C., Mendoza Beltran, A., van Vuuren, D.P., 2018. Uncertain environmental footprint of current and future battery electric vehicles. Environ. Sci. Technol. 52 (8), 4989–4995.

Del Duce, A., Gauch, M., Althaus, H.J., 2016. Electric passenger car transport and passenger car life cycle inventories in ecoinvent version 3. Int. J. Life Cycle Assess. 21 (9), 1314–1326.

Diekmann, J., et al., 2017. Ecological recycling of lithium-ion batteries from electric vehicles with focus on mechanical processes. J. Electrochem. Soc. 164, A6184–A6191.

Dotzauer, E., 2010. Greenhouse gas emissions from power generation and consumption in a Nordic perspective. Energy Policy 38, 701–704.

Dunn, J., et al., 2012. Impact of recycling on cradle-to-gate energy consumption and greenhouse gas emissions of automotive lithium-ion batteries. Environ. Sci. Technol. 46, 12704–12710.

Ecoscore. Available online: <http://www.ecoscore.be>.

EEA (European Environment Agency-EEA, 2017. Greenhouse Gas Emissions from Transportation <www.eea.europa.eu/data-and-maps/indicators/transport-emissions-of-greenhouse-gases/transport-emissions-of-greenhouse-gases-10>.

Ellingsen, L.A.-W., Majeau-Bettez, G., Singh, B., 2014. Lifecycle assessment of a lithium-ion battery vehicle pack. J. Indus. Ecol. 18, 113–124.

Ellingsen, L.A.W., Hung, C.R., Strømman, A.H., 2017. Identifying key assumptions and differences in life cycle assessment studies of lithium-ion traction batteries with focus on greenhouse gas emissions. Transp. Res. Part D: Transp. Environ 55, 82−90.

Environmental Energy Agency−EEA, 2018. Trends and projections in Europe 2018, Tracking progress toward Europe's climate and energy targets, Report No. 16/2018.

European Commission, 2017. White Paper on the Future of Europe: Reflections and Scenarios for the EU27 by 2025. European Commission: Brussels, Belgium.

European Commission, 2019a. 2030 Climate & energy framework. Available online: <https://ec.europa.eu/clima/policies/strategies/2030_en > (accessed 19.10.2019.).

European Commission, 2019b. 2050 Low-carbon economy. Available online: <https://ec.europa.eu/clima/policies/strategies/2050_en > (accessed October 19.).

Gaustad, G., 2018. Life-cycles of lithium ion batteries: understanding impacts from extraction to end-of-life <https://www.iea.org/media/workshops/2018/Session4GaustadRIT.pdf>.

Gradin, K., et al., 2018. Scrutinizing the electric vehicle material backpack. J. Clean. Product. 172, 1699−1710.

Hawkins, T.R., Singh, B., Majeau-Bettez, G., Strømman, A.H., 2012a. Comparative environmental life cycle assessment of conventional and electric vehicles. J. Ind. Ecol. 17 (1), 53−64 (2012).

Hawkins, T.R., Gausen, O.M., Stromman, A.H., 2012b. Environmental impacts of hybrid and electric vehicles—a review. Int. J. Life Cycle Assess. 17 (8), 997−1014.

Hawkins, T.R., Singh, B., Majeau-Bettez, G., Strømman, A.H., 2013. Corrigendum to: Hawkins, T.R., Singh, B., Majeau-Bettez, G., Strømman, A.H., 2012. Comparative environmental life cycle assessment of conventional and electric vehicles. J. Ind. Ecol. 17 (1), 158−160.

Goedkoop, M., Huijbregts, M., 2012. ReCiPe 2008 − A Life Cycle Impact Assessment Method Which Comprises Harmonised Category Indicators at the Midpoint and Endpoint Level, first edition (revised). Report 1: Characterization, PRé Scientific Publications, pp. 1−137.

Held, M., Graf, R., Wehner, D., Eckert, S., Faltenbacher, M., Weidner, S., et al., (2016). Abschlussbericht: Bewertung der Praxistauglichkeit und Umweltwirkungen von Elektrofahrzeugen. Berlin, Germany. <https://doi.org/10.1007/s13398-014-0173-7.2 >.

Helmers, E., Dietz, J., Hartard, S., 2017. Electric car life cycle assessment based on real-world mileage and the electric conversion scenario. Int. J. Life Cycle Assess. 22, 15−30.

Hischier, R., 2007. Ecoinvent Report No 18, Part V: Disposal of Electronic and Electric Equipment. Swiss Centre for Life Cycle Inventories, St-Gallen, Switzerland.

< https://phys.org/news/2019-01-science-polar-vortex-outbreaks.html>.

< https://www.pmel.noaa.gov/co2/story/Ocean + Acidification>.

International Energy Agency − IEA, 2017a. CO_2 Emissions From Fuel Combustion. Available from: <https://www.iea.org/publications/freepublications/publication/CO2EmissionsfromFuelCombustionHighlights2017.pdf>.

International Energy Agency − IEA, 2017b. Task 31: Fuels and Energy Carriers for Transport. Hybrid and Electric Vehicle Technology Collaboration Programme.

International Energy Agency − IEA, 2018. Energy balances of non-OECD countries.

IPCC, 2018. Special Report on Global Warming of 1.5°C, IPCC, Geneva, <www.ipcc.ch/sr15>.

ISO 14040, 1997. Environmental Management—Life Cycle Assessment—Principles and Framework. International Organization for Standardization, Geneva.

ISO ISO 14044, 2006. Environmental management Life cycle assessment Requirement and guidelines. International Organization for Standardization, Geneva.

Jochem, P., Babrowski, S., Fichtner, W., 2015. Assessing CO_2 emissions of electric vehicles in Germany in 2030. Trans. Res. Part A 78, 68−83.

Karaaslan, E., Zhao, Y., Tatari, O., 2018. Comparative life cycle assessment of sport utility vehicles with different fuel options. Int. J. Life Cycle Assess. 23 (2), 333−347.

Koroneos, C.J., Achillas Ch, Moussiopoulos, N., NanakiL, E.A., 2013. Life cycle thinking in the use of natural resources. Open Environ. Sci. 7, 1−6.

Kuchler, M., Bridge, G., 2018. Down the black hole: sustaining national socio-technical imaginaries of coal in Poland. Energy Res Soc Sci 41 (2018), 136−147.

Letnik, T., Marksel, M., Luppino, G., Bardi, A., Božičnik, S., 2018. Review of policies and measures for sustainable and energy efficient urban transport. Energy 163, 245−257.

Levitus, S., Antonov, J., Boyer, T., Baranova, O., Garcia, H., Locarnini, R., et al., 2017. NCEI ocean heat content, temperature anomalies, salinity anomalies, thermosteric sea level anomalies, halosteric sea level anomalies, and total steric sea level anomalies from 1955 to present calculated from in situ oceanographic subsurface profile data (NCEI Accession 0164586). Version 4.4. NOAA National Centers for Environmental Information. Dataset . Available from: https://doi.org/10.7289/V53F4MVP.

Lombardi, L., Tribioli, L., Cozzolino, R., Bella, G., 2017. Comparative environmental assessment of conventional, electric, hybrid, and fuel cell powertrains based on LCA. Int. J. Life Cycle Assess. 22 (12), 1989−2006.

Mai, Trieu, Jadun, Paige, Logan, Jeffrey, McMillan, Colin, Muratori, Matteo, Steinberg, Daniel, et al., 2018. Electrification Futures Study: Scenarios of Electric Technology Adoption and Power Consumption for the United States. National Renewable Energy Laboratory, Golden, CONREL/TP-6A20-71500. Available from: https://www.nrel.gov/docs/fy18osti/71500.pdf>.

Majeau-Bettez, G., et al., 2011. Life cycle environmental assessment of lithium-ion and nickel metal hydride batteries for plug-in hybrid and battery electric vehicles. Environ. Sci. Technol. 45, 4548−4554.

Matheys, J., van Autenboer, W., Timmermans, J.M., van Mierlo, J., 2007. Influence of functional unit on the life cycle assessment of traction batteries. Int. J. Life Cycle Assess. 12, 191−196.

Mathieux, F., et al., 2017. Critical Raw Materials and the Circular Economy. European Commission Joint Research Centre, Ispra, Italy.

McKone, T., Hertwich, E.G., 2001. The human toxicity potential and a strategy for evaluating model performance in life cycle assessment. Int. J. LCA 6 (2), 106−109.

Nanaki, E., Koroneos, C., 2013. Comparative economic and environmental analysis of conventional, hybrid and electric vehicles the case study of Greece. J. Clean. Product. 53, 261−266.

Nanaki, E.A., Koroneos, C., 2016. Climate change mitigation and deployment of electric vehicles in urban areas, Renewable Energy, Vol. 99. Elsevier, pp. 1153−1160.

Nanaki, E.A., Xydis, G.A., Koroneos, C.J., 2015. Electric vehicle deployment in urban areas. J. Indoor Built Environ. 25 (7). Available from: https://doi.org/10.1177/1420326X15623078.

National Aeronautics and Space Administration-NASA, 2017. <https://www.giss.nasa.gov/research/news/20170118/>.

National Aeronautics and Space Administration-NASA, 2018. <https://www.jpl.nasa.gov/news/news.php?feature = 7159>.

National Aeronautics and Space Administration-NASA, 2019. <https://data.giss.nasa.gov/gistemp/>.

National Oceanic and Atmospheric Administration, 2018. Trends in atmospheric carbon dioxide. [Online] Available at: <https://www.esrl.noaa.gov/gmd/ccgg/trends/data.html>.

National Snow and Ice Data Center World Glacier Monitoring Service, 2019a. <http://nsidc.org/sotc/glacier_balance.html>.

National Snow and Ice Data Center World Glacier Monitoring Service, 2019b. <http://nsidc.org/sotc/glacier_balance.htmlhttps://nsidc.org/cryosphere/sotc/sea_ice.html >.

Nerem, R.S., Beckley, B.D., Fasullo, J.T., Hamlington, B.D., Masters, D., Mitchum, G.T., 2018. Climate-change—driven accelerated sea-level rise detected in the altimeter era. PNAS, DOI: 10.1073/pnas.1717312115

Neubauer, J., et al., 2012. A Techno-economic Analysis of PEV Battery Second Use: Repurposed-Battery Selling Price and Commercial and Industrial End-user Value. SAE International, Warrendale, PA.

Nissan News, 2018. <https://global.nissannews.com/en/releases/release-487297034c 80023008bd9722aa069598-180326-01-e>.

Nordelöf, A., et al., 2014. Environmental impacts of hybrid, plug-in hybrid, and battery electric vehicles — what can we learn from life cycle assessment? Int. J. Life Cycle Assess. 19, 1866—1890.

Notter, D.A., Gauch, M., Widmer, R., et al., 2010. Contribution of Li-ion batteries to the environmental impact of electric vehicles. Environ. Sci. Technol. 44, 6550—6556.

OEKO, 2016. Electric mobility in Europe — Future impact on the emissions and the energy systems. Available at: <https://www.oeko.de/fileadmin/oekodoc/Assessing-the-status-of-electrification-of-the-road-transport-passenger-vehicles.pdf>.

Patterson, J., Alexander, M., Gurr, A., Greenwood, D. 2011. Preparing for a life cycle CO2 measure, doi: RD.11/124801.5

Richa, K., et al., 2017. Eco-efficiency analysis of a lithium-ion battery waste hierarchy inspired by circular economy. J. Indus. Ecol. 21, 715—730.

Rim, K., et al., 2013. Toxicological evaluations of rare earths and their health impacts to workers: a literature review. Saf. Health Work 4, 12—26.

Samaras, C., Meisterling, K., 2008. Life cycle assessment of greenhouse gas emissions from plug-in hybrid vehicles: implications for policy. Environ. Sci. Technol. 42 (9), 3170—3176.

Schippl, J., Gudmundsson, H., Sørensen, C.H., Anderton, K., Brand, R., Leiren, M.D., et al., 2016. Different pathways for achieving cleaner urban areas: a roadmap toward the white paper goal for urban transport. Transp. Res Procedia 14, 2604—2613.

Schweimer, G.W., Levin, M., 2000. Life Cycle Inventory for the Golf A4. Volkswagen AG, Wolfsburg, Germany.

Society of Environmental Toxicology and Chemistry (SETAC) and SETAC Foundation for Environmental Education Inc., 1991. A Technical Framework for Life — cycle Assessment, Washington, DC: Society of Environmental Toxicology and Chemistry and SETAC Foundation for Environmental Education Inc., Workshop held in Smugglers Notch, Vermont, August 18 — 83, 1990.

Swiss Centre for Life Cycle Inventories, 2014. Ecoinvent: The Life Cycle Inventory Data, Version 3.0. Swiss Centre for Life Cycle Inventories, Duebendorf.

Tagliaferri, C., Evangelisti, S., Acconcia, F., Domenech, T., Ekins, P., Barletta, D., et al., 2016. Life cycle assessment of future electric and hybrid vehicles: a cradle-to-grave systems engineering approach. Chem. Eng. Res. Des. 112, 298—309.

Tesla, <www.tesla.com>.

Tesla Motors. Available online: <http://www.teslamotors.com/blog2/?p = 39>.

The Copenhagen Diagnosis, 2011. Updating the World on the Latest Climate Science, Paperback ISBN: 9780123869999, Elsevier

Tobin, P., Schmidt, N.M., Tosun, J., Burns, C., 2018. Mapping states' Paris climate pledges: analysing targets and groups at COP 21. Glob. Environ. Change 48, 11—21.

United Nations Environment Programme — UNEP, 2011. Toward a Life Cycle Sustainability Assessment: Making Informed Choices on Products.

United States Environmental Protection Agency, US EPA, 2013. Application of Life-Cycle Assessment to Nanoscale Technology: Lithium-Ion Batteries for Electric Vehicles. Washington, DC.

USGCRP, 2017. Climate Science Special Report: Fourth National Climate Assessment, Volume I, Wuebbles, D.J., Fahey, D.W., Hibbard, K.A., Dokken, D.J., Stewart, B. C., Maycock, T.K. (Eds.). U.S. Global Change Research Program, Washington, DC, 470 pp.

Van Mierlo, J., Messagie, M., Rangaraju, S., 2017. Comparative environmental assessment of alternative fueled vehicles using a life cycle assessment. Transp. Res. Procedia 25, 3435–3445.

Wang, H, Zhang, X, Ouyang, M, 2015. Energy consumption of electric vehicles based on real-world driving patterns: a case study of Beijing. Appl. Energy 157, 710–719.

World Health Organization, 2016. Ambient Air Pollution: A Global Assessment of Exposure and Burden of Disease. World Health Organization, Geneva, Switzerland, ISBN 978-92-4-151135-3.

Wu, X., Freese, D., Cabrera, A., Kitch, W.A., 2015. Electric vehicles' energy consumption measurement and estimation. Transp. Res. Part D: Transp. Environ 34, 52–67.

Further reading

Ecoinvent, Ecoinvent Database. St-Gallen, 2009

European Environment Agency (EEA), EEA greenhouse gas –data viewer, September 12, 2019.

IPCC, 2014a. Fifth Assessment Report, Summary for Policymakers.

IPCC, 2014b. Climate Change 2014: Mitigation of Climate Change. IPCC, Paris, France, 2014; ISBN 9781107654815.

CHAPTER 6

Electric vehicle capitals — case studies

6.1 Introduction

The transportation sector is one of the primary contributors to global climate change and CO_2 emissions (International Energy Agency-IEA, 2018a,b). The reduction of carbon emissions is the driving force for the displacement of fossil fueled vehicles by alternative fuels. As cities are evolving, the need for an energy transition to a zero-carbon transportation system is a necessity in order to reduce air and noise pollution, preserving in this way both the health of their citizens as well as the natural environment. In this direction, cities, businesses, and governments around the world have recognized electric vehicles (EVs)—including full battery electric vehicles (BEVs) and plug-in-hybrid electric vehicles (PHEVs)—as an essential part of a smarter and more sustainable future. The latter is mainly attributed to their ability to deliver technical, environmental, societal, and health benefits, such as energy efficient improvement potential, energy security, reduction of harmful pollutants from road transport vehicles, decrease of greenhouse gas emissions (GHG) associated with conventional internal combustion engine vehicles (ICEVs), and noise reduction, as well as to industrial development.

In this context, various measures, regulations, incentive programs, as well as projects aiming to accelerate the development and adoption of EVs, seem to have paid off, given that in 2018 global EV sales reached 2 million, after having reached the 1 million mark in 2017 (International Energy Agency-IEA, 2019). This stands for a year-on-year growth in EV sales of 68% between 2017 and 2018, a strong rate comparable to 2015 (68%), after 2 years of weaker growth. However, a number of markets have considerably higher market penetration rates, reflecting the successful implementation of carefully tailored policies and measures at multiple levels toward the energy transition to zero-carbon cities.

Various studies in the past years have identified various aspects of EV deployment in urban areas, pointing out their significant roles. These

Electric Vehicles for Smart Cities
DOI: https://doi.org/10.1016/B978-0-12-815801-2.00003-4

include inter alia the studies of Perujo et al. (2011) and Trip and Konings (2014), who investigated the role of EVs within the urban context; as well as the studies of Newman et al. (2014), who provided a critical discussion on urbanism and EVs. The potential impacts of EVs on air quality in the Spanish cities Barcelona and Madrid as well as in the Greek city of Athens have also been investigated (Soret et al., 2014; Nanaki and Koroneos, 2016). Further to these, many studies focus on the public policies and knowledge which can trigger the development of electric mobility (e.g., Krause et al., 2013; Comodi et al., 2016). An assessment of leading EVs promotion activities (set on the state and city level) in US cities has also been carried out, providing useful input (Lutsey et al., 2015). However, a comparative casebook gathering useful data from different regions and cities around the world has not yet been published.

This chapter aims to provide a useful insight of the EV market, which embraces and embodies the concepts of electrification and sustainability. Therefore it focuses on the EV market of selected countries and cities around the world. The presented case studies are aiming to throw light on the transformation path each city has followed, so as to create opportunities for the acceleration of electric mobility. Furthermore, this chapter aims to illustrate the underlying local policies and the unique infrastructure and vehicle fleet solutions that have enabled the successful deployment of electromobility. Finally, the findings of this casebook chapter indicate that effective policies are important to decrease the upfront investment cost gap, to promote charging infrastructure, and to ensure a smooth integration of EV charging demands into power systems.

6.2 Global electric vehicle sales: a growing market

During the past year, the global EV market has significantly increased; in 2018 the global electric car fleet exceeded 5.1 million, up 2 million since 2017. China remains the world's largest electric car market (with nearly 1.1 million EVs sold in 2018, representing 55% of the global market), followed by Europe (with 385,000 units) and the United States (361,000 units). This trend is also highlighted in the first half (H1) of 2019 (Fig. 6.1), as China's EV industry recorded an increase of 66% in the sales of EVs year-on-year, and stood for 57% of global plug-in sales. In June, the EV share in all light vehicles sold was as high as 8.1%. In Europe, the increase in electric car sales in 2018 was 31% higher compared to 2017 (a growth rate lower than 2017 relative to 2016 (41%) and below the

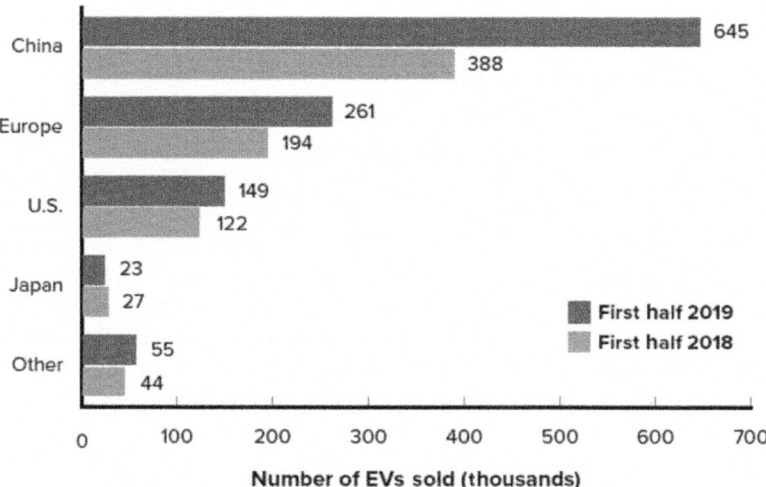

Figure 6.1 Electric vehicle sales during the first half of 2019 and 2018 (www.ev-volumes.com).

global average). Nonetheless, Europe hosts the countries with the largest penetration of electric car sales. For instance, Norway stands out as the global leader in terms of electric car market share reaching 50% in 2018, followed by Iceland (17.2%) and Sweden (7.9%). In terms of sales volumes, Norway is followed by Germany, the United Kingdom, and France (International Energy Agency-IEA, 2019).

In 2018 the sales of EVs in the United States increased by 82%, compared to 24% in 2017. This increase can be attributed to the release of the Tesla Model 3, with sales covering the additional 134,000 BEVs sold in 2018 compared to 2017 (Marklines, 2019). Japan is the only major electric car market where sales fell between 2017 and 2018 (−8%). These losses are related to the decline of Toyota Prius Plug-in sales and the transition of the Nissan Leaf to the 60 kWh version. Other markets where electric car sales dropped, such as India, South Africa, and Mexico, have much smaller electric car volumes.

With regard to the types of EVs sold, it is noted that globally the share of BEVs has increased from 50% in 2012 to 68% in 2018. The share of PHEVs in sales dropped in the United States from 47% in 2017 to 34% in 2018, due to strong BEV sales (EV volumes, 2019). As far as Europe is concerned, PHEV sales dominated in Finland (86%), Sweden (75%), and the United Kingdom (69%). Box 6.1 illustrates BEV and PHEV model availability and their sales during the first half of 2019.

BOX 6.1 Worldwide model availability and top 10 sales during the first half (H1) of 2019.

During the first half (H1) of 2019, global plug-in vehicles deliveries reached 1,134,000 units (46% higher compared to deliveries of the first half of 2018); 74% of sales were BEV and 26% were PHEV, a massive shift of 11% toward BEVs, compared to the first half of 2018. This was attributed to the Tesla Model-3, revised taxation/subsidy schemes, and the introduction in Europe of the more stringent WLTP (Worldwide Harmonized Light Vehicle Test Procedure) for CO_2 emissions, all leading to higher demand for pure EVs.

With regard to the models sold, it is noted that for the first half of 2019 Tesla was the world's best-selling plug-in vehicle. BAIC revived the EU-Series and ranked second. The BYD Yuan EV, a small SUV with 400 km e-range, sold 29,000 units in China since March 2019. The Mitsubishi Outlander PHEV, was an attractive substitute for all discontinued PHEVs, as with a battery of 12 kWh it stayed under the 50 g CO_2 limit even in the stricter WLTP. The BYD e5 and Geely Emgrand BEVs gained further volume.

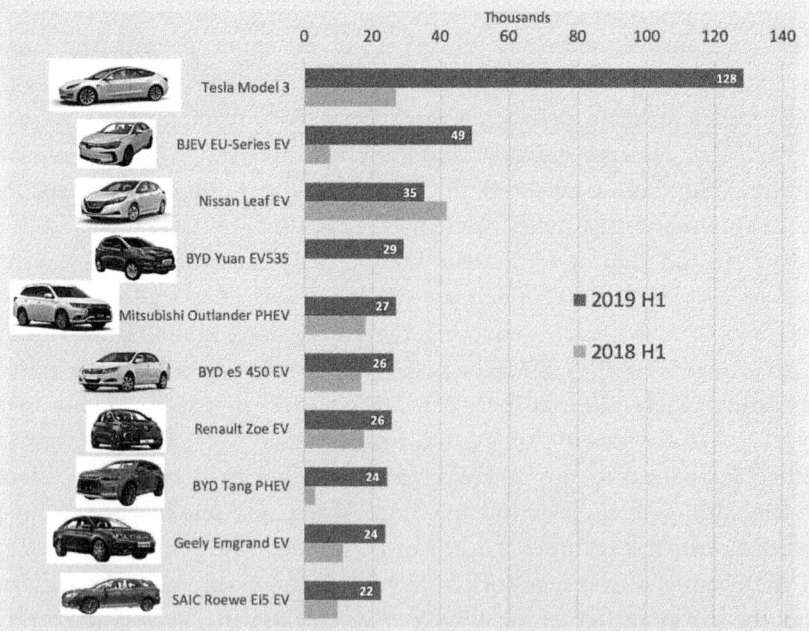

It is highlighted that only two out the top 10 sold EVs are PHEVs and they are both SUVs. This is attributed to the fact that PHEVs are more widely available in large size vehicles, with 60% of all models in the large car and SUV

(Continued)

BOX 6.1 (Continued)

segments, and with no PHEVs available in the small car segment. This trend is observed in all markets. The main reasons for the prevalence of PHEV in large cars are the presence of two powertrains is better suited to larger vehicles, and increased requirements for long-range capability for such vehicles. All major markets have a roughly similar number of PHEV models available, with Europe having most models and the United States having the least.

With regard to the sales of light commercial vehicles (LCVs), it is noted that in 2018 about 80,000 electric LCVs (mostly BEVs) were sold, almost entirely in China (54,000) and Europe (25,000). Overall global growth of electric LCV sales dropped in 2018 (24% from 94% in 2017).

Finally, the global stock of electric buses increased by 25% in 2018 compared to 2017, reaching about 460,000 vehicles, with China accounting for 99% of the global market; whereas BEV technology accounts for 93% of new electric bus registrations.

6.2.1 Charging infrastructure: recent developments

By the end of 2018, the number of charging points worldwide was estimated at 5.2 million, standing for a 44% increase compared to 2017. The latter is attributed to private charging points, which accounted for more than 90% of the 1.6 million installations in 2018. By the end of 2018, the number of installed publicly accessible fast chargers reached 144,000, whereas the number of slow chargers was 395,000 (International Energy Agency-IEA, 2019). It is noted that, slow chargers provide power less than or equal to 22 kilowatts (kW) and fast chargers provide power higher than 22 kW.

Charging stations can be classified into residential and nonresidential types, and can facilitate slow charging (level 1 and level 2) as well as fast charging (level 3 and DC) (Karali et al., 2017). The power output range of the charger (level), the socket and connector used for charging (type), and the communication protocol between the vehicle and the charger (mode) differentiate the chargers. The majority of EV charging involves residential charging with slow charging ports; nonetheless, several commercial charging stations with fast charging points (charging within an hour) have already been established (California Energy Commission, 2014). By the end of 2018, Tesla had established 1431 supercharger stations all over the world, of which 694 are located in North America, 442 in Europe, and 294 in the Asia—Pacific region (www.supercharge. info, 2018). Furthermore, the Canadian Automobile Association (CAA) has announced that with the cooperation of another charging infrastructure company 7906 charging stations (fast and slow charging) have been established in major cities of Canada (CAA electric vehicle charging station locator, 2018). Box 6.2 underscores the significance of mega chargers and their role in the energy transition to zero-carbon societies.

As far as the global number of publicly accessible chargers is concerned, it is noted that in 2018 it was 24% higher compared to 2017 levels, reaching 539,000. The growth rate of new installations of publicly accessible chargers is slowing in comparison to previous years (30% in 2017, 80% in 2016). In 2018 China remained the country with the largest installed publicly accessible charging infrastructure, accounting for half of the global total (International Energy Agency-IEA, 2019).

BOX 6.2 The necessity of mega chargers to future cities

During the past years, EVs have emerged as a prominent representative of zero-carbon emission vehicles and have set the future course of the auto industry. In this direction, as many manufacturers have expressed their interest in developing electric intercity buses, medium- and heavy-freight trucks (www. ttnews.com, 2018), mega chargers with the ability to charge at least 1 megawatt (MW) or above are going to be a necessity.

Tesla was the first company that used the label mega charger for the charging infrastructure employed for its semi heavy-freight truck (Tesla, 2017). Each Supercharger stall has a connector to supply electrical power at up to 72—250 kW via a direct current connection to the 400-volt car battery pack (Field, 2019). One pays for the electricity automatically with a credit card on file. Some older Tesla vehicles have 100—400 kWh, or unlimited, inclusive charging credit. At the beginning of 2012, the Tesla Supercharger network of fast charging stations was introduced; in October 2019 it consisted of 14,658 individual supercharger stalls at 1659 locations worldwide with an additional 115 locations under construction worldwide (of which 64 are in the United States) (Tesla, 2019). The Tesla Model S was the first car to be able to use the network, followed by the Tesla Model X and Tesla Model 3.

In 2018, ChargePoint, a US-based charger manufacturer and operator, presented a connector intended for both electric aircraft and heavy trucks that would use 4500 ampere interfaces with a maximum of 1000 volts, which would lead to a maximum combined power of 2 MW (ChargePoint, 2018).

The global number of publicly accessible chargers per electric car decreased from 0.14 in 2017 to 0.11 in 2018. This ratio remains higher than 1 charger per 10 electric cars, which is recommended by the European Union Alternative Fuels Infrastructure Directive (European Commission, EC, 2014). However, many leading countries in terms of electric car deployment remain below the global average of 1 charger per 10 electric cars (i.e., Norway and the United States have a ratio of 1 charger per 20 electric cars). On the other hand, the Netherlands and Denmark have a relatively high number of publicly accessible chargers per electric car (about 1 charger per 4—8 electric cars). Therefore it can be deducted that specific country features, such as population density, access to workplace charging infrastructure, and vehicle range play an important role for extensive publicly accessible charging infrastructure.

6.3 Electric vehicle adoption policies: recent developments

Sections 6.2 and 6.2.1 indicate that policies are of crucial importance to bridge both the cost gap between electric and conventional vehicles as well as to support the deployment of charging infrastructure. In this direction, many countries employ various means to promote EVs such as national targets, mandates, and regulations, financial incentives, and policies aiming to increasing the value proposition of EVs, public fleet procurement etc.

National targets enable policy makers to focus on the policy implementation of EV deployment. Mandates and regulations build on the definition of regulatory targets, so as to provide a clear signal to manufacturers and customers as they set a medium- to long-term vision for defining the evolution of vehicle characteristics. Most significant measures in this category include zero-emission vehicle (ZEV) mandates and fuel economy regulations. For instance, ZEV Alliance, including a number of US states, Canadian provinces, and European regions and countries have set a common vision to strive to make all passenger vehicle sales electric by 2050 (ZEV Alliance, 2015). In addition, a number of governments have announced bans on the sales of ICE cars or sales targets for 100% zero-emissions vehicle (Costa Rica, Denmark, Iceland, Israel, Portugal, and Spain). Norway has the most ambitious objectives that aim to have only ZEV sales in the light-duty vehicle (LDV) and public bus segments by 2025.

Financial incentives, including government subsidies as direct rebates, value-added tax (VAT), and vehicle registration tax exemptions, are the main policy mechanisms used to make EVs more appealing to both private and business customers. Their role is to provide financial support to EV users, so as to make EVs an attractive option in the automotive market.

Policies aiming to increase the value proposition of EVs: EV deployment can be supported by increasing the appeal of EVs over competing alternatives, providing advantages in terms of reduced fees, privileged access, and driving facilitations. These policies focus on the support of EV ownership and use, and consequently must be developed at a municipal level and be adapted to the unique local conditions of each urban area.

Public fleet procurement: The public authorities as well as the private sector can contribute significantly to the deployment of EVs by providing the market with demand signals, while exploiting their societal role; thus they could act as advocates of EV promotion through their staff and customers.

Based on the above, the deployment of EVs this early in such a premature EV market stage is policy driven. In this stage market sales are volatile and directly influenced by the annual developments of financial support policies applied in local markets. Policy strategies are also uncertain, as policy makers try to identify the transition to higher market maturity and consequently higher financial sustainability. Table 6.1 summarizes recent policy instruments and goals related to the deployment of EVs in urban areas by mid-2019.

BEV, battery electric vehicles; *EVs,* electric vehicles; *FCE,* Fuel Cell Electric Vehicles; *GHG,* greenhouse gas emissions; *ICE,* internal combustion engine vehicles; *NEDC,* new european driving cycle; *NEV,* new energy vehicles; *PHEV,* plug-in-hybrid electric vehicles; *ZEV,* zero-emission vehicle.

As far as public fleet procurement is concerned, it is highlighted that many cities at municipal levels have committed—via various strategies and declarations—to restrict and/or prohibit access to certain areas for ICE vehicles, aiming to abate climate change and the adverse effects on the urban environment. These include inter alia the following:

- *C40 Fossil Fuel Free Streets Declaration:* more than 20 cities around the world committed to procure more than 40,000 electric public buses by 2020 (C40, 2015). In this context, Paris, London, Los Angeles, Copenhagen, Barcelona, Mexico City, Tokyo, and Rome together with 19 other cities have committed to only purchase zero-emissions buses as from 2025, indicating that they will reach an all-electric fleet (battery electric or hydrogen fuel cell electric) fleet in the first half of the 2030s (C40, 2019a). Today these cities have combined bus fleets

Table 6.1 Update of EV deployment policies for light-duty vehicles in selected regions all over the world.

Targets	Key policy, mandates and targets	Announced (year)	References
Asia			
China	5 million EVs by 2020.	2012	Government of China (2012)
	12% NEV credit sales in passenger cars by 2020.	2015	Government of China (2015)
	Proposal for tightened fuel economy standard (4 L/100 km [NEDC] by 2025). (Current fuel economy standard until 2020).	2019	Government of China (2019)
Japan	20%–30% BEV and PHEV sales in PLDVs by 2030 (in addition to 40% HEVs and 3% FCEVs).	2014	Government of Japan (2014); Government of Japan (2018)
	Long-term goal ("by the end of 2050") of a reduction of 80% of GHG emissions per vehicle produced by Japanese automakers.	2018	Government of Japan (2018)
	Fuel economy target of 19.7% reduction in specific fuel consumption by 2020 compared to 2009 and an additional 23.8% between 2020 and 2030.	2011 & 2019	ECCJ Energy Conservation Center Japan (2011) and Government of Japan (2019a,b)
Korea	Targets of 430 000 BEVs and 67,000 FCEVs on the road by 2022.	2019	Government of Korea (2019)
	Subsides and rebates on national and local vehicle acquisition taxes, reduced highway toll fees and public parking fees.	2018	Korea Environment Corporation (2019)
Europe (selected countries)			
European Union	Emission standards for g CO_2/km of LDVs, requiring 15% reduction between 2021 and 2025 and 37.5% (30% for vans) by 2030, including incentives attached to 15% and 35% zero- and low-emissions vehicle shares.	2018	European Council (2019)
	Revision of the Clean Vehicles Directive on public procurement, including minimum requirements of 17.6% in 2025 and 38.5% in 2030.	2019	European Parliament (2019)
Denmark	1 million electrified vehicles stock in passenger light-duty vehicles by 2030.	2018	Government of Denmark (2018)

(Continued)

Table 6.1 (Continued)

Targets	Key policy, mandates and targets	Announced (year)	References
France	Multiply by five the sales of BEVs in 2022 compared to 2017.	2018	Government of France (2018)
	1 million BEVs and PHEVs in 2022.	2018	Government of France (2018)
	Ban on the sales of new cars emitting GHG in 2040.	2017	Government of France (2017)
Netherlands	100% ZEV sales by 2030.	2017	Kabinetsformatie (2017)
Norway	100% EV sales by 2025.	2016	Government of Norway (2016)
Spain	• 5 million EVs in light-duty vehicles, buses and two/three-wheelers.	2019	Government of Spain (2019)
	• 100% ZEVs sales by 2040.		
Sweden	• Reduction of CO_2 emissions from transport by 70% in 2030 compared to 2010.	2017	Government of Sweden (2017)
United Kingdom	• Net zero GHG emissions by 2045.		
	• 50%–70% EV sales by 2030.	2018	Government of the United Kingdom (2018)
	• Ban sales of new ICE cars from 2040.	2017	Government of the United Kingdom (2017)
North America			
Canada	• 10% ZEV sales from 2025.	2019	Government of Canada (2019)
	• 30% ZEV sales from 2030.		
	• 100% ZEV sales from 2040.		
United States (selected countries)	• 3.3 million EVs in eight states combined by 2025.	2014	• ZEV Program Implementation Task Force (PITF) (2014)
	• ZEVg mandate in 10 states: 22% ZEV credit sales in passenger cars and light-duty trucks by 2025.	2016	• ZEV Program Implementation Task Force (2014)
	• California: 1.5 million ZEVs and 15% of effective sales by 2025, and 5 million ZEVs by 2030.	2016	• State of California (2018, 2016), CARB (2016)

Adapted from International Energy Agency-IEA, 2019. Global EV Outlook 2018, Toward cross-modal modification.

of 80,000 vehicles and will drive market growth for electric buses in the coming years (C40, 2019b).

- The *California Air Resources Board (CARB)* has adopted a statewide regulation to convert all city buses added to the fleet to ZEVs by 2029 and all buses on the road by 2040 (CARB California Air Resources Board, 2018).
- Beijing aims for more than half of its bus fleet to be electric by 2020 (over 11,000 vehicles) (Beijing City Council, 2018).

6.4 Europe

Despite the fact that EU market is still dominated by petrol and diesel vehicles, the share of EVs is growing fast. The market share of electric cars in the EU was about 2% in the third quarter of 2018, around 30% higher than in 2017 (European Automobile Manufacturers Association-ACEA, 2018). In most Member States, hybrid car sales exceed fully electric car sales.

EU clean air policy and legislation requires the significant improvement of air quality in the EU, moving the EU closer to the quality recommended by the World Health Organization. Air pollution and its impacts on human health, ecosystems, and biodiversity should be further reduced with the long-term aim of not exceeding critical loads and levels. This requires strengthening efforts to reach full compliance with EU air quality legislation and defining strategic targets and actions beyond 2020.

In this direction, the acceleration of electromobility in the EU is supported by the following legal framework:

- Renewable Energy Directive 2009/28/EC (European Parliament and of the Council, 2009a), the Fuel Quality Directive 2009/ 30/EC (European Parliament and of the Council, 2009c), the Clean Vehicle Directive 2009/33/EC (European Parliament and of the Council, 2009b), the Regulations setting CO_2 standards for passenger cars (Regulation No. 443/2009; European Parliament and of the Council, 2009e) and LCVs (Regulation No. 510/2011; European Parliament and of the European Parliament and of The Council Regulation EU, 2011) are all key EU legislation regarding the promotion of sustainable, low-carbon fuels and low CO_2 emission vehicles.
- Directive 2009/28/EC by the European Parliament and the Council dated 23/04/2009 for the promotion of energy from renewable sources and amending and subsequently repealing Directives 2001/77/EC and 2003/ 30/EC12 set a target of 10% market share of renewables in transport fuels.

- The Commission Communication on a European alternative fuels strategy (European Commission Communication, 2013).

6.4.1 The Netherlands

By the end of December 2019 the number of passenger EVs registered in the Netherlands reached 203,636, out of which 107,536 were BEVs, 215 Fuel Cell Electric Vehicles (FCEVs), and 95,885 PHEVs (Netherlands Enterprise Agency, 2020). The total increase of BEV passenger cars in December 2019 reached 23,234, whereas the total increase of PHEVs in December 2019 was 403. It is noteworthy to mention that the share of EVs in new registrations of passenger cars in 2016 was 6.7%, whereas this share increased to 54.5% in 2019. With regard to charging infrastructure Fig. 6.2 highlights the development of required infrastructure to support the use of charging stations, and shows that during the past decade, regular public as well as semipublic charging stations increased steadily. In 2011 the volume of these charging stations amounted to a total of 1826; whereas in 2019 it increased to approximately 41,000 (Netherlands Enterprise Agency, 2020). The charging stations include:

- Regular public chargers are available 24/7: an increase from 400 stations in 2010 to 21,049 as of February 2019 was noticed.
- Regular semipublic, with limited accessibility: Semipublic charging points are interoperable (accessible by their owners) and can be found at shopping malls, office buildings, parking garages, etc. This type of charging station grew from 0 in 2010 to 17,059 in 2019.
- Regular public and semipublic.
- Fast charging points (Public and semipublic): An electric vehicle supply equipment (EVSE) is a charging point that may have several connectors, in order to accommodate different connector types, but only one can be used at the same time. Due to improvements in the data on fast chargers, from July 2019 onwards the number of EVSEs are being reported instead of connectors. Based on data from Aug. 2019, the number of fast charging connectors is approx. 25% more than the number of fast charging EVSEs (for instance, fast charging stations with two EVSEs and three connectors: not more than two connectors can be simultaneously used to charge electric cars).
- Fast charging locations refer to geographical location consisting of one or more chargers with an electric power of >22 kW.
- Private charging points.

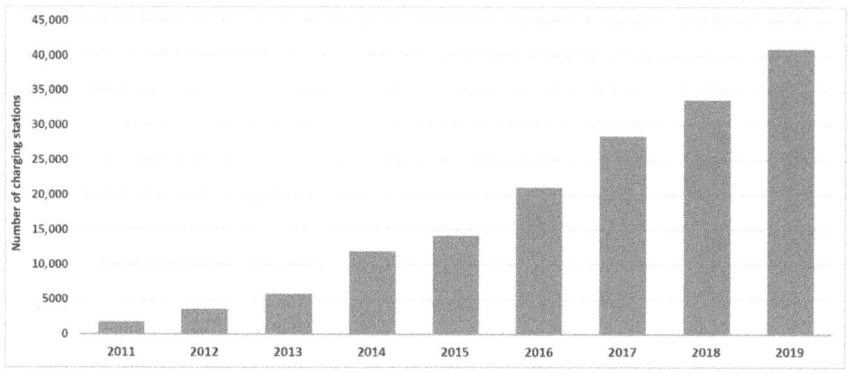

Figure 6.2 Number of charging stations in the Netherlands during the period of 2011–19 (Dutch Road Authority RDW, 2020).

Table 6.2 Dutch ambitions for the creation of zero-emissions transportation sector (Government of the Netherlands, 2017).

Ambition	
2020	10% of all new passenger cars sold will have an electric powertrain and a plug
2025	50% of all new passenger cars sold will have an electric powertrain and a plug, and at least 30% of these (15% of the total) will be fully electric
2030	100% of all new passenger cars will be fully electric

Based on the above, the *electric vehicle charger density* illustrates that the Netherlands tops the ranking with roughly 19 EV stations per 100 kms of paved road in 2017. To put it in perspective, the United Kingdom had 3.1 EV stations per 100 kms in 2017. As of December 2019, the city of Amsterdam comes first with 4320 charging points, followed by the city of Rotterdam (with 3172 charging points) and the city of Eindhoven (with 815).

Holland's ambitions for accelerating the shift to sustainable and smart mobility are summarized in Table 6.2.

6.4.1.1 Amsterdam

The city of Amsterdam has an area of 219 km^2 with a population of 862,965 (www.opendata.cbs.nl, 2019), out of which 4% walk, 22% use bike, 30% use the public transportation, and 44% use their passenger vehicles, with the average daily travel distance is 8 km. With regard to the energy mix, it is noted that this consists of (2017 data) 41% natural gas,

39% petroleum, and 12% coal; whereas approximately 8% comes from renewable sources, nuclear energy, and waste. Natural gas originates mainly from the Netherlands and is used to generate heat and electricity. A large proportion of crude oil and petroleum products are imported, and then reexported. Petroleum and petroleum products are used to produce fuels and products such as plastics (www.longreads.cbs.nl, 2019).

Amsterdam is one of the European cities that is considered to be a pioneer in the deployment of electromobility, taking into consideration that through 2016, 20,000 cumulative EV sales were recorded, with 3000 EV sales in 2016, and 5% electric share of new LDVs sales in 2016 (Hall et al., 2017). In this direction, as foreseen by its Clean Air Action Plan (Box 6.3), Amsterdam aims to intensify the effort for the energy transition to a zero-emission transportation sector by 2030. The goals for the creation of a carbon-free city, are envisioned to Amsterdam's new Clean Air Action Plan, which not only aims to ban all petrol and diesel vehicles from town by 2030 (citylogistics.info, Amsterdam's Clean Air Action Plan, 2019), but also to proceed with an electric energy transition on every transportation level, including public transit.

Amsterdam currently has five Low Emission Zones (LEZ), where vehicle use is restricted, so as to limit tailpipe emissions. LEZ are considered a popular air quality measure in many European cities, with approximately 200 in existence [i.e., England, Italy, Sweden, and Holland (Holman et al., 2015)]. Restrictions typically apply to heavy duty vehicles, which usually run on diesel, but some LEZ also include other types of vehicles, such as very old, polluting cars. In the case of Amsterdam, these zones are going to be expanded and the regulations tightened, in order to become by 2030 zero-emission zones, where petrol, diesel, or gas vehicles are going to be banned.

Policies and promotion measures, for the acceleration of electromobility in Amsterdam, consist of:

- Priority to EV drivers for parking permits (they obtain free public parking spots), while the waiting list for other vehicles can last years.
- Free charging in public parking spaces. Information on their location and availability is accessible in real-time via an open API, making Amsterdam the first city in the world to provide such information in this manner.
- Subsidies: The National Government offers through the Ministry of Infrastructure and the Environment a € 5000 subsidy on the purchase of all-electric taxis or delivery vans. An additional subsidy is offered by

BOX 6.3 Clear air action plan milestones (www.citylogistics. info, Amsterdam's Clean Air Action Plan, 2019)

Clean Air Action Plan: A carbon free city by 2030

- From 2020, diesel vehicles with a Euro 3 engine will be banned within the A10 ring road;
- From 2022, only public transport buses and private coaches with electric or hydrogen engines will be allowed in the city center. Goods traffic will only be allowed in the environmental zone with a zero-emission or Euro 6 diesel engine;
- From 2025 onwards, only zero-emission taxis, scooters, buses, trucks and vans will be allowed to enter the area inside the A10 ring road. The same applies for passenger and pleasure vessels and public transport ferries. Further to this, only electric scooters and mopeds will be allowed in the built-up area of Amsterdam.
- From 2030, the entire built-up area of Amsterdam will be emission-free for all forms of transport, including cars and motorbikes. In addition, the planned initiatives include:
- The introduction of a government funded subsidy for the purchase of privately owned electric cars valued at € 6000 per EV, beginning in 2021. The subsidy would then be lowered in steps until it reaches € 2200 euros by 2030.
- Electric vehicles would be freed from value-added and motor vehicle taxes starting in 2025, alongside initiatives to strengthen the used car market for EVs, as well.
- Publicly used EVs will also be subject to purchase subsidies: The initiatives would include € 2030 per vehicle starting in 2021, with a drop to € 1830 by 2024. On the other hand, in order to make the purchase of combustion vehicles a less attractive alternative, the taxes for gasoline and diesel will be increased by one cent per liter in 2020, with another cent, for a total of a two-cent increase, in 2023.
  https://video.news24.com/show/176812

several local governments for the purchase of full electric taxis and vans, € 5000.
- Introduction of a scrappage program (in 2014) to remove old polluting vehicles.

6.4.2 Spain

The total number of EVs (including BEVs and PHEVs) registrations in Spain in 2019 reached 41,460 units, out of which 24,180 were BEVs.

This figure represents an increase of more than 11,000 registrations compared to 2018, when BEVs reached 16,407 units and PHEVs 12,295 (European Alternative Fuels Observatory—EAFO, 2020). In 2012 the volume of these charging stations amounted to a total of 400; whereas in 2019 it increased to 8820 (European Alternative Fuels Observatory—EAFO, 2020); out of which, 7576 were normal charging points ($< = 22$ kW) and 1244 fast charging points (> 22 kW).

Spain aligned with EU's legislation, has put in force measures related to the use of EVs. To be more specific, the promotion of the use of EVs in Spain is supported by indirect technology support (e.g., tax incentives), direct technology support (e.g., grants) and public purchasing incentives (including tax exemptions). In this context, the following legislative framework supports the uptake of EVs:

- Royal Decree 648/2011, which foresees the provision of financial aid for the purchase of EVs (Ministerio de Industria, Turismo y Comercio, 2011b), in the form of a bonus up to 25% of the sales price of the vehicle before tax, with a maximum of € 6000 per unit.
- Royal Decree 647/2011 (Ministerio de Industria, Turismo y Comercio, 2011a), which regulates the load operator defined by Law 54/1997 of the Electricity Sector (Jefatura del Estado, 1997) as a consumer qualified to sell electricity to recharge consumer vehicles. In this Decree, a supervalley rate for recharging EVs in a specific time tract is also introduced.
- Royal Decree 294/2013 (Ministerio de Industria, Turismo y Comercio, 2013), constitutes an updated version of Royal Decree 648/2011, and it concerns changes to the amount of the subsidy, which can reach up to € 5500 per vehicles that are full electric power operated, with a driving autonomy greater than 90 km.

Table 6.3 sums up relative policy measures to promote electromobility in Spain.

6.4.2.1 Barcelona

The city of Barcelona, is the capital of the autonomous community of Catalonia and the second most populous municipality of Spain; having a population of 1.6 million within city limits (Instituto Nacional de Estadística, 2016) its urban area extends to numerous neighboring municipalities within the Province of Barcelona and is home to around 4.8 million people, making it the sixth most populous urban area in the European Union. The city has a high population density and its transport

Table 6.3 Policy measures for the promotion of electromobility in Spain (Cansino and Yñiguez, 2018).

Financial incentives	Grant of tax incentives of € 2000−7000 for the purchase of EVs and other eco-friendly vehicles
Research financing	€ 140 million for industrialization support and R&D; € 173 million to priority R & D lines
Infrastructure	• "Movele program" (2008−11, investments ca. € 10 million): targeted the ramp-up of infrastructure and dispersion of EVs in Barcelona, Madrid, and Seville • € 35 million investment in electric grid related communication systems
Financial support of public authorities	For municipalities with ≥ 50,000 inhabitants (=145 cities) 20% subvention for the purchase of EVs (€ 6000 max/unit)
Consumer perception	Private consumer interest in EVs is currently low, due to high purchasing cost, low vehicle autonomy, recharging models, and battery issues.

is mostly public, thanks to integrated multimodal pricing that allows the use of bus, metro, tram, and train. Nonmotorized transport comes up to 41.7%, attributed partially to Bicing, a public bike system, with 35,000 daily uses. Powered two-wheelers account for 40% of private travel within the city.

With regard to the energy mix, it is noted that this consists of (2019 data): 36.8% renewable technologies; whereas 58.6% of the electricity produced in Spain during 2019 was obtained using technologies that produce zero CO_2 emissions. Combined cycle, with 21.9% of the total national generation, has been the technology that most contributed to the generation mix in 2019, followed by nuclear (21.2%), wind (20.6%), cogeneration (11.4%), and hydro (9%). Behind these is coal, with 5% of the total national generation (Red Eléctrica de España, 2020).

The number of EVs and motorcycles currently registered in Barcelona remains below 2000. To be more specific, Barcelona has more than 280 plug-in electric and hybrid vehicles in its fleet. The uptake of the EV in Barcelona is higher compared to other Spanish cities; it is highlighted that in 2014, 30% of the vehicles sold were EVs (425 BEV/FEV and PHEV/E-REV); whereas currently the number of EV users comes up to 530 (https://meet.barcelona.cat/en/visit-barcelona/get-around-the-city/electric-vehicles). It should be highlighted that Barcelona is the European city with the most electric motorcycles; with 150 recharging points for these vehicles. Furthermore, Barcelona is leading the introduction of electric taxis and is currently working toward the introduction of a new way of renting cars, based on car sharing, using 100% EVs. With regard to the charging infrastructure in Barcelona city and surroundings, currently there are 300 public free-of-charge recharging points and 180 more points at municipal-vehicle depots.

According to Barcelona's Electric Mobility Strategy 2018−24 (Ajutament de Barcelona, 2018), which sets ambitious targets for the acceleration of electromobility, by 2024 80% of the municipal fleet should be electric—electric buses should reach 100 in number and electric taxes 800. Further to this, the strategy aims to increase the number of electric private cars and motorcycles up to a combined total of 24,000. The axes of these targets set are:

- *Public procurement*: increase the share of EVs in the municipal fleet from 35% in 2018, to 50% in 2020 and to 80% in 2024. It should be noted that the municipal fleet consists of about 1500 vehicles.
- *Public transport*: the target is to have 25 fully electric buses of Transportes Metropolitanos de Barcelona (TMB) by 2020 and 100 by 2024.
- *Taxis:* as of 2019 no new taxi licenses will be issued for diesel vehicles, whereas from 2024 onwards only electric taxis can apply for a taxi license. At the same time, the strategy foresees an increase in the number of (exclusive) charging points for taxis throughout the city. It is expected that the measures will make it possible to meet the target of 200 electric taxis in 2020 and 800 in 2024.
- *Promotion of private use of EVs*: the number of public charging points will be tripled at underground public parking spaces, providing EVs free access to these spaces.

6.4.3 Norway

Despite the fact that Norway is not part of the European Union, it is closely connected through the European Economic Area agreement; for this reason, the successful implementation of electromobility in the city of Oslo is presented as a case study. The BEV development in Norway has evolved since the 1970s as follows (Figenbaum and Kolbenstvedt, 2013): concept development phase (1970−90); Testing (1990−99); Early Market (1999−2009); Market introduction (2009−12); and Market expansion (2013).

During the past decade, Norway has become a global forerunner in the field of electromobility, as the number of EVs usage has been increasing, with the stock of EVs to reach 342,367 units at the end of June 2019, consisting of 237,710 all-electric passenger cars and vans and 104,657 plug-in hybrids (The Norwegian Electric Vehicle Association, 2019). It is highlighted that in 2010 there were only 3347 registered electric cars; with the highest number in the Norwegian counties of Akershus, Oslo, and Hordaland. Especially for the case of BEVs it is pointed out that the BEV market share surpassed 50% for the first time in March 2019 (with share of 58.4%), whilst during the first quarter of 2019 the BEV market share was also higher than ever, reaching 48.4%.

The best-selling BEV in 2018 was the Nissan Leaf, which also became the best selling model overall, regardless of its propulsion system. The BEV fleet grew 41% between 2018 and 2017. The most numerous BEVs in the fleet are Nissan Leaf (49,823), Volkswagen e-Golf (31,883), BMW i3 (19,749), and Tesla Model S/X (30,106) (The Norwegian Electric Vehicle Association, 2019). The abovementioned statistics reflect the strong incentives provided by the Norwegian government for the purchase and ownership of EVs (Fridstrøm and Østli, 2017). The lucrative incentives, such as tax reductions and subsidies, as well as free parking and lower annual fees, have made the country keen on electric driving. EVs are exempt from the annual road tax, public parking fees, and toll payments (including domestic ferries), exempt from 25% VAT on sales, and are given access to bus lanes. Table 6.4 summarizes the broad range of incentives, including fiscal incentives, direct subsidies, fuel cost savings, and others that have been currently employed in Norway for the acceleration of EVs.

The findings of Table 6.4 reflect the coordinated efforts of the Norwegian government for the promotion of zero emission vehicles (ZEVs) as it aims to ban selling of petrol or diesel vehicles in the country from 2025 onwards (Norwegian Ministry of Transport and Communications, 2017). However, apart from the significant number of incentives, Norway seems to have all the ingredients for a successful EV acceleration: electricity is relatively cheap (Hovland, 2018), with high level of security of supply, and there are beneficial conditions for regular charging at home, given that 78% of Norwegians live in detached, semi-detached, or row houses (Statistics Norway, 2019a). Further to this, as 99% of Norway's energy production comes from renewable energy sources (the hydropower share reached 93.5% and wind power 3.7% in

Table 6.4 Overview of battery electric vehicles incentives in Norway.

Type of incentive	Incentives	Introduction year	What it means for the BEV user	Targets
Fiscal	Exemption from registration tax	1990/1996	The tax is based on ICEV emissions and weight (i.e., VW Up € 3000; VW Golf: € 6000−9000).	Until 2020
	VAT exemption	2001	Vehicles competing with BEVs are levied a VAT of 25% on sales price minus registration tax.	Until 2020
	Reduced annual vehicle license fee	1996/2004	BEVs and hydrogen vehicles € 52 (2014 figures). Diesel rate: € 360−420 with/without particulate filter.	To be continued indefinitely
	Exemption from the re-registration tax	2018	A tax is levied on the change of ownership of ICEVs and PHEVs. 0−3 year old vehicles above 1200 kg: € 610, 4−11 years € 370. BEVs have an exemption.	2018−onwards
Direct subsidies to users	Free toll roads	1997	In Oslo-area saved costs come up to € 600−1000 € per year. Some places exceed € 2500.	Law revised: Rates for BEVs in toll roads and ferries will be decided by local governments (up to a maximum rate of 50% of the ICEV rate).
	Reduced fares on ferries	2009	Similar to toll roads saving money for those using car ferries.	
	Financial support for normal charging stations.	2009	Reduced investors risk, reduced users range anxiety, expand usage	National plan for charging infrastructure to be developed.
	Financial support for fast charge station	2011	More fast charging stations influences BEV km driven & market shares	ENOVA[a] support program to establish fast charging along major transport corridors. City fast charging is left to commercial actors.
User privileges	Access to bus lanes	2003/2005	Time efficiency: driving to work in the bus lane during rush hours.	Local authorities have the authority to introduce restrictions if BEVs delay buses.
	Free parking	1999	Users get a parking space where these are scarce or expensive and save time looking for a space.	Local authorities have the authority to introduce rates up to 50% of the ICEV rate

BEV, battery electric vehicles; ICEV, internal combustion engine vehicles; PHEV, plug-in-hybrid electric vehicles VAT, value-added tax.
[a]Enova SF is owned by the Ministry of Climate and Environment and contributes to reduced GHG emissions, development of energy and climate technology, and a strengthened security of supply.
Adapted from Norwegian Ministry of Transport and Communications, 2017, National Transport Plan 2018−2029, Available at: <https://www.regjeringen.no/contentassets/7c52fd2938ca42209e4286fe86b28bd/en-gb/pdfs/stm201620170033000engpdfs.pdf>.

May 2019) (Statistics Norway, 2019b), the use of EVs is a very attractive option also from a life cycle point of view (see Chapter 5: Climate Change Mitigation and Electric Vehicles). Despite the impressive EV acceleration, several complaints have arisen with regard to the high public subsidies as compared to the value of the reduced carbon footprint of EVs; the travel mode shift by people who buy an EV as a second car instead of taking buses and trains; the potential traffic congestion in Oslo's bus lanes due to the increasing number of electric cars; the loss of revenue for some ferry operators due to the large number of electric cars exempted from payment; and shortage of parking spaces for owners of conventional cars due to preference to electric cars and lack of a cap on parking time.

As far as the charging infrastructure is concerned, it is highlighted that the majority of BEV owners can charge their vehicle at home in a private parking space and 42% use a dedicated wall box EVSE for charging, whereas only 9% of PHEV owners use this type of charging connection (Figenbaum and Kolbenstvedt, 2016). Based on the above percentages, the installed number of private wall box EVSE charge stations passed 90,000 by the end of 2018.

Public charging consists of:

- AC level 2 chargers with type 2 connectors rated for 3.6—22 kW charge power;
- Limited number of older installations with Schuko domestic type sockets.

Most fast chargers are equipped with both a Combined Charging System (CCS)[1] and a CHAdeMO [2]cable, but only one of these can be used at a time. A small number of fast chargers are single standard CHAdeMO or CCS. The best estimate is therefore that there are 1100 fast chargers in Norway, of which about 95% are dual standard CCS CHAdeMO chargers (www.ieahev.org).

6.4.3.1 Oslo

The municipality of Oslo has a population of 672,061 (as of July 1, 2017), whereas the population of the city's urban area is 1,000,467 (as of December

---

[1] Combined Charging System (CCS) covers charging electric vehicles using the Combo 1 and Combo 2 connectors at up to 350 kilowatts.

[2] CHAdeMO is the trade name of a quick charging method for battery electric vehicles delivering up to 62.5 kW by 500 V, 125 A direct current via a special electrical connector. A revised CHAdeMO 2.0 specification allows for up to 400 kW by 1000 V, 400 A direct current.

BOX 6.4 Measures that are going to be effected in the city of Oslo

Planned measures for the city of Oslo

- A car-free city center (inner city)
- New low-emission zones (greater Oslo)
- Residential parking zones with free parking for EVs (greater Oslo)
- Congestion tax (none for EVs) (the whole city)
- Increased numbers of toll gates/road throughout the city, with free passage for EVs
- A fossil-free city 2024 (greater Oslo)
- Only zero-emission taxis from 2022 (the whole city)
- Ban on sales of diesel and gasoline vehicles (all of Norway from 2022)
- Temporary bans on diesel cars on the most polluting days (the whole city from 2017)

3, 2018) (Statistics Norway, 2015; Hagesæther Pål Vegard, 2018). In 2019 Oslo was announced as the European Environmental Capital[3] of the year; receiving in this way recognition for the city's efforts to reduce emissions from the transportation within the urban area. The ambitious goals made by the City Government of Oslo is that by the year 2020 "the CO_2 emissions should be reduced by 50%, and by the year 2030, it should be reduced by 95%." To be able to reach this ambitious goal, the citizens of Oslo need to change from fossil to EVs. The aim is to convince people to change to EVs, where EVs have no fees or taxes, which could help a user save "at least 10,000 Euros" (Portvik, 2019). In this context, the public transport operator (public transport is controlled by provincial authorities through tenders that private bus companies compete for) in Oslo, Ruter, announced a rollout of 70 battery electric buses in the city center in 2019. In addition, the City Council has decided to electrify three large ferries that traffic the inner parts of the Oslofjord; two battery electric ferries were put into use for a fully battery electric car ferry service on the west coast of Norway, and more than 60 electric ferries are under development. Box 6.4 lists a number of measures that are going to be effected in the city of Oslo, with the aim to achieve a zero-emissions transportation system.

In Oslo more than 50% of new cars sold in 2017 were either fully battery electric (37.5%) or plug-in hybrid (14.1%). The exponential growth

---

[3] https://www.youtube.com/watch?v = 9s-lC1vjumE

of EV sales in Oslo is continuing, with a 53% sales share for EVs in 2018 and a percentage of 16% of total cars in Oslo, with 9% fully electric cars and 7% plug-in hybrids (OFV, 2018). Nonetheless, despite the increase in sales of EVs, the required infrastructure for charging points and rapid chargers has not been developed at the same speed, given that there are only 1450 municipal charging stations. As a reference, it is noted that in 2018 over 12,000 new EVs were registered in Oslo, while during the same period only 19 new charging stations were installed (Badallaj, 2019).

Table 6.5 illustrates the charging points in Oslo, which can be categorized into the following types: Schuko (type 1 chargers), type 2-chargers, and CHAdeMO/CCS combo ("superchargers"). Some of the chargers are public, meaning that every EV-user has access to them, and some of them are private and restricted to each central district, i.e., only users who live in that district are allowed to use chargers in that district.

Since 2008, the city of Oslo has been engaged in EVSE development (e.g., creating its own CPO and installing more than 1300 public charging stations), and it plans to further install fast chargers and parking garages equipped with EVSE outlets, so as to deal with the shortage of the number of available charging points per vehicle (one charger per 10 cars) (Portvik, 2019). The EVSE deployment target for 2018 was to install 600 (three times the average annual number of 200) publicly accessible EVSE (200 slow chargers and 400 fast chargers). The municipality further incentivizes EVSE installation in sport clubs, commercial centers, and parking (50% of the installation costs).

Oslo also adopted a measure in 2017 to strengthen the availability of private charging infrastructure. This regulation mandates that new buildings must have at least 50% of the parking facilities equipped for electric car charging. The grid capacity must also be designed to charge at 3.6 kW all of the vehicles in the building without any need for smart charging to prevent local power shortages.

Table 6.5 Types of chargers in Oslo (Badallaj, 2019).

Type of charger	Amount
Schuko/ Schuko CEE 7/4	1100
Type 2	722
Type 2 + Schuko	224
CHAdeMO/CCS Combo	139
Total	2185

6.4.4 United Kingdom

As of February 1, 2020 the United Kingdom is no longer part of the European Union; nonetheless the efforts made until now to create a zero-emission future are noteworthy. At the end of Q1 2014 the number of licensed ultra low emission vehicles (ULEVs) in the United Kingdom increased from 9500 at the end of Q1 2010 to 200,000 at the end of Q4 2018 (an increase of 1732%). Currently cars account for around 93% of all licensed ULEV vehicles. Other ULEVs include vans and scooters (Department for Transport's Vehicle, 2020).

A surge of plug-in car sales took place in the UK at the beginning of 2014. Total registrations went from 3586 in 2013, to 37,092 in 2016, and rose to 59,911 in 2018. The market share of the plug-in segment went from 0.16% in 2013 to 0.59% in 2014, and achieved 2.6% in 2018. In 2019 an average of almost 6100 plug-in models were registered each month, compared to less than 5000 a month in 2018 and fewer than 4000 each month in 2017 (Society of Motor Manufacturers and Traders—SMMT, 2019). Compared to 2018 Q3, the number of battery electric cars more than tripled (+234%), affected by the release of Tesla Model 3 and strong growth for other popular models. Hybrid electric cars increased by 22% over that period, whereas the number of plug-in hybrid electric cars decreased by 27%.

As of September 2018, the Mitsubishi Outlander P-HEV is the all-time top-selling plug-in car in the UK (with 7,000 units registered), followed by the Nissan Leaf (with 24,000 units). Ranking third is the BMW 330e with more than 13,000 units, followed by the BMW i3 with 11,000 units. However, despite the rise in the number of EVs their proportion in the UK vehicle fleet remains small. In 2018 around 59% of licensed cars were petrol, 39% diesel, and 0.5% were either a plug-in hybrid, battery electric, range-extended electric, or fuel cell electric car.

In this direction, the UK government has supported measures to encourage the acceleration of EVs through different policies, targets, and grants and incentives to individuals buying new vehicles. The Road to Zero Strategy (Department for Transport, 2018) sets out several new measures and targets, including:

- ULEVs to reach a percentage of at least 50%—and as much as 70%—of new car sales by 2030, alongside up to 40% of new vans.
- Charge points to be installed in new build homes and new lampposts to include charging points.

Table 6.6 Types of chargers in UK (ZapMap, 2019).

Type of charger	Amount
AC level 2 chargers	1225
CHAdeMO	1717
CCS	1457
TESLA	339
Inductive charging	0
Total	4738

- Funding to new and existing companies that produce and install charge points.
- Grant of £500 to EV owners to put in a charge point in their home through the EV homecharge scheme.
- Ban the sale of new petrol and diesel cars and vans by 2040. By 2040, it is expected the majority of new cars and vans sold will be 100% zero emission and all new cars and vans will have significant zero-emission capability.

In addition, from September 2020 an ultra-low emissions zone will be created requiring all cars, motorcycles, vans, minibuses, coaches, and heavy goods vehicles to meet strict emission standards or pay a daily charge. In advance of these requirements, all private hire taxi vehicles licensed for the first time from January 1, 2018 must be zero-emission capable.

With regard to charging infrastructure, it is noted that the number of EV charge points per 100 km of road in the United Kingdom has increased from 42 in 2011 to 570 in 2019 (EAFO, 2020); with the majority of them to have a charge rate of less than or equal to 22 kW. In January 2020 in Great Britain there were (ZapMap, 2020):

- 10,500 public charging points
- 16,900 devices
- 29,500 connections

Table 6.6 summarizes the type of chargers in UK in May 2019.

It should be noted that the UK Government has provided £40 million (€ ~ 47 million) of funding via the Go Ultra Low City scheme to eight cities across the UK to support the uptake of ULEVs.

6.4.4.1 London

London is the capital and largest city of England and of the United Kingdom. Greater London encompasses a total area of 1583 km^2, an area which had a population of 8,787,892 in 2016 and a population density of 4542 inhabitants per km^2 (www.ons.gov.uk). With regard to the energy mix, it is noted that this consists of (2019 data): 41% gas; 22% wind, wave, and solar PV; 19% nuclear; and 9% of the electricity produced in the UK during 2018 was obtained using thermal technologies, 5% coal, and 3% from other sources (National Statistics, Department of Business, Energy and Industrial Strategy, 2019).

London has been declared as one of 25 EV capitals with half of all EVs worldwide (Hall et al., 2017). Sales of EVs, both BEV and PHEV, in London have increased during the past years. In 2018, EVs accounted for 2.81% of sales in London—higher than the UK average of 2.13%.

The number of EVs in London has grown significantly during the last 5 years; nonetheless their percentage is still low compared to petrol cars, as EVs make up less than 0.4% of the 2,863,600 cars registered in London. EVs in London are supported by a range of charging infrastructure, ranging from rapid DC chargers, to slow to fast AC chargers. Rapid chargers are costly per unit but offer the fastest charge time, whereas slow to fast AC chargers cost considerably less to purchase and install, but require more time to charge. At October 1, 2019, there were 4360 EV charging devices, out of which 323 were rapid charging devices (Department for Transport's Vehicle, 2020). During the same period, the ratio of charging devices per 100,000 population was 49; whereas the rapid devices per 100,000 population was 3.6.

It is highlighted that during the past years there has been significant public investment in charge points in London from the origins of London's first public charging network, Source London in 2011 to the lamppost and freestanding charge points being installed today via the Go Ultra Low City Scheme (www.goultralow.com). Transport for London has also committed to installing 300 rapid chargers by the end of 2020. Apart from the efforts of the public sector the private sector is investing as well, and the commercial case is set to improve further, with growing zero-emission fleets of taxis, private hire, and other key user groups.

6.5 United States of America

As of October 2019, more than 1.3 million EVs were sold in the United States; the EV share of new car sales grew to 2.6% in October 2019 (hybrid-cars.com). The EV share is highest in the major West Coast markets. To be more specific, in 2017 the San Jose area had the highest share at 10%, followed by other California areas (4%−6%) and markets in Colorado, Hawaii, Oregon, Vermont, and Washington (2%−4%). Overall, the share of new vehicles that are plug-in electric in these 50 areas is 1.2%, about three times the proportion in the rest of the United States. EV sales in the United States grew substantially between 2010 and 2017. A major driver behind the growth has been the ZEV regulation, adopted by California and nine other states, along with the many complementary local actions in the adopting states (Box 6.5). In California, 5% of new vehicle sales were electric in 2017, compared with 1.2% in other ZEV markets, and 0.6% in the rest of the country.

As of December 31, 2018, there were 1,046,840 EVs (BEV and PHEV) in the United States and through April 5, 2019 there were 21,324 charging locations and 62,153 charging connections. Table 6.7 illustrates the number of EVs sold through December 31, 2018 as well as the relative market share within each State.

BOX 6.5 Zero-emission vehicles (ZEV) alliance.

ZEV sale market mechanisms can function in the absence of federal legislation (Abuelsamid, 2018). In 2013 nine states (California, Connecticut, Maryland, Massachusetts, New Jersey, New York, Oregon, Rhode Island, and Vermont) signed a ZEV Memorandum of Understanding (MOU), in order to enact policies that will ensure the deployment of 3.3 million ZEVs by 2025, through involvement in a ZEV Program Implementation Task Force. Individual states are responsible for their respective implementation, but they are following California's lead by requiring automakers to produce ZEVs.

ZEV Action Plan (ZEV Program Implementation Task Force, 2014): In 2014 an action plan, which identified 11 priority actions to accomplish the goals of the MOU was published. The plan also included a research agenda, which included further research and relative actions. On an annual basis, each state must provide a report regarding the number of registered ZEVs, the number of public EVSE and hydrogen fueling stations, as well as any available information regarding workplace fueling for ZEVs.

ZEV Task Force Multi-State ZEV Action Plan 2018−21:

In June 2018 a new ZEV action plan (ZEV Task Force, 2018) was published for 2018−21. The 2018 action plan, which is based on the 2014 action plan recognizes the needs in five priority areas:
- Raising consumer awareness and interest in EV technology;
- Building out a reliable and convenient residential, workplace and public charging/fueling infrastructure network;

(Continued)

BOX 6.5 (Continued)
- Continuing and improving access to consumer purchase and nonfinancial incentives;
- Expanding public and private sector fleet adoption; and
- Supporting dealership efforts to increase ZEV sales.

International ZEV Alliance:
International ZEV Alliance is a global initiative between 16 North American (British Columbia, Canada; California, USA; Connecticut, USA; Maryland, USA; Massachusetts, USA; New York, USA; Oregon, USA; Québec- Canada; Rhode Island, USA; Vermont, USA) and European national and subnational governments (Germany, Netherlands, Norway, United Kingdom) to accelerate the global transition to ZEVs. Their goal is to:
- Accelerate the adoption of ZEVs (electric, plug-in hybrid, and fuel cell vehicles.
- Make all passenger vehicles sales in their jurisdictions ZEVs by no later than 2050 and to collaboration on policies and actions to achieve their ZEV targets.
- Unlock GHG reductions of over 125 million tons CO_2 per year in 2030, and over 1.5 billion tons CO_2 per year in 2050, in climate change mitigation when including life cycle impact of EVs
- Meet regularly to support their ongoing policy and technology developments in their respective jurisdictions and direct new work to establish global best practices to support ZEVs.
- Improve EV policy, incentives, and infrastructure activities

6.5.1 California

California includes six of the 50 largest US metropolitan areas by population (Los Angeles, San Francisco, Riverside, San Diego, Sacramento, and San Jose) and was among the top eight markets nationally in 2017 in terms of EV sales share. Since 2011 the state of California has accounted for half of the plug-in electric vehicles (PEVs) sold in the United States; in particular, California has the largest stock of PEVs in the United States, with cumulative sales of over 500,000 by the end of November 2018 (Szczesny, 2018). Fig. 6.3 illustrates nine of the top 10 California counties ranked by registered light-duty EVs per capita. Among registered light-duty EVs in Silicon Valley, 39% are Teslas, 23% are Chevrolets (Volt and Bolt), 14% are Nissan (LEAF), 8% are Toyota (Prius), and 6% are Ford (Fusion and Focus). Statewide, California has a

Table 6.7 Number of EVs sales in United States during 2017—18 (Autoalliance, 2019).

State	EV sales 2017	EV sales 2018	2018—17 YOY sales increase	2018 EV market share within state
Alabama	381	866	127.30%	0.41%
Alaska	85	155	82.35%	0.59%
Arizona	2976	7086	138.10%	1.84%
Arkansas	187	435	132.62%	0.35%
California	94,873	153,442	61.73%	7.84%
Colorado	4156	7051	69.66%	2.61%
Connecticut	2304	3415	48.22%	2.02%
Delaware	401	627	56.36%	1.27%
District of Columbia	398	761	91.21%	3.34%
Florida	6573	13,705	108.50%	1.03%
Georgia	2427	6004	147.38%	1.18%
Hawaii	1934	2296	18.72%	2.59%
Idaho	241	497	106.22%	0.77%
Illinois	3812	7357	93.00%	1.20%
Indiana	933	2036	118.22%	0.82%
Iowa	433	917	111.78%	0.70%
Kansas	452	943	108.63%	0.96%
Kentucky	360	787	118.61%	0.53%
Louisiana	283	613	116.61%	0.28%
Maine	464	799	72.20%	1.13%
Maryland	3244	6299	94.17%	1.91%
Massachusetts	4632	8990	94.08%	2.53%
Mean	3686	6434	94.78%	1.33%
Median	933	2036	94.08%	0.96%
Michigan	2742	3571	30.23%	0.59%
Minnesota	1398	2853	104.08%	1.14%
Mississippi	128	231	80.47%	0.22%
Missouri	1150	2268	97.22%	0.73%
Montana	143	274	91.61%	0.47%
Nebraska	260	628	141.54%	0.73%
Nevada	1068	2325	117.70%	1.62%
New Hampshire	788	1123	42.51%	1.16%
New Jersey	5033	9230	83.39%	1.59%
New Mexico	369	705	91.06%	0.81%
New York	10,090	15,752	56.11%	1.56%
North Carolina	2055	4712	129.29%	1.02%
North Dakota	39	95	143.59%	0.24%

(*Continued*)

Table 6.7 (Continued)

State	EV sales 2017	EV sales 2018	2018−17 YOY sales increase	2018 EV market share within state
Ohio	2091	4456	113.10%	0.74%
Oklahoma	691	2683	288.28%	0.35%
Oregon	3988	5976	49.85%	3.41%
Pennsylvania	3346	6063	81.20%	0.92%
Rhode Island	433	619	42.96%	1.26%
South Carolina	562	1170	108.19%	0.53%
South Dakota	79	135	70.89%	0.35%
Tennessee	791	1994	152.09%	0.73%
Texas	5419	11,764	117.09%	0.78%
Utah	1163	2295	97.33%	1.60%
Vermont	871	824	−5.40%	1.92%
Virginia	2932	6375	117.43%	1.67%
Washington	7068	12,650	78.98%	4.28%
West Virginia	113	218	92.92%	0.27%
Wisconsin	1576	1956	24.11%	0.79%
Wyoming	51	92	80.39%	0.35%
Total	187,985	328,118	74.54%	1.96%

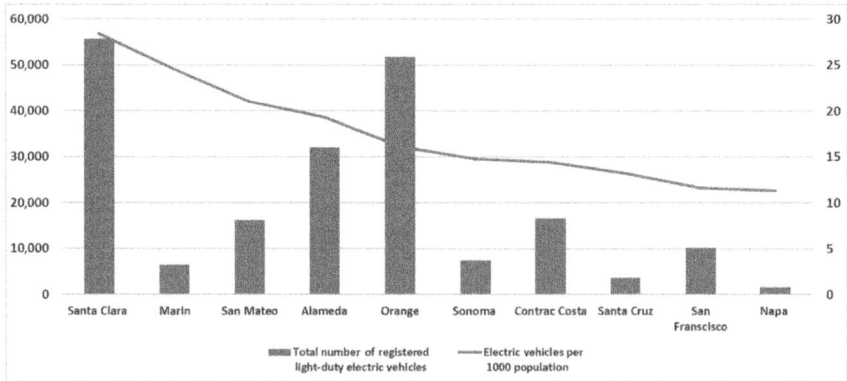

Figure 6.3 Top 10 California counties with regard to electric vehicles per capita in 2018. *Data adapted from https://jointventure.org/news-and-media/news-releases/1776-silicon-valley-sets-pace-for-electric-vehicle-adoptionnew-data-shows-region-accounts-for-nearly-20-of-electric-vehicles-in-california.*

similar breakdown by maker with a smaller share of Nissans and a larger share of Toyotas and Fords.

In 2018 California's plug-in car market share reached 7.8% (with a national share of 1.1%); the state's plug-in segment market share surpassed the take-rate of conventional hybrids (4.1%) for the first time (California New Car Dealers Association, 2019). During the first half of 2019 the sales of new EVs in California shot up 63.7%, to 51,750 units, attributed mainly to the sales of the Tesla Model 3 (about 33,000 Model 3 s were sold in California in the first half of 2019, followed by Chevrolet's Bolt EV, at 4482 units, and by the Tesla Model X at 3690 units). It should be noted that Tesla's market share in California is nearly 3.5 times its 1.2% share across the entire United States (California New Car Dealers Association, 2019). However, the EV market share in the state reached 5.5% during the first nine months of 2019.

The Government of California has been supporting the adoption and deployment of electromobility, by placing a number of both financial and nonfinancial incentives. As part of the state's government incentives, in addition to the existing federal tax credit, PEVs and FCEVs are eligible for a purchase rebate of up to US$2500 through the Clean Vehicle Rebate Project (Clean Vehicle Rebate Project CVRP, 2014). In addition, applicants that purchased or leased battery electric vehicles or a plug-in hybrid meeting California's Enhanced Advanced Technology Partial Zero-Emission Vehicle (Enhanced AT PZEV) were entitled to a clean air sticker allowing the vehicle to be operated by a single occupant in California's carpool or high occupancy vehicle lanes (HOV) up until January 1, 2019. Further to the abovementioned incentives, the South Coast Air Quality Management District and the San Joaquin Valley Air Pollution Control District provide additional incentives to residents of their district through the Enhanced Fleet Modernization Program (EFMP Plus Up) (California Air Resources Board, 2017). Residents of these districts can receive between $2500 and $4500 for replacing an old vehicle with a cleaner one, depending on their level of income.

California's ambitious targets—with regard to the creation of a zero-emission transportation sector—were initiated in 2012, with the establishment of the goal of getting 1.5 million ZEVs by 2025 (Lagos, 2014); this was updated in January 2018, when a new goal of getting a total of 5 million ZEVs by 2030 was set (Box 6.6).

Currently, about 29% of California's electricity is produced from renewable sources (solar and wind), 36% from natural gas, and only 4%

> **BOX 6.6 California plug-in electric collaborative**
> The California Plug-In Electric Vehicle Collaborative (PEV Collaborative) is a public–private partnership, launched in 2010, with the main objective of advancing the PEV market in California and globally. The PEV collaborative convenes, collaborates, and communicates on emerging PEV market trends and addresses barriers to PEV market growth. It consists of 47 members, including the California state government, local government entities, global automakers, utilities, research and environmental NGOs, and third-party charging providers.

from coal, most of which is generated outside the state (California Energy Commission, 2017). To be more specific, in 2018 California ranked first in the nation as a producer of electricity from solar, geothermal, and biomass resources and fourth in the nation in conventional hydroelectric power generation. In 2018 large- and small-scale solar PV and solar thermal installations provided 19% of California's net electricity generation.

With regard to the charging infrastructure, it is noted that there are about 21,000 charging stations statewide. To be more specific, by the end of June 2019 the number of public chargers reached 20,653, including (California Governor's office of Business and Economic Development—Go-Biz, 2019):

- Level 1 (4–5 miles of range per hour, 367 chargers at 169 sites)
- Level 2 (12–70 miles of range per hour, 17,216 chargers at 4764 sites)
- DC Fast (3–20 miles of range per minute, 3070 chargers at 685 sites)

A fair share of power outlets is still privately owned in homes or workplaces, with the latter playing a large role in attracting commuters toward EVs. With faster charging and cheaper, more efficient batteries, long distance travel becomes possible with plug-in EVs. It should be highlighted that not all public connectors serve all plug-in EVs and not all connectors can be used simultaneously. Tesla, for example, operates a network of chargers dedicated to Tesla vehicles.

6.5.1.1 Los Angeles

The County of Los Angeles is the most populous county in the United States, as per the 2010 US Census, according to which its population reached 9,818,605. The city of Los Angeles, is the most populous city in California, and the second most populous city in the United States, after New York City, with an estimated population of nearly four million people. The city is characterized by automobile dependency, given that about 86% of all workers commute to work by private vehicle, either driving alone or carpooling (McKenzie, 2015).

Los Angeles, is considered the largest single market by sales volume, where area residents purchased more than 38,000 new EVs in 2017, constituting more than one-fifth of the entire US EV market. In terms of cumulative EV sales, the Los Angeles metropolitan area accounted for more than 200,000 sales from 2010 to 2018; during the same period, EV sales in the San Francisco and San Jose metropolitan areas exceeded 71,000 and 54,000, respectively. It should be noted that despite the fact that EVs accounted for 1% of the national LDV market, EV sales reached 5% in Los Angeles, constituting one of the largest US EV markets by sales share and by annual sales volume (Joint Venture Silicon Valley, 2019).

Los Angeles has established an ambitious plan for the reduction of transport emissions under its Zero Emissions 2028 Roadmap 2.0 (Transportation Electrification Collaboration-LACI, 2018), which aims to achieve an overall 25% reduction in GHG emissions and air pollution by 2028. Los Angeles Green New Deal involves a number of measures as illustrated in Box 6.7.

The charging stations in Los Angeles (offered by Blink, Greenlots, Tesla, ChargePoint, and SemaCharge) are plentiful in Beverly Hills, Hollywood, the Financial District, and along the highways. In 2016 the city of Los Angeles replaced a distance of 7242 km lampposts with LED lights instead. With this in effect, power centrals can use the energy savings to power up to 100 new charging stations. Following this progressive change, 30 of these charging stations using the surplus energy have been installed in 2016. It should be noted that Los Angeles with a 5% share of EV sales, has more than twice the US average of charging stations. Los Angeles also wants to install 10,000 publicly available EV chargers by 2022; and 28,000 chargers by 2028. In addition, the Los Angeles Police Department has recently added 100 electric BMW i3 to its fleet. Currently 2661 level 2 charging stations and 234 level three charging stations are installed within 10 miles of Los Angeles (Alternative Fuels Data Center, 2020).

6.5.1.2 Silicon Valley—San Jose

San Jose is a growing city of more than 1 million people in the heart of Silicon Valley, which grew by about 130,000 people between 2000 and 2016 (U.S. Census Bureau, 2000, 2016). Residents of Santa Clara

BOX 6.7 LA's green new deal (https://plan.lamayor.org/sites/default/files/pLAn_2019_final.pdf)

This involves a commitment to uphold the Paris Climate Agreement; aiming to deliver environmental justice and equity through an inclusive green economy. It incorporates initiatives from 44 partner organizations, employing a unique, collaborative, multisector approach to meeting the goals for the creation of a sustainable city. In this direction, the deal incorporates basic actions, aiming to eradicate emissions coming from energy consuming sources such as the residential, transportation, and energy sector. The New Deal targets include inter alia:

1. The creation of a zero-carbon electricity grid—reaching the accelerated goal of 80% renewable energy supply by 2036; aiming to 100% renewables by 2045.
2. The creation of 300,000 green jobs by 2035 and 400,000 by 2050.
3. Zero emissions buildings by 2050.
4. Zero waste future by phasing out styrofoam by 2021, ending the use of plastic straws and single-use takeout containers by 2028, and phase out the use of landfills by 2050.
5. Recycling 100% of wastewater by 2035; sourcing 70% of water locally.
6. Planting and maintaining at least 90,000 trees—which will provide 61 million square feet of shade—citywide by 2021 and increasing tree canopy in low-income, severely heat impacted areas by at least 50% by 2028.

Transportation sector

With regard to the road transportation sector, the targets include:

Increase the percentage of ZEVs in the city to 25% by 2025; 80% by 2035; and 100% by 2050.

100% zero-emission school buses in Los Angeles.

Introduction of 155 new electric DASH buses.

Implementation of an updated Clean Truck Program with prioritization to zero-emission trucks.

County, of which San Jose is the largest city, spend an average of 28 minutes commuting to work and 75% drive alone; while 86% also work within the county (U.S. Census Bureau, 2017). As per California Department of Motor Vehicles (2017) about 82% of the vehicles registered in the county are autos, while trucks make up 12% of registered vehicles. The total number of registered EVs in Silicon Valley was 83,440 (63% battery electric and 37% plug-in hybrid vehicles) in 2018. Metropolitan San Jose is one of the nation's top markets for EV sales share, with EVs accounting for more than 13% of new vehicle sales in 2017 (Lutsey, 2018).

It is pointed out that, despite the fact that sales of EVs in 2018 reached 1% of the national light-duty vehicle market, in San Jose the sales of EVs reached 13%, making the city one of the largest EV markets by sales share and by annual sales volume. With regard to vehicles' fuel mix, it is noted that 88% of the registered LDVs are fueled by gasoline, 6% are hybrids, and 3% are EVs (2% all-electric and 1% plug-in hybrids). In comparison, only 2% of LDVs registered throughout the state are EVs (Joint Venture Silicon Valley, 2019). Tesla is the most popular EV in San Jose with more than 10% of Tesla registrations throughout the state. The Santa Clara County, has the highest per capita EV adoption, with 28.4 EVs per 1000 residents. Among registered light-duty EVs in Silicon Valley, 39% are Teslas, 23% are Chevrolets (Volt and Bolt), 14% are Nissan (LEAF), 8% are Toyota (Prius), and 6% are Ford (Fusion and Focus).

With regard to the charging infrastructure, the two main charging networks in operation are ChargePoint and SemaConnect and the following charging stations can be distinguished (Alternative Fuels Data Center, 2020):

- 1552 Level 2 charging stations; and
- 215 Level 3 charging stations.

Since 2012 the citizens of San Jose can also apply for private charging stations online. To facilitate access to these permits, an online application service has been put in place, allowing anyone to acquire a permit to install a level 2 charging station in the comfort of their home.

6.5.2 New York City

The state of New York, with a population of 19.8 million people and a gross domestic product (GDP) of $1.5 billion in 2016 (U.S. Bureau of Economic Analysis, 2017) is the fourth most populous state in the United States. The state is committed, through its PlaNY initiative, to shift toward cleaner, locally sourced energy, including a 2030 vision for the city to obtain 50% of the power mix from renewable energy sources, while reducing GHGs by 40% relative to 1990 levels (New York Public Service Commission-PSC, 2016). New York's Clean Energy Standard was revised in 2019, according to which New York State's Green New Deal requires 100% carbon-free electricity by 2040. The cornerstone of this newly proposed mandate is a significant increase of New York's successful Clean Energy Standard to 70% renewable electricity by 2030.

As part of the unprecedented ramp-up of renewable energy, New York has already invested $2.9 billion into 46 large-scale renewable projects across the state as it significantly increases its clean energy targets, such as quadrupling New York's offshore wind target to a nation-leading 9000 MW by 2035; doubling distributed solar deployment to 6000 MW by 2025; and deploying 3000 MW of energy storage by 2030. In addition, New York participates in the Regional Greenhouse Gas Initiative, an emissions cap-and-trade program which sets a limit on GHG emissions and operates a regional market for trading acceptable energy certificates (NYSERDA, 2019).

With regard to energy consumption by sector, it is noted that in 2017, 30.5% was attributed to the transportation sector; whereas 30.4% was attributed to the commercial sector; 28.7% and 10.5% to the residential and industrial sectors, respectively (U.S. Energy Information Administration EIA, 2019). As far as the state's energy mix is concerned, it is noted that in 2018, 29% of New York's in-state generation at both large- and small-scale facilities came from renewable sources; whereas one-third of its electricity came from nuclear power plants[4]. During the past years, the state of New York has established a number of initiatives—as illustrated in Box 6.8, for the promotion of EVs.

EV sales in New York increased by 63% in 2018, as the number of EVs on the road jumped to 36,854 in 2018, up from 24,551 in 2017. During the period of 2011—18, EV registrations within New York increased significantly, nonetheless they still remains small as a share of total registered vehicles. It is pointed out that the penetration of hybrids in New York appears to have peaked between 2% and 3% of all vehicles. Since 2011 EV registration on a cumulative basis has grown to over 16,000 vehicles (New York Department of Motor Vehicles NYDMV, 2019). This remains small relative to all registered vehicles, which totaled 11,368,939 in the state in 2016 (New York Department of Motor Vehicles NYDMV, 2019).

As of December 31, 2018, there were more than 3200 EV charging stations installed statewide. As per Alternative Fuels Data Center (2020) the number of charging stations in New York come up to 1716. Many of the charging stations are located in public parking garages, and there is usually a small fee for charging. Apartment dwellers who park in a local

---

[4] The state includes nuclear power as a zero-emissions resource that counts toward New York's 2040 emissions reduction goals.

BOX 6.8 New York State incentives for the promotion of electromobility (New York State Energy Research and Development — NYSERDA, 2018)

Alternative Fuel Vehicle Research and Development Funding: The New York State Energy Research and Development Authority's (NYSERDA) Clean Transportation Program provides funding for projects that enhance mobility, improve efficiency, reduce congestion, and diversify transportation methods and fuels through research and development of advanced technologies.

Alternative Fueling Infrastructure Tax Credit: An income tax credit is available for 50% of the cost of alternative fueling infrastructure, up to $5000. Qualifying infrastructure includes EV supply equipment and equipment to dispense fuel that is 85% or more natural gas, propane, or hydrogen. Unused credits may be carried over into future tax years. The credit expires December 31, 2022.

Electric Vehicle Emissions Inspection Exemption: Vehicles powered exclusively by electricity are exempt from state motor vehicle emissions inspections.

EVSE Rebate: The NYSERDA Charge Ready New York program offers rebates for public and private entities toward the purchase and installation of Level 2 EVSE at public parking facilities, workplaces, and multi-unit dwellings. Rebates are available for $4000 per port.

Heavy-Duty Alternative Fuel and Advanced Vehicle Purchase Vouchers: NYSERDA provides incentives for alternative fuel trucks and buses, based on a staggered schedule and are distributed based on specific criteria. Eligible vehicles must be in operation 70% of the time and be garaged in the program area.

High Occupancy Vehicle (HOV) Lane Exemption: Through the Clean Pass Program, eligible plug-in EVs may use the Long Island Expressway HOV lanes, regardless of the number of occupants in the vehicle. Vehicles must display the Clean Pass vehicle sticker, which is available from the New York State Department of Motor Vehicles. This exemption expires September 30, 2025.

Plug-In Electric Vehicle (PEV) Rebate Program: The NYSERDA provides rebates of up to $2000 for the purchase or lease of a new eligible PEV. Rebate amounts vary based on a vehicle's all-electric range and manufacturer's suggested retail price.

Workplace EVSE and Plug-In Electric Vehicle (PEV) Incentives: NYSERDA is offering employers in the greater New York City region $8000 rebate per dual-connector EVSE installed. Employees of organizations that receive the rebate are eligible for a $500 rebate toward the purchase or lease of a qualified PEV.

ZEV and Fueling Infrastructure Rebates for Municipalities: The New York State Department of Environmental Conservation's Municipal ZEV Rebate Program offers rebates to cities, towns, villages, counties, and New York City boroughs for the purchase or lease of eligible ZEVs and the installation of

(Continued)

BOX 6.8 (Continued)

eligible ZEV fueling infrastructure. To qualify, ZEVs must be purchased or leased on or after May 1, 2018, at a dealership within the state, and leases must be at least 36 months in length. ZEV fueling infrastructure must be installed primarily for public use. Maximum rebate amounts for the purchase or lease of ZEVs reach either $5000 per vehicle (50 miles or greater electric range) or $2500 per vehicle (10—50-mile electric range) and $250,000 per facility of EVSE. A single municipality may receive up to 50% of the total available funds toward ZEVs and EVSE, and up to 75% of the total available funds for hydrogen fueling infrastructure.

garage are able to charge while the car is not in use. The city also offers the possibility to people living in single family homes to install their own Level 2 chargers. The city of Manhattan in New York, United States, has 1462 public charging station ports (Level 2 and Level 3) within 15 km; 93% of the ports are Level 2 charging ports and 33% of the ports offer free charges for your electric car. The two main charging networks in operation are Tesla and ChargePoint.

6.5.3 Seattle, Washington

Seattle, also known as the Emerald City, is a seaport city located on the West Coast of the United States, and is the seat of King County, Washington. Seattle with an estimated 744,955 residents as of 2018, is the largest city in both the state of Washington and the Pacific Northwest region of North America. The Seattle metropolitan area's population stands at 3.94 million, and ranks as the 15th largest in the United States (Balk, 2018).

Road transportation was responsible for 66% of Seattle's GHG emissions in 2014. Out of these, 50% were attributed to passenger vehicles (cars, light-duty trucks, SUVs, and buses), and 16% to freight transport including medium- and heavy-duty trucks (City of Seattle, 2018). With regard to its energy mix, it is highlighted that as it borders the Pacific Ocean almost 90% of the electricity is derived from hydropower. To be more specific, in 2018 86% of the produced electricity came from hydropower, whereas 8% from renewable energy sources (wind and biogas) and 5% from nuclear power (www.seattle.gov, 2020). Therefore the city's abundance of hydropower is beneficial to the adoption of electromobility in the city.

Since 2009 Seattle has been working toward EV adoption, aiming to provide streamlining for charging infrastructure, incorporating EVs into the municipal fleet, developing a regional infrastructure network, and promoting outreach and consumer awareness. As far as the electrification of the private sector is concerned, this was accelerated by a number of federal, state, and local actions. The State of Washington partnered with Oregon, California, and British Columbia to create the West Coast Electric Highway (www.westcoastgreenhighway.com), installing DC/Fast Charging stations every 25—50 miles along the I-5 corridor and other major roadways in the Pacific Northwest. From 2011 to 2013 the City operated a pilot program to provide public access to charging infrastructure in City-owned or managed parking garages.

In 2013, the City of Seattle set an ambitious goal to be carbon neutral by 2050. In this direction, in 2016, the City set a goal to increase electric light-duty vehicle ownership to 30% by 2030. To meet this goal, Mayor Murray launched the Drive Clean Seattle Initiative (Seattle Office of Sustainability & Environment, 2017) aiming to electrify the transportation sector at scale. The implementation steps included an Executive Order 18-01 on State Efficiency and Environmental Performance directing City departments to reduce fleet-related climate pollution by purchasing low-emission or EVs, using other clean fuels, and prohibiting idling. In 2019 the City of Seattle updated its Green Fleet Action Plan (Saunders, 2019) focusing on electrification, cleaner fuels, increased efficiency, and a green fleet standard for fleet procurement. Box 6.9 highlights the specific actions foreseen to accelerate the EV charging infrastructure.

BOX 6.9 Seattle's incentives for the promotion of electromobility (Saunders, 2019)

Electric Vehicle Charging Infrastructure Planning Specific Actions
- Install EVSE infrastructure 2019 through 2025.
- Any capital departments doing major renovations, remodels or new construction will evaluate the need for EVSE and incorporate into the project.
- Determine costs for all fleet department vehicle(s) by parking spot and location for EVSE needs in 2019—25.
- Install contingency generators for EVSE sites (emergency management teams will assist in determining best locations).
- Incorporate EV charging needs in the Emergency Fuel Contingency Plan.

The number of EVs (both BEVs and PEVs) in King County in February 2020, reached 29,968, out of which 22,095 were BEVs and 7873 were PEVs (data.wa.gov, 2020). Currently, Seattle is ranked as one of the top US markets for EVs with an EV sales share that is four times the national average. As of the end of 2015, Seattle ranked seventh of the 50 largest US cities in both highest EV sales share (second highest outside of California) and most extensive public electric charging infrastructure (third highest outside of California). In 2016 plug-in EV registrations reached 1236, whereas in March 2017, there were 359 additional EV registrations in Seattle, bringing the total to 5143. As of the end of February 2020, the number of EVs in the city of Seattle reached 10,505 (data.wa.gov, 2020). Currently, EV buyers in Seattle can take advantage of both the federal tax credit of up to $7500 and the Washington State and local sales tax exemption of up to about $3100. The total available financial incentive depends on the type of vehicle and local sales tax rates. Furthermore, the City operates over 125 on-road EVs (20% of the light-duty fleet), 71 pieces of electric off-road equipment, and over 500 conventional hybrids. In addition to the city's central motor pool, EVs are deployed in most city departments including police, fire, transportation, parks, and both municipal utilities.

With regard to charging infrastructure, the city is characterized by a strong concentration of 905 level 2 charging stations and 65 level 3 charging stations (DC fast charging stations or DCFC) (Alternative Fuels Data Center, 2020). Seattle's charging infrastructure provides charging stations from various networks such as Blink, Greenlots, Tesla, EVgo, ChargePoint, and SemaCharge.

6.6 China

China is the world's most populous country with a rapidly growing economy (China's GDP grew at about 10% annually between 2000 and 2010) and is considered to be the world's second largest oil consumer after the United States, and the largest global energy consumer, according to the International Energy Agency (International Energy Agency -IEA, 2019). According to China Petroleum Group Economic and Technical Research Center, the oil consumption of China is as high as 625 million tons in 2018, and over 60% of this is for transportation; moreover, China's reliance on imported oil reached 69.8% of total demand in 2018, and has exceeded 50% for 11 consecutive years (Liu and Jiang, 2018).

China is the largest producer and consumer of coal in the world and is the largest user of coal-derived electricity. However, since 2014 coal as a percentage of the energy mix has fallen, declining from 64% in 2015 to 62% in 2016 (DW, 2017). In 2018 64.1% of China's generated electricity came from coal, 3.1% from natural gas, 4.2% from nuclear energy, 17.1% from hydropower, and the rest from renewable energy sources: wind, solar, and biomass (National Energy Administration, 2018).

In light of energy and environmental concerns, the Chinese government has introduced several policy initiatives for the support of the uptake of EVs. In view of the above mentioned, China's EV market has become one of the largest worldwide with about half of the world's new EV sales with 2.61 million cumulative light-duty EVs sold through 2018; and the number is projected to reach 80 million by 2030. Fig. 6.4 shows the best selling passenger vehicles in China in 2017.

In 2018 the percentage of EV sales in the Chinese leading major markets of Beijing, Shanghai, and Shenzhen, represented 5%−11% of new vehicle sales. It is noted, that the term of new energy vehicles (NEVs) is used by the Chinese government, in order to describe vehicles eligible for public subsidies, and includes BEVs, PHEVs, and FCEVs (PRTM Management Consultants Inc, 2011). However, it should be mentioned that the sales of NEVs in China decreased by 54.5% in January 2020; whereas the overall sales of vehicles, including passenger cars, trucks, and commercial vehicles fell 18% year on year to 1.94 million units (China Association of Automobiles Manufacturers, 2020); this could be attributed to the outbreak of Covid-19, the disease caused by the coronavirus (Ren, 2020).

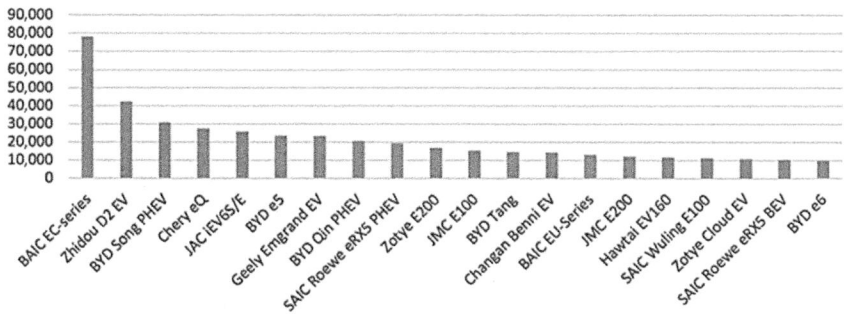

Figure 6.4 Best selling vehicle models in 2017 (Clean Technica, 2018).

With regard to the adopted policy framework, it is mentioned that several branches of the national government are involved in this process. These include the Ministry of Science and Technology, the National Development and Reform Commission (NDRC), the Ministry of Industry and Information Technology, and the Ministry of Finance, which are responsible for R&D, strategic policy, long-term investment issues, standards, and subsidy policy in the EV industry. In addition, several other ministry-level organizations are involved in the development of the EV industry, such as the Environmental Protection Agency, the State Planning Commission, the Electric Vehicle Standardization Committee, the State Economic and Trade Commission, and the CAA. During the past years, China's government's political support for the adoption of EVs has four goals:

- the creation of a world-leading industry that would produce jobs and exports;
- ensuring energy security, so as to reduce its oil dependence;
- the reduction of urban air pollution; and
- the reduction of its carbon emissions

In this direction, in June 2012 the State Council of China published an energy saving and NEV industry development plan (2012–20) (State Council, 2012), which set a target for cumulative PEV sales of 5 million by 2020. As during the period of 2014–15, passenger PEV sales increased sharply, with an annual growth rate of more than 300%, China's State Council issued the Guidance on Accelerating the Promotion and Application of NEVs in 2014 (State Council, 2014). The Chinese government launched in 2009 two rounds of NEV demonstration projects, in order to promote their commercialization. The first round (2009–12), which covered a total of 25 pilot cities (including Beijing, Shanghai, Hangzhou, Dalian, Shenzhen, etc.) focused firstly on the public transportation (buses, special vehicles), and then to private transportation. Given that the results of the first founded demonstration project did not meet the expectations set by the NEV plans, the Chinese government issued the Notice on the Continued Work to Promote the Development of NEVs, deciding to continue the demonstration project until 2015 covering 39 cities.

The provided policy initiatives for the acceleration of EV uptake include government-directed subsidies (i.e., purchase subsidies and tax exemption) as well as regulatory incentives (i.e., free parking, access to bus lanes, and toll waivers). EV drivers are given access to bus lanes, are exempted from the access restrictions at peak times; while they may also charge and park free of charge in many places. In Beijing, Shanghai, and Chongqing, all new residential buildings must be prewired for charging equipment in their parking spaces. For larger public parking lots, a minimum of 10% of parking spaces must be equipped with charging stations. Another important advantage for EV drivers are total or partial waivers from license plate availability restrictions. Moreover, automakers need to obtain 10% of sales credits from EVs from 2019 onwards. Compliance is obligatory for companies with annual sales of over 30,000 units.

In 2019 the number of public charging stations for EVs owned and operated by its members came up to 495,488 (189,000 AC charging stations, 206,000 DC and 488 of both types). During 2019, 365,000 charging facilities were installed, representing an increase of 29.5% compared to the corresponding period of 2018 (Zhihua, 2019). According to China Electric Vehicle Charging Infrastructure Promotion Association, at the end of November 2019 the number of charging facilities throughout the country reached 1174 million units, up 61.2% on an annual basis. The public charging infrastructure network remained concentrated, with the cities of Beijing and Shanghai, together with Guangdong, Jiangsu, Shandong, Zhejiang, Anhui, Hebei, Hubei and Fujian provinces, accounting for 74.0% of all such facilities. In November 2019 charges throughout the country totaled 535 million kWh, up 45 million kWh compared to October 2019. Buses and passenger vehicles were the big users of the charging facilities, while other types of vehicles such as taxis and sanitation vehicles were light users.

As of November 2019 there were eight Chinese companies (representing 90.0% of all stations in operation across the country) that own and operate at least 10,000 EV charging stations, including:

- Qingdao Teld New Energy: 144,000 units
- Star Charge: 112,000 units
- State Grid Corporation of China: 88,000 units
- Jiangsu YKC New Energy Technology: 33,000 units
- EV Power: 25,000 units
- AnYo Charging: 18,000 units
- Potevio: 14,000 units
- Shenzhen Car Energy Network: 12,000 units

Furthermore, as of November 2019 China had 306 battery swapping stations. Beijing ranked first with 126 stations, followed by Guangdong province with 63 stations, whereas Fujian (17) and Zhejiang (13) provinces ranked third and fourth, respectively. The two main operators of battery swapping stations in China are Aulton New Energy (183) and NIO (123).

Charging infrastructure incentives (public and private) include the construction of municipal charging stations by the central government as well as financial incentives, requirements with respect to new building construction, and other policies, such as:

- The city of Shenzhen offers purchasers of EVs subsidies of up to RMB 20,000 for vehicle insurance and installation of charging equipment (Shiqi Ou et al., 2017).
- In 2014 Guangzhou adopted a requirement that new buildings must have 18% of parking spots either equipped with EV charging or enabled for future installation (Guangzhou City Government, 2014).
- In 2017 the Beijing municipal government began mandating that all parking spots in new residential developments are set aside space for EV chargers, with new government or state-owned enterprise buildings required to install chargers at 25% of parking spots.

Box 6.10 summarizes the policy guidelines of the Chinese government regarding the charging infrastructure.

BOX 6.10 Timeline of charging infrastructure policy guidelines in China

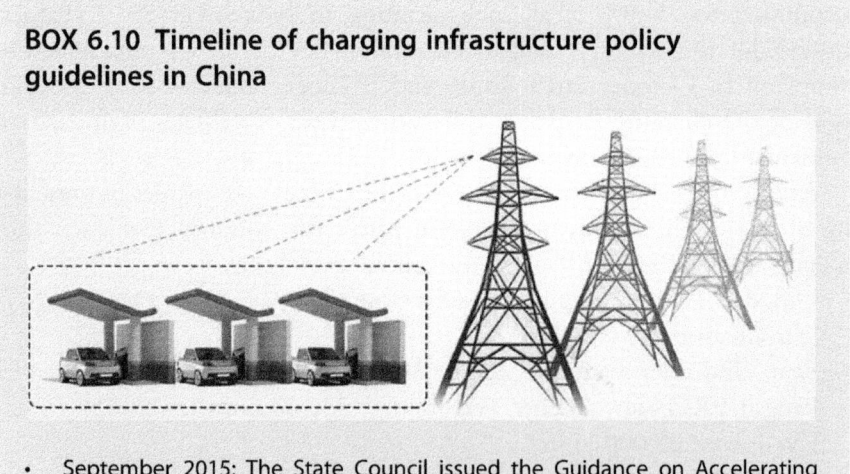

- September 2015: The State Council issued the Guidance on Accelerating the Construction of EV Charging Infrastructure (State Council, 2015), according to which, charging infrastructure should be sufficient for 5 million EVs by 2020, all new residential construction should be equipped with EV charging, 10% of parking spaces in large public buildings to be
(Continued)

BOX 6.10 (Continued)

available for EV charging, and at least one public charging station for every 2000 EVs.

- October 2015: China National Development and Reform Commission-NDRC issued the Guidelines for Developing EV Charging Infrastructure (2015–20), according to which least 120,000 EV charging stations and 4.8 million EV charging posts should be built by 2020. The guidelines divide China into three regions with varying degrees of EV infrastructure promotion and call for establishing a grid of EV-charging-enabled highways covering the most populous coastal provinces of East China (China National Development and Reform Commission- NDRC, 2015).

- January 2016: the National Energy Administration (NEA) released a notice summarizing five new national standards for EV charging interfaces and communications protocols (China National Energy Administration-NDRC, 2016a).

- January 2016: The Ministry of Finance, Ministry of Science and Technology, Ministry of Industry & Information Technology, NDRC, and NEA published the 13th Five Year Plan for NEV Infrastructure Incentive Policies (Ministry of Science and Technology, 2016). The plan included RMB 90 million in funding for installation of charging infrastructure, specifying that charging stations should have a minimum number of charging posts, chargers would be installed at government buildings, and the procurement of chargers would be open to any charging manufacturer.

- July 2016: NDRC published a *Notice on Accelerating Residential EV Charging Infrastructure Construction*, setting out standards and procedures for residential charging as well as designating the Jing-Jin-Ji, Yangtze River Delta, and Pearl River Delta regions as demonstration zones for residential charging infrastructure development (National Development and Reform Commission-NDRC, 2016b).

6.6.1 Beijing

Beijing is the capital of the People's Republic of China, and the world's third most populous city. The city, located in northern China, is governed as a municipality under the direct administration of the central government with 16 urban, suburban, and rural districts (National Statistical Yearbook of China, 2017).

The number of NEVs in Beijing has increased during the past years, from 13,370 sales in 2015 (Qiu et al., 2019) the sales of new registered NEVs reached 60,600 in 2018 (Kingdom of the Netherlands, 2018). In 2019, there was an increase of 17,000 units of BEVs. Around 140,000 out of a total of 188,000 were purchased by individuals and companies, while the remaining 48,000 were used in the public sector (China Association of Automobiles Manufacturers CAAM, 2020). Furthermore, the stock number of new energy buses has been rising on an annual basis; by 2018, almost 7882 public electric buses were operating in various services, including Foton Ouhui electric buses and Yinlong electric buses, which were almost exclusively used as public buses, whereas only a few were used as touring coaches.

With regard to charging infrastructure, it is noted that by the end of 2016, Beijing had built 612 charging stations and approximately 60,000 charging piles (both public and private). In particular, 23 charging operators had access to the public management platform and more than 6000 charging piles were available; while more than 5000 communities had installed a total of 26,000 self-use charging piles. Additionally, Beijing Municipal Commission of Housing and Urban—Rural Development collaborated with State Grid, in order to enhance the charging conditions in 327 communities. Two providers are responsible for the charging infrastructure in Beijing: State Grid and China Potevio.

With regard to local policies, Beijing has promoted the uptake of NEVs, since 2015 with the provision of local subsidies (only for the purchase of BEVs) that were up 100% that of central subsidies. In 2016 Beijing Municipal Commission of Development and Reform (BMCDR) published the "Beijing electric vehicle charging infrastructure planning (2016—2020 years)," aiming to cover the charging demand brought by the increasing number of EVs (Beijing Municipal Commission of Development and Reform, 2016). According to this plan, the target of realizing "one charging pile for one vehicle" was set, so as to facilitate the charging of private users.

In addition, the Beijing Municipal Science and Technology Commission, together with the Beijing Municipal Economic Information Commission, the Beijing Municipal Finance Bureau, the Beijing Municipal Urban Management Commission, and the Beijing Municipal Transportation Commission, implemented the "Measures for Promotion and Application of New Energy Vehicles in Beijing" and took the lead nationwide in abolishing the preregistration system for NEVs. In July 2018 the Beijing Municipal Finance Bureau and other relevant authorities jointly issued a new notice to subsidize NEVs (including BEVs and FCEVs). In 2019 Beijing implemented new rules that remove subsidies for EVs with a range below 155 miles, while more expensive EVs will have incentives slashed by as much as 60%. It has also banned companies from building BEV plants unless they have a minimum capacity of 100,000 units—a blow to EV startups.

Under the "Action Plan for the Promotion and Application of New Energy Smart Vehicles in Beijing 2018–2020," Beijing's target was to double the fleet to 400,000 BEV units sold. To achieve this, the city of Beijing has set a number of measures, including:

- Increase of the percentage of the number of EV's in taxis (80% of new taxis to be plug-ins), public transport (all buses used in central urban areas and the sub-center will all be replaced by EVs); logistics distribution (vehicles under 4.5 tons will be largely replaced with EVs). It is mentioned that Beijing has succeeded in its goal to introduced 4500 electric public transport buses by the end of 2017 and is now aiming to reach 10,000 in 2020 (Xinhua, 2018).
- Usage of EVs in its airport green traffic demonstration area, the sub-center low-carbon demonstration area, and the Winter Olympics demonstration area, among others.

Finally, the provided benefits from the usage of NEVs in the city of Beijing, include:

- Exemption from vessel and vehicle tax.
- Charging fee reductions.
- Exemption from purchase restrictions.
- Light-duty ICEV are exempted from entering Beijing's fifth ring road during weekdays.
- Taxi purchase and usage fee reductions.

6.6.2 Shanghai

Shanghai is located on the southern estuary of the Yangtze, and the Huangpu River flows through it. With a population of 27,058,000 as of 2020, a 2.82% increase from 2019 (macrotrends.net), it is the most populous urban area in China and the second most populous city in the world.

Shanghai is one of the 25 pilot cities that was selected by the Chinese government to demonstrate energy efficient and NEV deployment and one of the six pilot cities for subsidy of private NEV purchase. In 2006 the city established the New Energy Vehicle Promotion Office of Shanghai, so as to facilitate the industrialization of NEVs. In 2009 NEVs were listed as one of the nine new high-technology industrialization projects in Shanghai. In 2011 they designated a strategic new industry with priority to policy and financial support.

The number of NEVs in Shanghai has increased during the past years, from 28,714 sales in 2015 (Qiu et al., 2019) the sales of new registered NEVs reached 66,321 in 2018 (Kingdom of the Netherlands, 2018). Nonetheless, since 2016 the growth speed of private vehicles in Shanghai slowed down, reaching 5.11 million in 2018, a year-on-year increase of 420,000 (CAAM, 2020). Moreover, during the period of 2017−19 nearly 60,000 electric light trucks and vans have been deployed for urban freight movement, representing about 35% of the city's overall fleet of urban delivery vehicles (Kingdom of the Netherlands, 2018). With cumulative sales of 178,658 NEVs during 2010−18 and 127,700 charging points (public and private), Shanghai is considered to be the NEV capital of the world. By the end of 2016, Shanghai had built 227 pubic fast charging stations, 22 fast charging stations on expressways, 12 bus charging stations, two public charging stations for energy storage, and a total number of 5084 charging piles.

Its purchase subsidies for private consumers and fleets used to favor PHEVs but are increasingly focusing on BEVs. PHEVs can get up to 30% of central subsidies, while BEVs get up to 50% (Bloomberg, 2018a,b). The NEV license plate is often cited as the most important driver of NEV adoption as it bypasses Shanghai's expensive license plate auction system. Apart from the above, users of NEVs in Shanghai enjoy the following privileges:

- Free parking in Shanghai's city center.
- Discounted public charging fees (NEV owners pay only 32 CNY or 4 € when charging their car at a public station).
- Exemption for vessel and vehicle tax.
- Taxi purchase and usage fee reductions.
- Battery recycle subsidies (up to 1.000 CNY or 127 € per battery for OEMs).

In addition, Shanghai provides the largest NEV car-sharing program; with the company EV Card owning more than 30,000 NEVs (the majority of which are found in Shanghai) for shared use in some 40 cities.

6.6.3 Shenzhen

Shenzhen is a city of 12 million, located on the central coast of southern Guangdong province in the People's Republic of China; bordering Hong Kong across the Sham Chun River to the south, Huizhou to the northeast, and Dongguan to the northwest. Shenzhen hosts many digital and high-tech companies, such as Huawei and TenCent, as well as the world's largest manufacturer of NEVs, BYD, and the vast majority of China's lithium-ion battery producers.

Shenzhen is one of the Chinese cities to promote the uptake of NEVs and is considered to be a leader in the field of alternative public transportation, given that by the end of 2017 all buses (16,359 units) were electric (World Resources Institute, 2018). As a matter of fact, the city was the first in the world to successfully electrify its entire bus fleet. With regard to EV sales, it is noted that in 2018, the EV population in Shenzhen reached 153,146 units, out of which 61,857 are logistics EVs and 91,289 are EVs (Crow et al., 2018). With regard to charging infrastructure, it is pointed out that the number of slow charging piles in Shenzhen by the end of July reached 27,146 (static.nfapp.southcn.com, There Will Be Charging Piles for Every Kilometer in Downtown Shenzhen, 2017).

Shenzhen has placed a number of incentives for the acceleration of EVs, including (1421 Consulting, 2018):
- Purchase subsidies up to 50% of central subsidies
- License plate incentives
- Equipment investment subsidies for companies
- R&D subsidies
- Service trade subsidies
- Import subsidies
- First-hour free parking for NEVs
- Charging fee cap at 0.45 CNY (0.6 €) per kilowatt (which is even lower than what Shanghai offers)
- Onetime vehicle usage subsidy in addition to the purchase subsidy of 10,000−20,000 CNY (€ 1275−2545)
- Subsidies for public charging infrastructure
- Road restrictions on vehicles with internal combustion engines
- Battery recycling subsidies based on battery capacity

It is highlighted that in 2019 Shenzhen built the largest electric taxi charging station in the world, which has the ability of accommodating almost 5000 NEVs per day, using a total of 160 MWh of energy on average. The station is operated by the Chinese power company Southern Power Grid, in collaboration with state-owned Potevio and China's largest maker of electric cars, BYD (Schmidt, 2019).

6.6.4 Tianjin

Tianjin is one of the four municipalities under the direct administration of central government of the PRC and is located in Northern China on the shore of the Bohai Sea. It is one of the four largest municipalities and the largest harbor in North China. By the end of 2014 its population reached 15.5 million, placing the city as one of the six megacities (population exceeding 10 million) in China (National Bureau of Statistics of China NBS, 2014).

The city's economic prosperity as well as its rapid urbanization led to a significant increase of the number of private vehicles (from 0.2 in 1999 to 2.3 million in 2015), posing an environmental burden (Liu et al., 2017). Together with Beijing and 10 other cities in Hebei province, Tianjin was listed in the first batch of 28 cities and areas to formally initiate the NEV demonstration program in 2013. To be more specific, in 2013 the city of Tianjin was selected as an EV adoption pilot city; resulting in the provision of central government subsidies, local government subsidies of matching value, as well as total maximum subsidies of almost 100,000 CNY. The implementation of the abovementioned measures had as a result the adoption of 39,192 NEVs in 2017. According to the Promotion and Implementation Plan for NEVs in Tianjin (2016−20), Tianjin aims to increase its EV stock to 50,000 by the end of 2020.

With regard to charging infrastructure, 43 high-speed charging stations featuring 191 charging poles have been built, according to the local State Grid Tianjin Electric Power Company. The 13 major expressways crossing Tianjin have all been installed with charging poles, allowing drivers from Beijing, Tianjin, and Hebei to charge on-demand. In 2018, the average daily amount of electricity on Tianjin's high-speed charging stations was 2300 kWh, a year–on–year increase of 201.44%.

6.7 Japan

Japan has launched, during the past years, several R&D projects, aiming to accelerate the uptake of EVs. Furthermore, Japan, has launched several projects, such as the "Next generation vehicle charging infrastructure deployment," in order to expand the number of charging stations. This program involved the cooperation of local governments, highway operators, and other players, who received subsidies for charging equipment and up to two-thirds of the installation costs.

Japan aims to increase the share of next generation vehicles in new vehicle sales to 50%—70% by 2030, of which BEVs and PHEVs should account for 20%—30% and HEVs for 30%—40%. Additional goals include the installation of two million ordinary chargers and 5000 quick chargers and the achievement of a 50% market share for Japanese companies in the global storage battery market.

With regard to Japan's energy mix, this is largely dependent on fossil fuels such as oil, coal, and liquefied natural gas (LNG). In particular, in 2018 the share of the domestic supply of primary energy was as follows: 39% oil, 23.4% LNG, 25.1% coal, 7,6% renewable energy sources, 3.5% hydroelectric power, and 1.4% nuclear power. Despite the fact that EVs could reduce the GHG emissions, Japan's long-term low-carbon strategy does not foresee the phase out of coal and relies mainly on CO_2 capture and storage technologies in its power plants (Government of Japan, 2019c), thus hindering the environmental benefits of the use of EVs— from a life cycle point of view. As a reference, it is highlighted that 30 coal-fired power plants are either in the planning stage or under construction (Sauer, 2019). Nonetheless it should be pointed out that after the nuclear disaster in Fukushima in March 2011, Japan committed itself to using renewable energy and further increasing its energy efficiency. Within the framework of a decentralized electricity supply system and a "Smart Community Concept," the batteries of plug-in hybrids and EVs could be used as buffer storage (reservoir for surplus green electricity as well as a source of energy during electricity shortages) for locally generated electricity from renewable energy sources.

In December 2018 the cumulative light-duty plug-in EV sales in Japan reached 257,300 units since 2009 (International Energy Agency—IEA, 2018c); whereas the newly registered EVs reached 26,500. It is noted that by the end of 2017 the Japanese stock consisted of 104,490 BEVs standing for 50.9% and 100,860 PHEVs standing for 49.1% (International Energy Agency—IEA, 2018c). In 2018 the top selling model was the Nissan Leaf, which was ranked as the all-time top selling plug-in EV in the country, with over 100,000 units sold since December 2010 (Global Nissan News, 2018).

The country's charging infrastructure in 2018 included approximately 22,000 slow chargers publicly available; whereas the number of fast chargers reached only about 7700 stations. To be more specific, Japan, during the past 10 years, has installed 7700 CHAdeMO DC fast chargers (40% of the total in the world) as well as more than 20,000 AC Level 2 charging stations. The majority of CHAdeMo chargers (mostly around 50 kW) in Japan are installed at:

- dealerships—2300
- convenience stores—1000
- shopping malls—400
- along highways—nearly 400

The increase in the number of EV charging stations in Japan falls under efforts to support the rising number of EVs resulting from the introduction of government subsidies for EV buyers. It is noted that the government's goal is to have a fast charger every 9.3 miles (15 km) or within every 19-mile (30-km) radius. To support BEVs, operators can get subsidies of ¥5 million ($47,000) per charger and up to ¥45 million ($420,000) for construction costs (Insideevs, 2019).

6.7.1 Goto Islands

The Gotō Islands are Japanese islands in the East China Sea, off the western coast of Kyūshū and constitute part of Nagasaki Prefecture. In 2009 the Nagasaki Prefecture established the Nagasaki EV&ITS Consortium, a collaborative effort set by industry, academia, and government to promote EVs and intelligent transportation systems (ITS) throughout Nagasaki. The goal of the EV&ITS project was to create "Driving Tours of the Future" by incorporating EVs and ITS technology into the local tourism industry. Agriculture, fishing, and tourism are the main industries of the islands (Nagasaki Perfecture, 2011).

Taking into consideration the fact that on average the number of inhabitants per km^2 is 100; while the number of passenger cars per 1000 inhabitants reaches 620, it evident that the vehicle density is higher compared to the Japanese average (approx. 453 passenger cars per 1000 inhabitants), while the population density is well below the Japanese average (approx. 337 inhabitants per km^2). The implementation of the project resulted in around 55 EVs per 10,000 households. As per the latest available info (World EV Cities & Ecosystems, 2014) 177 EVs are in operation on the Goto Islands. With regard to Goto's energy production, it is noted that during 2010 over half of the electricity consumed was generated from locally produced renewable sources (wind and solar power, biogas). In addition, there is an underwater power line that connects to the Japanese mainland. There are approximately 20 fast charging stations available for charging.

With regard to driving tours, 100 EVs are available for use at publicly accessible parking areas. The navigation system provides users with a wide array of technical information about the vehicles, parking, and charging systems, as well as tourist information about sightseeing, restaurants, and hotels. Sensors at the rental stations and selected points on the tour feed updated information into the system.

6.7.2 Tokyo

Tokyo is the capital of Japan and constitutes part of the Kantō region, including the Izu and Ogasawara Islands; with a population of over 13.9 million in 2019; whereas the metropolitan area is the world's most populous with over 38 million people (Tokyo Metropolitan Government Bureau of Statistics Department, 2018).

The city of Tokyo has funded projects in major cities and along major traffic routes for the acceleration of the use of EVs. Since 2012 a carbon tax has been applied in order to improve the competitiveness of EVs: €6.39 kL^{-1} for oil and petroleum products, €6.56 t^{-1} for hydrocarbons, and €5.63 t^{-1} for coal (Ministry of Environment, 2017). Further to this, Tokyo is one of the 20 cities that signed the C40 declaration of intent on clean buses and commits to replacing all of its buses and its municipal fleet with hydrogen vehicles. In March 2012 there were 2381 vehicles deployed (1975 EVs and 407 PHVs). The cumulative sales of EVs reach almost 60,000 units (Lutsey, 2018). Regarding chargers, the target was to install 80 quick chargers by 2012. By February 2013 there were already 117 chargers.

The Metropolitan Government of Tokyo in 2018 engaged in a "Zero Emission Tokyo Strategy," which foresees carbon-free buildings and vehicles by 2050. The road map also sets a 2030 midterm target, according to which 30% of Tokyo's energy is to be generated by renewable sources, bolstered by the installation of 1.3 GW of solar power equipment. Other midterm targets include a 25% reduction in single-use plastics by 2030—part of a national target—a 50% reduction in food waste compared to 2000, the installation of 1000 high-speed charging stations for EVs, and the construction of 150 hydrogen charging stations. The strategy acknowledges the impacts of weather-related disasters on both a global and nationwide scale, in particular highlighting the 2018 floods in western Japan, which caused ¥1.158 trillion in damage, the 95,000 cases of heat-related illnesses last year, and more recently the

90,000 homes damaged by Typhoon Hagibis in October 2019 (Zero Emissions Tokyo Strategy, 2018).

6.8 Comparative analysis of cities

The adoption of electromobility is a complex and sometimes unpredictable process. The case studies presented in previous sections identify some of the major impact factors for the broader dissemination of EVs in urban areas. In this section a comparative analysis of the 13 cities presented through Sections 6.4–6.7 is employed, based on data from statistical data and literature references (as these were stated in abovementioned sections). It should be noted that data refer to 2019 EV sales.

In Europe, the cities taken into consideration include Amsterdam, Barcelona, Oslo, and London; in the United States: Los Angeles, San Jose, New York City, and Seattle; in China: Shanghai, Beijing, Tianjin, and Shenzhen; and in Japan: Tokyo. All these cities—as presented—are interested in the reduction of transport-related emissions and have already implemented different national and local measures, which support the acceleration of the usage of EVs. Fig. 6.5 depicts the cities under study as well as their EV sales for 2019.

6.8.1 Electric vehicle sales and charging infrastructure availability

As shown in Fig. 6.6, the number of EVs (both BEVs and PEVs) sold in 2019 was highest in Shanghai, Beijing, and Los Angeles.

Figure 6.5 Cities under examination and relative EV sales. The bubble size indicates different sales volumes.

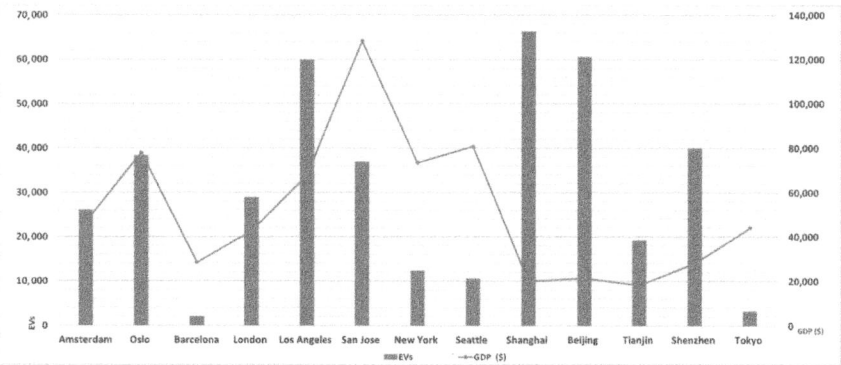

Figure 6.6 Sales of EVs per capita in 2019, for cities under study.

Data points in Fig. 6.6, corresponding to the right axis, present each city's GDP per capita, expressed in US$ per capita (2019 data) and are used as a comparative benchmark; whereas data points on the left axis stand for the number of EV sold in each city in 2019. Data indicate that cities in China led the 2019 EV market, with Shanghai, Beijing reaching sales over 60,000 units and Shenzhen with sales reaching approximately 40,000 units. Most likely it would be expected that cities of lower GDP would have a slower adoption of EVs due to lack of available funds needed for investments for faster development of EV market; nonetheless in the case of Chinese cities it is noted that despite the low GDP, EV uptake is high. This is mainly attributed to policies and incentives provided for EV's purchase as well as to investments into charging infrastructure (Section 6.6). It can be also concluded that even in countries with higher GDPs the EVs market adoption is not as high as expected (with the exception of Norway). On the other hand, in cities in the United States, such as San Jose and New York, despite the high GDP, the market sales of new EVs in 2019 did not follow this trend. This is attributed mainly to the provision of different financial and nonfinancial incentives, model availability, and consumer preferences.

It should be highlighted that the city of Oslo in Norway continues to experience far greater EV sales shares than any other market, with 61% of passenger vehicle sales being electric in 2018, compared to 49% for Norway nationally. Following these were Shenzhen and San Jose with a percentage of 21% each and Tianjin with 18%.

EV charging infrastructure plays a crucial role in the energy transition to low-carbon transportation systems. As the adoption of electromobility moves from the stage of early adoption to an early majority, the percentage of people with access to home charging is expected to decrease, thus increasing the reliance on public charging. A lack of available public charging stations will likely suppress the demand. In this context, the available charging infrastructure in each city under study is assessed using several metrics, including the absolute number of public charge points, the number of charge points per million population, and the number of electric passenger vehicles per public charge point. Charging infrastructure includes public charging stations (due to the availability of data). Despite the fact that the majority of EV users charge their vehicles at home, public charging remains an important element to ensure EVs are as convenient as conventional vehicles. In dense urban settings where home charging is typically less available, public charging plays a particularly crucial role.

Fig. 6.7 indicates that the Chinese cities of Shenzhen, Shanghai, and Beijing are leaders in public charging infrastructure construction. Shenzhen, has more public charge points compared to the other cities under study (both in Europe and the United States).

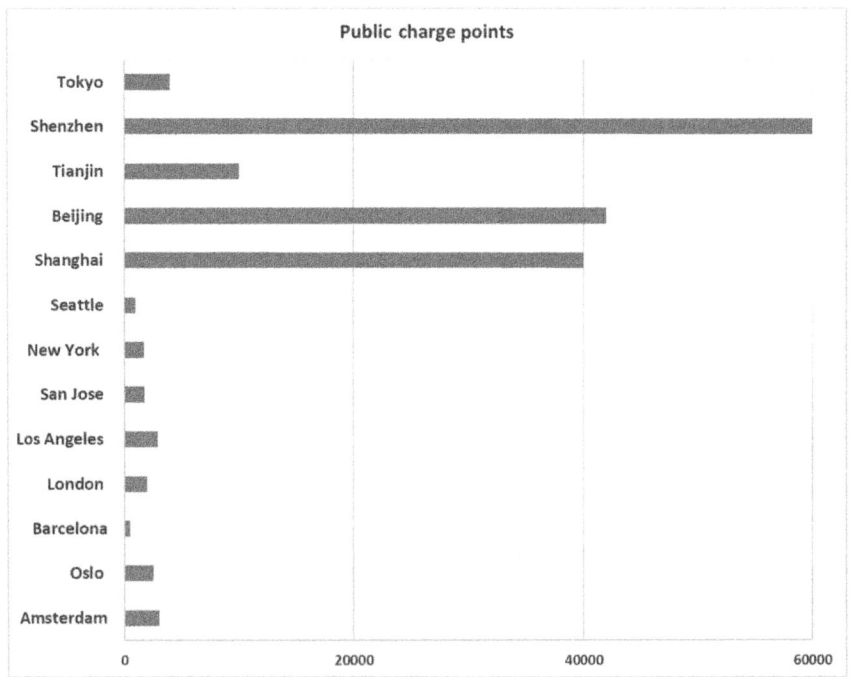

Figure 6.7 Public charge points in cities under study.

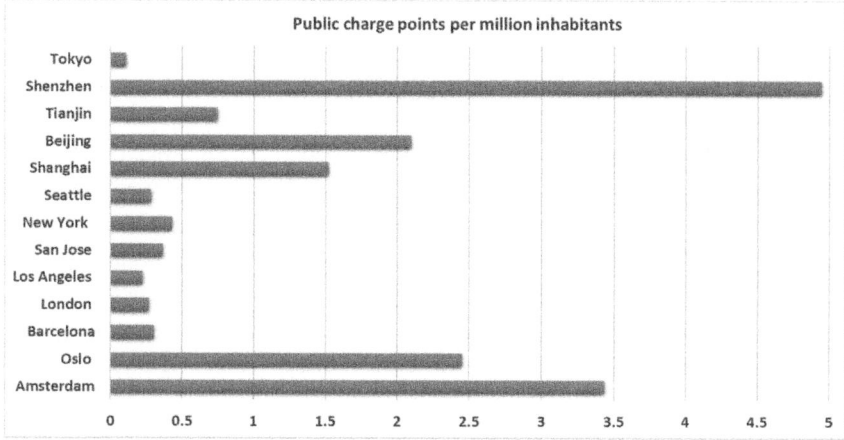

Figure 6.8 Public charge points per million inhabitants in 2019.

Fig. 6.8 shows that in 2019 Shenzhen's charging density with over 4500 charge points per million residents ranked first; while Oslo, Amsterdam, and Beijing were the next highest with over 2000. Cities in the United States tend to have fewer public charging points per inhabitants and have the highest ratio of EVs to public charge point (Fig. 6.9), as more drivers there have access to private home charging. Many cities also have substantial workplace charging installed. San Jose has the highest amount of workplace charging among US cities at almost 900 charge points per million population.

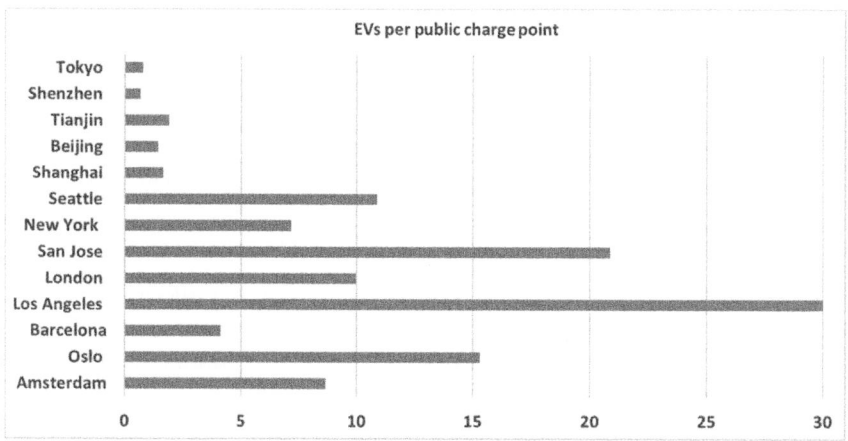

Figure 6.9 Electric vehicless per public charge point in cities under study in 2019.

Furthermore, Fig. 6.9, shows that the Chinese cities have eight or fewer EVs for each public charge point; in Shenzhen the ratio is lowest at three to one. This is also the case for the cities of Amsterdam and London with 10 or fewer EVs for each public charge point. It is highlighted that in 2019 the ratios of EVs to public charging network in the US cities of Los Angeles and San Jose were closer to 30 to 1, indicating the public charging network may not be keeping pace with EV market growth, but also reflecting the widespread availability of private home and workplace charging. Within California, the highest EV market shares of 2019 new registrations were the ones with the most extensive public charging network. This includes San Jose with a 10% EV market share, and Los Angeles with 5% EV market share.

The findings of Fig. 6.9 suggest that a high ratio of EVs per public charge station is not synonymous with a low EV market share (as an example the case of Shenzhen is mentioned); The above can be attributed to a number of economic factors, such as financial incentives and tax abatement, which have a significant impact on the market uptake. The differences in the correlation across the cities indicate that other factors also affect the EV adoption, such as federal mandates or incentives, and that these factors have varying influence in different national contexts.

6.9 Concluding remarks

The energy transition to a low-carbon transportation sector requires a fundamental change in the nature and structure of the overall transport sector. This transition requires technology developments and behavioral changes, as well as a major policy push. In general, policies need to take into consideration the following dimensions in an integrated way:

- the availability of energy carriers/fuels produced from renewable energy sources;
- the deployment of vehicles that can use renewable energy fuels; and
- the development of infrastructure for energy and fuel distribution.

The countries and cities leading in electric mobility use a variety of measures such as fuel economy standards coupled with incentives for zero- and low-emissions vehicles and use economic instruments for their employment. Further to this they set targets and are engaged both at a political and strategic level in their implementation, aiming to achieve a zero-carbon energy future. The case studies reveal that policy and regulations; finance innovation; resources and capacity building; as well as products and services innovation are of crucial importance for the successful deployment of electromobility in urban areas. In addition, the cities presented in this chapter reveal that greater EV adoption faces barriers of model availability, cost, convenience, and consumer preferences.

What are the qualities and factors that determine the leading markets of tomorrow? Why is the transition to electromobility concentrated in specific areas? The answer to this is that the cities under study employ an integrated approach to a coherent and coordinated set of policies, in order to reach a zero-carbon transportation system. Measures are taken at various levels of jurisdiction—within multicountry regional blocs, at national and subnational levels, and within cities—aiming to support EV investment, deployment, and availability. Consumer incentives ensure that EVs are affordable in the near term, as their costs are expected to decrease. Governments and utilities are helping to build out the necessary charging infrastructure to ensure the convenience of EVs is fully realized. The California cities exemplify the broad approach across state and local agencies, electric power utilities, private companies, and nonprofit organizations.

On the other hand, integrating EVs into the grid is a key challenge for policy makers. The balance between charging demand and capacity is a challenge that policy makers will have to overcome not only for EVs to be scaled at the levels envisioned but also to support a clean transportation economy. In addition, policy makers should also take into consideration the fact that the transport sector plays a large role in the decarbonization of the energy system, as long as the grid is powered by renewable energy sources.

However (at the time of writing this chapter) the outbreak of the COVID-19 pandemic is expected to seriously affect the uptake of EVs in cities during the upcoming period. As it is still unclear when the virus is going to be contained, the adverse economic impact could be detrimental to EV industry. This could affect consumer confidence and relative expenditure. Further to this, taking into consideration the fact that EV batteries are primarily manufactured by Chinese and Korean suppliers such as CATL, Samsung HDI, and LG Chem, their supply could be limited. In addition, the economic impact of COVID-19, which has led to falling oil prices and lower government subsidies, could be of crucial importance for the demand of EVs.

References

1421 Consulting, 2018, March 6. Subsidies for foreign companies in Shenzhen Area. <https://www.1421.consulting/2018/03/subsidies-foreign-companies-shenzhen-area>.

Abuelsamid, S., 2018. GM's push for a U.S. electric car program could be dead on arrival. Forbes. <https://www.forbes.com/sites/samabuelsamid/2018/10/26/gm-push-for-us-ev-program-could-be-dead-on-arrival/#1393ed3e5521>.

Ajutament de Barcelona, 2018. L'Estratègia per la Mobilitat Elèctrica 2018−2024 a la ciutat de Barcelona. <https://ajuntament.barcelona.cat/premsa/2018/03/14/lestrategia-per-la-mobilitat-electrica-2018-2024-a-la-ciutat-de-barcelona/>.

Alternative Fuels Data Center, 2020. <https://afdc.energy.gov/stations/#/find/nearest?location = los%20angeles%20&fuel = ELEC>.

Amsterdam's Clean Air Action Plan, 2019. <http://www.citylogistics.info/wp-content/uploads/2019/05/RD63-Handout-Lyon-EVS32_A4-3.pdf>.

Autoalliance, 2019. Energy and environment. Advanced Technology Vehicle Sales Dashboard. <https://autoalliance.org/energy-environment/advanced-technology-vehicle-sales-dashboard/>.

Badallaj, V., 2019. How many charging stations for electric-cars are needed in Oslo by 2020? Thesis submitted for the degree of Master in Informatics: Programming and Network. University of Oslo.

Balk, G., March 26, 2018. Seattle just one of 5 big metros last year that had more people move here than leave, census data show. The Seattle Times. <https://www.seattletimes.com/seattle-news/data/seattle-just-one-of-5-big-metros-last-year-that-had-more-people-move-here-than-leave-census-data-show/>.

Beijing City Council, 2018., Half of Beijing's buses to be electric driven by 2020. <www.ebeijing.gov.cn/BeijingInformation/BeijingNewsUpdate/t1568532.htm>.

Beijing Municipal Commission of Development and Reform, 2016. Beijing electric vehicle charging infrastructure planning (2016−2020 years).

Bloomberg, 2018a. In a change of heart, China is said to keep local EV subsidies. <https://www.bloomberg.com/news/articles/2018-02-12/in-a-change-of-heart-china-is-said-to-keep-local-ev-subsidies>.

Bloomberg, 2018b. In a change of heart, China is said to keep local EV subsidies, February 12.

C40, 2015. C40 Clean Bus Declaration urges cities and manufacturers to adopt innovative clean bus technologies. <www.c40.org/blog_posts/c40-clean-bus-declaration-urges-cities-andmanufacturers-to-adopt-innovative-clean-bus-technologies>.

C40, 2019a. Fossil-fuel-free streets declaration. <www.c40.org/other/fossil-fuel-free-streets-declaration>.

C40, 2019b. Network overview C40 cities. <www.c40.org/networks/zero-emission-vehicles>.

CAA electric vehicle charging station locator, 2018. <http://www.caa.ca/evstations/>.

California Air Resources Board, 2017. Enhanced fleet modernization program.

California Department of Motor Vehicles, 2017. Estimated vehicles registered by county <https://www.dmv.ca.gov/portal/wcm/connect/add5eb07-c676-40b4-98b5-8011b059260a/est_fees_pd_by_county.pdf?MOD = AJPERES>.

California Energy Commission, 2014. California electric vehicle fast charging stations.

California Energy Commission, 2017. Renewable energy − overview.

California Governor's Office of Business and Economic Development−Go-Biz, 2019. Electric vehicle charging station permitting guidebook. <http://businessportal.ca.gov/wp-content/uploads/2019/07/GoBIZ-EVCharging-Guidebook.pdf>.

California New Car Dealers Association, 2019. 15 (4), <https://www.cncda.org/wp-content/uploads/Cal-Covering-3Q-19.pdf>.

Cansino, J.M., Yñiguez, R., 2018. Promoting electro mobility in Spain. Public measures and main data (2007−2012). Transp. Res. Part D Transp. Environ. 38, 59.

CARB, 2016. Zero-Emission Vehicle Standards for 2018 and Subsequent Model Year Passenger Cars, Lighttrucks, and Medium-Duty Vehicles. California Air Resources Board. <www.arb.ca.gov/msprog/zevprog/zevregs/1962.2_Clean.pdf>.

CARB (California Air Ressources Board), 2018. California transitioning to all-electric public bus fleet by 2040. <www.arb.ca.gov/news/california-transitioning-all-electric-public-bus-fleet-2040>.

ChargePoint, 2018. ChargePoint reveals new concept design for high-powered charging of electric aircraft and semitrucks. <www.chargepoint.com/about/news/chargepoint-reveals-new-conceptdesign-high-powered-charging-electric-aircraft-and-semi>.

China Association of Automobiles Manufacturers, 2020. <http://www.caam.org.cn/chn/21/cate_463/list_1.html>.

China National Development and Reform Commission- NDRC, October 19, 2015. <https://www.ndrc.gov.cn/zcfb/zcfbtz/201511/ W020151117576336784393.pdf>.

China National Energy Administration —NDRC, January 5, 2016a. <http://www.nea.gov.cn/2016-01/05/c_134978578.htm>.

City of Seattle, 2018. Mayor J.A. Durkan, Seattle Climate Action. <http://greenspace.seattle.gov/wp-content/uploads/2018/04/SeaClimateAction_April2018.pdf>.

Clean Technica, 2018. 2017 China electric car sales blow world out of the water—BAIC EC-series is a superstar. <https://cleantechnica.com/2018/01/29/2017-china-electric-car-sales-blow-world-water-baic-ec-series-superstar/>.

Clean Vehicle Rebate Project (CVRP), March 2014. Eligible vehicles. California Center for Sustainable Energy. <https://ww3.arb.ca.gov/msprog/aqip/cvrp/cvrp_final_report_fy1314.pdf>.

Comodi, G., Caresana, F., Salvi, D., Pelagalli, L., Lorenzetti, M., 2016. Local promotion of electric mobility in cities: guidelines and real application case in Italy. Energy 95, 494—503.

Crow, A., Mullaney, D., Liu, Y., Wanga, Z., 2018. New EV Horizon: Insights From Shenzhen's Path to Global Leadership in Electric Logistics Vehicles. Rocky Mountain Institute.

Department for Transport, 2018. The road to zero next steps toward cleaner road transport and delivering our industrial strategy. <https://assets.publishing.service.gov.uk/government/uploads/system/uploads/attachment_data/file/739460/road-to-zero.pdf>.

Department for Transport's Vehicle licensing statistics dataset, 2020. <https://www.gov.uk/government/collections/vehicles-statistics>.

Dutch Road Authority (RDW), 2020. <https://www.rdw.nl/over-rdw/dienstverlening/open-data/handleidingen>.

DW, 2017. China coal consumption declines for third straight year. <https://www.dw.com/en/china-coal-consumption-declines-for-third-straight-year/a-37755092>.

ECCJ (Energy Conservation Center Japan), 2011. Final report of joint meeting between the automotive evaluation standards subcomittee, energy efficiency standards subcommittee of the advisory committee for natural resources and energy and the automobile fuel efficiency standards subcommittee. <www.eccj.or.jp/top_runner/pdf/tr_passenger_vehicles_dec2011.pdf>.

European Alternative Fuels Observatory—EAFO, <www.eafo.eu > (accessed 25.01.20).

European Automobile Manufacturers Association—ACEA, 2018. New passenger car registrations by fuel type in the European Union. <https://www.acea.be/uploads/press_-releases_files/20181108_PRPC_fuel_Q3_2018_FINAL.pdf>.

European Commission Communication, 2013. Clean power for transport: A European alternative fuels strategy, COM (2013) 17 final, 2013, Brussels.

European Commission, EC, 2014. <https://eur-lex.europa.eu/legal-content/EN/TXT/PDF/?uri = CELEX:32014L0094&from = EN>.

European Council, 2019. CO2 emission standards for cars and vans: Council confirms agreement on stricter limits, <www.consilium.europa.eu/en/press/press-releases/2019/01/16/co2-emissionstandards-for-cars-and-vans-council-confirms-agreement-on-stricter-limits/>.

European Parliament, 2019. JD-review of the clean vehicles directive legislative train schedule: resilient energy union with a climate change policy, <www.europarl. europa.eu/legislativetrain/theme-resilient-energy-union-with-a-climate-change-policy/file-jd-clean-vehicles-directivereview>.

European Parliament and of The Council, 2009a. Directive 2009/28/Ec on the promotion of the use of energy from renewable sources and amending and subsequently repealing Directives 2001/77/EC and 2003/30/EC, 2009, OJL140, 5.6.2009, p. 16.

European Parliament and of The Council, 2009b. Directive 2009/30/EC, amending Directive 98/70/EC as regards the specification of petrol, diesel and gas-oil and introducing a mechanism to monitor and reduce greenhouse gas emissions and amending Council Directive 1999/32/EC as regards the specification of fuel used by inland waterway vessels and repealing Directive 93/12/EEC, 2009,OJL 140,5.6.2009, p. 8.

European Parliament and of The Council, 2009c. Directive 2009/33/EC, on the promotion of clean and energy-efficient road transport vehicles, 2009, OJL140, 15.5.2009, p. 5.

European Parliament and of The Council Regulation (EU) No 510/2011 of 11 May 2011, on setting emission performance standards for new light commercial vehicles as part of the Union's integrated approach to reduce CO_2 emissions from light-duty vehicles, 2011, OJ L 145, 31.5.2011, p. 1.

Field, K., 2019. Tesla's V3 Superchargers Deliver 250 kW Charging & 1,722 km/hr. Cleantechnica (accessed 12.12.19.).

Figenbaum, E., Kolbenstvedt, M., 2013. Electromobility in Norway - Experiences and Opportunities with Electric Vehicles. Transportøkonomisk institutt, Oslo, TØI report 1281/2013.

Figenbaum, E., Kolbenstvedt, M., 2016. Learning from Norwegian Battery Electric and Plug-in Hybrid Vehicle users. Results from a Survey of Vehicle Owners. Institute of Transport Economics, TØI report 1492/2016.

Fridstrøm, L., Østli, V., 2017. The vehicle purchase tax as a climate policy instrument. Transp. Res. Part A Pol. Pract. 96, 168—189. Available from: https://doi.org/ 10.1016/j.tra.2016.12.011.

Global Nissan News, 2018.Nissan LEAF sales surpass 100,000 in Japan (Press release). Yokohama: Nissan. April 20. <https://global.nissannews.com/en>.

Government of Canada, 2019. Interim report from the advisory council on climate action. <www.canada.ca/en/environment-climate-change/services/climate-change/advisory-councilclimate-action/interim-report.html>.

Government of China, 2012. [Energy-saving and new energy vehicle industry development plan (2012—2020)], <www.gov.cn/zwgk/2012-07/09/content_2179032.htm>.

Government of China, 2015. [Electric vehicle charging infrastructure development guidelines 2015—2020], National Energy Administration, <www.nea.gov.cn/ 134828653_14478160183541n.pdf>.

Government of China, 2019. [Publicly solicited opinions on the mandatory national standards living vehicle fuel consumption limits and pedestrian vehicle fuel consumption evaluation methods and indicators draft for comment], Ministry of Industry and Information Technology, <www.miit.gov.cn/n1146295/n1652858/n1653100/n3767755/c6616494/content.html>.

Government of Denmark, 2018. Together for a greener future. Ministry of Energy, Utilities and Climate, <https://en.efkm.dk/news/news-archive/2018/oct/together-for-a-greener-future/>.

Government of France, 2017. Climate Plan 2017, Ministry of Europe and Foreign Affairs, <https://lc.ambafrance.org/Climate-Plan-2017>.

Government of France, 2018. Contrat strategique de la filiere automobile 2018—2022 [Strategic contract of the automotive sector 2018—2022]. <www.pfa-auto.fr/wp-content/uploads/2018/06/DP-SCFAutomobile.pdf>.

Government of Japan, 2014. Auto vehicle industry strategy 2014. Ministry of Economy Trade and Industry. <www.meti.go.jp/press/2014/11/20141117003/20141117003-A.pdf>.

Government of Japan, 2018. METI releases interim report by Strategic Commission for the new era of automobiles, Ministry of Economy Trade and Industry. <www.meti.go.jp/english/press/2018/0831_003.html>.

Government of Japan, 2019a. (New fuel consumption standard values of passenger cars were presented). <www.meti.go.jp/press/2019/06/20190603003/20190603003.html>.

Government of Japan, 2019b. New fuel efficiency standards for trucks and buses formulated, Ministry of Economy, Trade and Industry. <www.meti.go.jp/english/press/2019/0329_003.html>.

Government of Japan, 2019c. Low carbon energy plan. <https://www.kantei.go.jp/jp/singi/ondanka/kaisai/dai40/pdf/senryaku.pdf>.

Government of Korea, 2019. (Ministry of Environment's policy briefing on promoting environment friendly vehicles in 2019). Ministry of Environment. <www.me.go.kr/home/web/board/read.do?boardMasterId = 1&boardId = 935880&menuId = 286>.

Government of Norway, 2016. National transport plan 2018−2029, Avinor, Jernbaneverket (Norwegian National Rail Administration), Kystverket (Norwegian Coastal Administration), Statens Vegvesen (Norwegian Public Roads Administration). <www.ntp.dep.no/English/_attachment/1525049/binary/1132766?_ts = 1571e02a3c0>.

Government of Spain, 2019. Borrador del plan nacional integrado de Energia y clima 2021−2030 (Draft of the national plan including energy and climate), Ministry of Ecologic Transition. <www.miteco.gob.es/es/cambio-climatico/participacionpublica/documentoresumendelborradorplannacionalintegradodeenergiayclima2021-2030_tcm30-487345.pdf>.

Government of Sweden, 2017. The Swedish climate policy framework. <www.government.se/495f60/contentassets/883ae8e123bc4e42aa8d59296ebe0478/the-swedishclimate-policy-framework.pdf>.

Government of the Netherlands, 2017. p. 43. <https://www.kabinetsformatie2017.nl/binaries/kabinetsformatie/documenten/verslagen/2017/10/10/coalition-agreement-confidence-in-the-future/coalition-agreement-2017-confidence-in-the-future.pdf>.

Government of the United Kingdom, 2017. Air quality plan for nitrogen dioxide (NO_2) in Government of the United Kingdom (2017), Department for Environment, Food & Rural Affairs and Department for Transport. <www.gov.uk/government/publications/air-quality-plan-for-nitrogen-dioxide-no2-in-uk-2017>.

Government of the United Kingdom, 2018. The road to zero—next steps toward cleaner road transport and delivering our industrial strategy, Department of Transport. <https://assets.publishing.service.gov.uk/government/uploads/system/uploads/attachment_data/file/739460/road-to-zero.pdf>.

Guangzhou City Government, November 28, 2014. <http://zwgk.gd.gov.cn/007482532/201412/t20141209_559123.html>.

Hagesæther Pål Vegard, December 2, 2018. Nå bor det over én million i Stor-Oslo. Aftenposten.

Hall, D., Cui, H., Lutsey, N., 2017. Electric vehicle capitals of the world: What markets are leading the transition to electric? The International Council on Clean Transportation. <https://theicct.org/sites/default/files/publications/World-EV-capitals_ICCT-Briefing_08112017_vF.pdf>.

Holman, C., Harrison, R., Querol, X., 2015. Review of the efficacy of low emission zones to improve urban air quality in European Cities. Atmos. Environ. 111, 161−169.

http://www.ev-volumes.com/.

https://longreads.cbs.nl/trends18-eng/economy/figures/energy/.

< https://opendata.cbs.nl/statline/#/CBS/nl/dataset/37230ned/table? ts = 1578685738191>.

< https://www.macrotrends.net/cities/20656/shanghai/population> (accessed 29.02.20.).

https://www.seattle.gov/light/fuelmix/

Battery-powered cvs could represent trucking's future, but many questions—and hurdles—remain, 2018. <https://www.ttnews.com/articles/electric-trucks-advance>.

https://www.zap-map.com/.

Insideevs, 2019. Japan's EV infrastructure is massive, electric car sales not so much <https://insideevs.com/news/338290/japans-ev-infrastructure-is-massive-electric-car-sales-not-so-much/>.

Instituto Nacional de Estadística, 2016. Barcelona: Población por municipios y sexo. International Council on Clean Transportation, San Francisco, CA.

International Energy Agency—IEA, 2018a. Global energy & CO_2 status report 2017.

IEA, 2018b. Global EV Outlook 2018: Toward Cross-Modal Electrification. IEA.

International Energy Agency—IEA, 2018c. Clean energy ministerial, and electric vehicles initiative (EVI) (May 2018). Global EV Outlook 2017: 3 million and counting (PDF). IEA Publications. See pp. 9−10, 19−23, 29−28, and Statistical annex, pp. 107−113 (accessed 02.01.19.).

International Energy Agency—IEA, 2019. Global EV Outlook 2018, Toward cross-modal modification.

Jefatura del Estado, ley 54/1997, de 27 de noviembre del sector eléctrico, 1997, BOE n° 285 de 28.11.1997, p. 35097.

Joint Venture Silicon Valley, April 20, 2019. Silicon Valley sets pace for electric vehicle adoption. <https://jointventure.org/news-and-media/news-releases/1776-silicon-valley-sets-pace-for-electric-vehicle-adoptionnew-data-shows-region-accounts-for-nearly-20-of-electric-vehicles-in-california> (accessed on 22.02.20.).

Kabinetsformatie, 2017. Coalition agreement 'Confidence in the Future'. <www.kabinetsformatie2017.nl/documenten/verslagen/2017/10/10/coalition-agreement-confidencein-the-future>.

Karali et al., 2017. Vehicle-grid integration Lawrence Berkeley National Laboratory.

Kingdom of the Netherlands, 2018. New Energy Vehicles, Developments in China, the Netherlands and prospects for Sino-Dutch cooperation in the field of commerce and policy. <http://zakendoeninchina.org/wp-content/uploads/2018/10/Chinas-New-Energy-Vehicles-developments-report-sept-2018.pdf>.

Korea Environment Corporation, 2019. 전기차 세제혜택 [EV Portal − Electric vehicle tax benefit], <www.ev.or.kr/portal/saletex?pMENUMST_ID = 21548>.

Krause, R.M.S., Carley, R., Lane, B.W., Graham, J.D., 2013. Perception and reality: public knowledge of plug-in electric vehicles in 21 U.S. cities. Energy Policy 63, 433−440.

Lagos, M., September 22, 2014. Brown signs several clean-air vehicle bills. San Francisco Chronicle. https://www.sfgate.com/bayarea/article/Brown-signs-several-clean-air-vehicle-bills-5771184.php (accessed 2.2.20.).

Liu, Z.Q., Jiang, X.F., 2018. Domestic and foreign oil and gas industry development report, China Petroleum Group Economic and Technical Research Center, China. Chinese electric vehicle ownership will reach 80 million by 2030, China EV100 chairman says. <https://www.yicaiglobal.com/news/chinese-electric-vehicle-ownership-will-reach-80-million-2030-china-ev100-chairman-says>.

Liu, X., Li, G., Ma, S., Tian, J., Liu, L., Zhu, W., 2017. Urban road traffic scale analysis from the perspective of atmospheric environmental indicators in Tianjin, China. Ecol. Indicat. 82, 392−398.

Lutsey, N., 2018. California's Continued Electric Vehicle Market Development.

Lutsey, N., Searle, S., Chambiss, S., Bandivadekar, A., 2015. Assessment of leading electricity vehicle promotion activities in United States cities. The International Council on Clean Transportation, July 2015. White paper.

Marklines, 2019. Marklines. <www.marklines.com/portal_top_en.html> (accessed December 19.).

McKenzie, B., August, 2015. Who drives to work? Commuting by automobile in the United States: 2013. American Community Survey Reports. <https://www.census.gov/hhes/commuting/files/2014/acs-32.pdf>.

Ministerio de Industria, May 10, 2011b. Turismo y Comercio, Real Decreto 648/2011, de 9 de mayo, por el que se regula la concesión directa de subvenciones para la adquisición de EVs durante 2011, en el marco del Plan de acción 2010-2012 del Plan integral de impulso al EVs en España 2010-2014, BOE n° 111.

Ministerio de Industria, May 23, 2011a. Turismo y Comercio, Real Decreto 647/2011, de 9 de mayo, por el que se regula la actividad de gestor de cargas del sistema para la realización de servicios de recarga energética. BOE n°122.

Ministerio de Industria, April 27, 2013. Turismo y Comercio, Real Decreto 294/2013, de 26 de abril, por el que se regula la concesión directa de subvenciones para la adquisición de EVs en 2013, en el marco de la Estrategia integral para el impulso del EVs en España 2010—2014. BOE n° 101, p. 32072.

Ministry of Science and Technology, January 20, 2016. <https://www.most.gov.cn/tztg/201601/t20160120_123772.html>.

Nagasaki Perfecture, 2011. <http://www.pref.nagasaki.jp/ev/ev&its/en/eng_ev&its5.pdf>.

Nanaki, E.A., Koroneos, C., 2016. Climate change mitigation and deployment of electric vehicles in urban areas, Renewable Energy, Vol. 99. Elsevier, pp. 1153—1160.

National Bureau of Statistics of China (NBS), 2014. China Statistical Yearbook, 2014.

National Development and Reform Commission—NDRC, September 2016b. <http://www.ndrc.gov.cn/zcfb/zcfbtz/201609/t20160912_818178.html>.

National Energy Administration, 2018. Detailed electricity statistics (accessed 7.02.20.).

National Statistics, Department of Business, Energy and Industrial Strategy, 2019. Digest of United Kingdom, Energy Statistics. <https://assets.publishing.service.gov.uk/government/uploads/system/uploads/attachment_data/file/840015/DUKES_2019_MASTER_COPY.pdf>.

National Statistical Yearbook of China, 2017. Figures based on 2006 statistics.

Netherlands Enterprise Agency, 2020. Statistics Electric Vehicles in the Netherlands (up to and including December 2019). <https://www.rvo.nl/sites/default/files/2020/01/Statistics%20Electric%20Vehicles%20and%20Charging%20in%20The%20Netherlands%20up%20to%20and%20including%20December%202019.pdf>.

Newman, D., Wells, P., Donovan, C., Nieuwenhuis, P., Davies, H., 2014. Urban, suburban or rural: where is the best place for electric ehicles? Int. J. Automot. Technol. Manage 14 (3/4).

New York Department of Motor Vehicles (NYDMV), 2019. Vehicle, snowmobile, and boat registrations. Open Data NY. <https://data.ny.gov/Transportation/Vehicle-Snowmobile-and-Boat-Registrations/w4pv-hbkt/data>.

New York Public Service Commission—PSC, 2016. Order adopting a clean energy standard. <https://www.nyserda.ny.gov/All-Programs/Programs/Clean-Energy-Standard>.

New York State Energy Research and Development—NYSERDA, May 31, 2018. Governor Cuomo announces $250 million initiative to expand electric vehicle infrastructure across New York State. <https://www.governor.ny.gov/news/governor-cuomo-announces-250-million-initiative-expand-electric-vehicle-infrastructure-across>.

New York State Energy Research and Development — NYSERDA, April 23, 2019. Governor Cuomo announces record number of electric vehicle sales with 63 percent increase in 2018.

<https://www.nyserda.ny.gov/About/Newsroom/2019-Announcements/2019-04-23-Governor-Cuomo-Announces-Record-Number-of-Electric-Vehicles>.

Norwegian Ministry of Transport and Communications, 2017. National Transport Plan 2018−2029, <https://www.regjeringen.no/contentassets/7c52fd2938ca42209e4286-fe86bb28bd/en-gb/pdfs/stm201620170033000engpdfs.pdf>.

Open data portal for the State of Washington, <https://data.wa.gov/Demographics/General-Statistics-about-the-Electric-Vehicle-Popu/57rq-7t96 > (accessed 28.02.20.).

Perujo, A., Thiel, C., Nemry, F., 2011. Electric vehicles in an urban context − environmental benefits and techno-economic barriers. In: Soylu, S. (Ed.), Electric Vehicles the Benefits and Barriers. InTech .

Portvik, S., 2019. Oslo−The EV capital of the world. <https://www.mhsr.sk/uploads/files/usKtg8Oh.pdf>.

PRTM Management Consultants, Inc., 2011. The China new energy vehicles program − challenges and opportunities. World Bank. <http://siteresources.worldbank.org/EXTNEWSCHINESE/Resources/3196537-1202098669693/EV_Report_en.pdf>.

Qiu, et al., 2019. Assessing the effectiveness of city-level electric vehicle policies in China. J. Energy Policy 130, 22−31.

Red Eléctrica de España, 2020. <https://www.ree.es/en/press-office/news/press-release/2019/12/spain-closes-2019-10-more-installed-renewable-power-capacity>.

Ren, D., 2020. China's new energy vehicle sales more than halved in January, as Covid-19 weighs on world's largest car market. <https://www.scmp.com/business/companies/article/3050513/chinas-new-energy-vehicle-sales-more-halved-january-covid-19>.

Sauer, N., 2019. Japan sets carbon neutral goal with focus on capturing emissions. Climate Home News, <https://www.climatechangenews.com/2019/06/12/japan-says-will-carbon-neutral-fails-set-timeline/>.

Saunders, P., 2019. Department of finance and administrative services, fleet management, green fleet action plan − an updated action plan for the city of Seattle. <https://www.seattle.gov/Documents/Departments/FAS/FleetManagement/2019-Green-Fleet-Action-Plan.pdf>.

Schmidt, 2019. World's largest charging station in Shenzhen powers all-electric taxi fleet. <https://thedriven.io/2019/05/24/worlds-largest-charging-station-in-shenzhen-powers-all-electric-taxi-fleet/>.

Seattle Office of Sustainability & Environment, 2017. Drive Clean Seattle, implementation strategy. <https://www.seattle.gov/Documents/Departments/Environment/ClimateChange/Drive_Clean_Seattle_2017_Report.pdf>.

Shiqi Ou, et al., 2017. A Study of China's Explosive Growth in the Plug-in Electric Vehicle Market. Oak Ridge National Laboratory.

Society of Motor Manufacturers and Traders—SMMT, January 2019. <https://www.smmt.co.uk/vehicle-data>.

Soret, A., Guevara, M., Baldasano, J.M., 2014. The potential impacts of electric vehicles on air quality in the urban areas of Barcelona and Madrid (Spain). Atmos. Environ. 99, 51−63.

State Council, 2012. Energy Saving and NEV Industry Development Plan (2012−2020). No. (22nd ed.), State Council, Beijing.

State Council, 2014. Guidance on accelerating the promotion and application of NEVs (35rd ed.), State Council, Beijing.

State Council, September 15, 2015. Guiding opinions on accelerating the construction of electric vehicle charging infrastructure, <http://www.gov.cn/zhengce/content/2015-10/09/content_10214.htm>.

State of California, 2016. 2016 ZEV action plan. <www.gov.ca.gov/wpcontent/uploads/2017/09/2016_ZEV_Action_Plan.pdf>.

State of California, 2018. Governor Brown takes action to increase zero-emission vehicles, fund new climate investments. <www.gov.ca.gov/2018/01/26/governor-brown-takes-action-to-increase-zeroemission-vehicles-fund-new-climate-investments>.

Statistics Norway, 2015. Population and population changes, Q2 2015. Statistics Norway. August 20, 2015.

Statistics Norway, 2019a. Boforhold, registerbasert. <https://www.ssb.no/boforhold>.

Szczesny, J., December 11, 2018. Sales of electric vehicles growing steadily in California. The Detroit Bureau. <http://www.thedetroitbureau.com/2018/12/sales-of-electric-vehicles-growing-steadily-in-california/ > (accessed 13.12.19.).

Tesla, 2017. Tesla Semi & Roaster unveil, Tesla, <www.tesla.com/semi>.

Tesla, January 28, 2019. Superchargers. Tesla (accessed 24.01.19.).

Tesla supercharger station locator, 2018. <https://supercharge.info/>.

The Norwegian Electric Vehicle Association, 2019. Statistikk for elbilsalget og antall ladestasjoner i Norge. https://elbil.no/elbilstatistikk (accessed 04.02.20.)

There Will Be Charging Piles for Every Kilometer in Downtown Shenzhen. <http://static.nfapp.southcn.com/content/201709/08/c662645.htm>.

Transportation Electrification Collaboration-LACI, 2018. Zero emissions 2028 roadmap. <https://laincubator.org/roadmap/>.

Trip, J.J., Konings, R., 2014. Supporting electric vehicles in freight transport in Amsterdam. E-mobility NSR, file nr. 35-2-6-11.

U.S. Census Bureau, 2016. American community survey 1-year estimates U.S. Bureau of the Census 2016.

U.S. Census Bureau, 2017. American community survey 5-year estimates U.S. Bureau of the Census 2017.

U.S. Energy Information Administration, EIA, 2019. New York state profile and energy estimates. <https://www.eia.gov/state/?sid = NY#tabs-2>.

World EV Cities & Ecosystems, 2014. <http://www.worldevcities.org/data/#ev_ev_status/goto_islands>.

World Resources Institute, 2018. How did Shenzhen, China build world's largest electric bus fleet? <https://www.wri.org/blog/2018/04/how-did-shenzhen-china-build-world-s-largest-electric-bus-fleet>.

Xinhua, 2018. Electric buses run on Beijing street. <http://www.xinhuanet.com/english/2017-10/22/c_136698327.htm>.

Zero Emissions Tokyo Strategy, 2018. <https://www.kankyo.metro.tokyo.lg.jp/en/about_us/zero_emission_tokyo/strategy.files/Zero_Emission_Tokyo_Strategy.pdf>.

ZEV (Zero Emissions Vehicle), 2014. Multi-state ZEV action plan 2014. ZEV program implementation task force. <www.ct.gov/deep/lib/deep/air/electric_vehicle/path/multi-state_zev_action_plan_may2014.pdf>.

ZEV Alliance, 2015. <http://www.zevalliance.org/wp-content/uploads/2015/12/ZEV-Alliance-COP21-Announcement_12032015.pdf>.

ZEV Program Implementation Task Force, 2014. Multi-state ZEV action plan. <www.nescaum.org/documents/multi-state-zev-action-plan.pdf>.

ZEV Task Force, 2018. Multi-state ZEV action plan: 2018—2021—accelerating the adoption of zero emission vehicles. <https://www.zevstates.us/>.

Zhihua, L., 2019. Charging stations for electric vehicles spread across China. <http://www.chinadaily.com.cn/a/201907/11/WS5d26ff7ba3105895c2e7cfac.html>.

東京都の人口（推訊）— Population of Tokyo. Tokyo Metropolitan Government Bureau of Statistics Department, 2018. Archived from the original on October 2, 2018.

Index

CPI Antony Rowe
Eastbourne, UK
November 04, 2020